Cat Astrology

Cat Astrology

Matthew Petchinsky

CONTENTS

Cat Astrology: Feline Mysteries of the Cosmos

By: Matthew Petchinsky

Introduction to Cat Astrology: Feline Mysteries of the Cosmos

Welcome to *Cat Astrology: Feline Mysteries of the Cosmos*, a journey into the fascinating world where the ancient wisdom of astrology meets the enigmatic and beloved creatures we share our lives with—cats. This book is designed to help you unlock the cosmic secrets that influence your feline companions, providing insights into their behaviors, moods, and personalities. Whether you're a seasoned astrologer, a devoted cat lover, or simply curious about the mystical connections between the stars and our pets, this book offers a unique perspective on understanding and nurturing the cats in your life.

Purpose of the Book

The purpose of this book is to explore how the planetary movements, zodiac signs, moon phases, and celestial events influence the behavior and characteristics of cats. By delving into the cosmic patterns that shape your cat's nature, you can gain a deeper understanding of their needs, preferences, and quirks. This knowledge can help you foster a stronger bond with your feline friends, improve their well-being, and create a harmonious environment that aligns with their natural rhythms.

Astrology has long been used to interpret human behavior, guiding us in relationships, career choices, and personal growth. But what about our pets? Cats, with their mysterious and often inscrutable behaviors, are particularly well-suited to astrological interpretation. This book bridges the gap between the human-centric practice of astrology and the animal kingdom, offering a comprehensive guide to applying astrological principles to your cat's life.

Structure of the Book

Cat Astrology: Feline Mysteries of the Cosmos is structured into six distinct parts, each focusing on a different aspect of astrology and its influence on cats:

- **Part I: The Planets and Cats**: This section explores the influence of each planet in our solar system on your cat's personality and behavior. From the Sun's role in shaping vitality to Pluto's impact on transformation, each chapter provides detailed insights into how these celestial bodies affect your feline friend.
- **Part II: Zodiac Signs and Feline Traits**: Here, you'll find a deep dive into the twelve zodiac signs and how they manifest in cats. Each chapter covers the specific traits, behaviors, and

needs of cats born under each sign, offering guidance on how to care for them based on their astrological profile.

- **Part III: Celestial Bodies and Their Influence on Cats**: Beyond the traditional planets, this section examines the roles of asteroids, the North and South Nodes, and other celestial bodies in your cat's life. These chapters reveal the more subtle and esoteric influences that shape feline behavior.
- **Part IV: Moon Phases and Feline Behavior**: The Moon's phases have a powerful effect on all living creatures, and cats are no exception. This section discusses how each phase of the Moon influences your cat's moods, energy levels, and behavior, providing tips on how to align their routines with lunar cycles.
- **Part V: Celestial Events and Their Impact on Cats**: Celestial events such as eclipses, retrogrades, and meteor showers can have profound effects on your cat's behavior. This part of the book explores these phenomena and offers advice on how to navigate their impact on your feline companions.
- **Part VI: Integration and Practical Applications**: The final part of the book brings all the astrological insights together, offering practical advice on creating cat horoscopes, understanding feline compatibility, and using astrology to enhance your cat's health and well-being.

Each section is designed to build upon the previous one, guiding you from a foundational understanding of astrological principles to more advanced applications. By the end of the book, you'll have a comprehensive toolkit for interpreting and responding to your cat's astrological influences.

The Significance of Astrology in Understanding Feline Behavior

Why should we consider astrology when it comes to our cats? Unlike humans, cats can't communicate their thoughts and feelings in words. They express themselves through subtle behaviors, body language, and sometimes through more dramatic actions. Astrology offers a framework for understanding these behaviors in the context of broader cosmic patterns.

For example, have you ever noticed your cat becoming unusually energetic during certain times of the month? Or perhaps they seem more aloof and distant at others. These shifts can often be explained by astrological factors such as the Moon's phase or the influence of a particular planet. By paying attention to these astrological cues, you can better anticipate your cat's needs and create an environment that supports their natural rhythms.

Astrology also helps us appreciate the individuality of each cat. Just as no two humans are exactly alike, no two cats share the same astrological makeup. Even cats of the same breed can exhibit vastly different behaviors depending on their astrological profile. By understanding your cat's unique astrological chart, you can tailor your care to suit their specific needs, leading to a happier and more fulfilled feline companion.

In conclusion, *Cat Astrology: Feline Mysteries of the Cosmos* invites you to explore the celestial connections that influence your cat's life. Through this journey, you'll discover new ways to understand and appreciate the mysterious and magical nature of cats, all while deepening the bond you share with your feline friends. So, let's embark on this cosmic adventure together, and unlock the astrological secrets that make your cat the unique and beloved creature they are.

Part I: The Planets and Cats

Chapter 1: The Sun and Your Cat

The Sun is the center of our solar system, and in astrology, it is considered the core of our identity. Just as the Sun provides the energy that sustains life on Earth, it also symbolizes the life force, vitality, and essence of every living being. In the context of feline astrology, the Sun represents the fundamental personality of your cat—their innate character, how they express themselves, and their overall energy levels. Understanding the influence of the Sun on your cat can provide invaluable insights into their behavior, preferences, and needs.

The Role of the Sun in Astrology

In astrological terms, the Sun is associated with the self, identity, and ego. It governs the essential traits that define who we are at our core, including our basic personality, willpower, and life purpose. For cats, the Sun similarly reflects their core personality traits, determining how they interact with the world around them, their natural energy levels, and their overall sense of vitality.

The position of the Sun in your cat's astrological chart is determined by the time, date, and location of their birth. This placement reveals the zodiac sign your cat was born under, often referred to as their "Sun sign." Each zodiac sign imbues the Sun's energy with specific qualities, shaping your cat's general demeanor and approach to life.

How the Sun Influences Your Cat's Personality

The Sun's position at the time of your cat's birth plays a crucial role in shaping their personality. Just as in humans, the Sun sign is the most prominent aspect of a cat's astrological profile. It provides a broad overview of their character, highlighting key traits that are likely to be dominant throughout their life.

For instance, a cat with the Sun in Aries may exhibit boldness, curiosity, and a love for adventure. They might be more inclined to explore new environments, show assertiveness in their interactions with other pets, and display a fiery spirit. On the other hand, a cat with the Sun in Taurus might be more laid-back, preferring the comforts of home, enjoying routine, and being affectionate in a steady, reliable manner.

These personality traits, influenced by the Sun, are often evident in a cat's daily behavior. Observing your cat in various situations—whether they are playing, interacting with other animals, or simply lounging in the sun—can offer clues about how their Sun sign shapes their actions and reactions.

Energy Levels and Vitality

The Sun is the primary source of energy for all living things, and in astrology, it symbolizes the life force that drives us. For cats, the Sun's placement in their astrological chart can indicate their natural energy levels and overall vitality.

A cat with a strong Sun placement, such as in the fire signs (Aries, Leo, Sagittarius), is likely to be highly energetic, playful, and active. These cats often have a zest for life that is palpable—they are the ones who chase after toys with relentless enthusiasm, climb to the highest perches, and demand attention with their vibrant personalities. Their vitality is usually high, and they thrive on physical activity and interaction.

Conversely, a cat with the Sun in a more subdued sign, such as Taurus or Cancer, might have a calmer, more relaxed energy. These cats may prefer to conserve their energy, choosing to spend more time resting, cuddling, or observing their surroundings from a comfortable spot. Their vitality is expressed in a more measured way, with a focus on maintaining comfort and security.

It's important to note that while the Sun's position provides a general indication of a cat's energy levels, it interacts with other planetary influences in their chart, which can modify or enhance these traits. For example, a Taurus cat with a strong Mars placement might display more energy than a typical Taurus, balancing their natural tendency for relaxation with bursts of activity.

The Sun and Your Cat's Health

The Sun's influence extends beyond personality and energy—it also plays a role in your cat's overall health and well-being. A strong and well-placed Sun in your cat's astrological chart is often associated with robust health, a strong immune system, and a natural resilience to illness. These cats are usually able to recover quickly from minor ailments and maintain a vibrant, healthy appearance.

However, if the Sun is poorly aspected or weakened by its placement in the chart (for instance, if it's in a sign where it's considered "in detriment" like Aquarius), there may be a tendency towards health issues related to the areas governed by the Sun. For example, cats with a weakened Sun might experience issues with energy regulation, leading to lethargy, or they might be more prone to conditions that affect their vitality, such as chronic fatigue or immune system weaknesses.

Monitoring your cat's behavior and health, particularly in relation to their energy levels, can provide early indicators of when something might be amiss. By understanding the Sun's role in your cat's astrological chart, you can take proactive steps to support their health—whether that means ensuring they get enough physical exercise, providing a diet that supports their vitality, or creating an environment that aligns with their natural energy rhythms.

The Sun and Seasonal Influences

The Sun also governs the seasons, and changes in the Sun's position throughout the year can have a significant impact on your cat's behavior and energy levels. Just as humans experience shifts in mood and energy with the changing seasons, so too do cats.

During the summer months, when the Sun is strongest, you may notice your cat becoming more active, playful, and sociable. The increased sunlight can boost their energy levels, making them more eager to explore their environment and engage in outdoor activities. On the other hand, during the winter months, when the Sun's presence is less dominant, your cat might become more withdrawn, preferring to sleep more and conserve energy.

Understanding these seasonal influences can help you adjust your cat's routine and environment to better suit their needs. For example, providing a warm, sunny spot for them to lounge in during the winter can help them maintain their energy levels, while ensuring they have plenty of opportunities for outdoor play during the summer can keep them engaged and active.

How to Support Your Cat's Sun Sign

Each Sun sign has specific needs and preferences that, when met, can enhance your cat's well-being and happiness. Here are some tips on how to support your cat based on their Sun sign:

- **Aries**: Provide plenty of stimulation and opportunities for adventure. Aries cats thrive on excitement, so interactive toys, puzzles, and outdoor exploration are key to keeping them happy.
- **Taurus**: Focus on comfort and routine. Taurus cats appreciate stability and luxury, so create a cozy environment with plush bedding, regular meal times, and consistent daily routines.
- **Gemini**: Engage their curiosity and social nature. Gemini cats love variety and interaction, so rotate their toys regularly, introduce new experiences, and spend time playing with them.
- **Cancer**: Offer security and affection. Cancer cats are sensitive and home-loving, so ensure they have a safe, quiet space to retreat to and give them plenty of cuddles and attention.

- **Leo**: Shower them with attention and praise. Leo cats love being the center of attention, so make sure they feel special with plenty of affection, playtime, and perhaps even a few regal accessories.
- **Virgo**: Maintain cleanliness and order. Virgo cats are fastidious and may be more sensitive to dirt and disarray, so keep their environment tidy and their litter box clean.
- **Libra**: Create a harmonious and aesthetically pleasing environment. Libra cats appreciate beauty and balance, so consider their surroundings—comfortable beds, soft lighting, and a peaceful atmosphere.
- **Scorpio**: Respect their privacy and intensity. Scorpio cats can be intense and secretive, so provide them with hiding spots and respect their need for solitude at times.
- **Sagittarius**: Encourage exploration and freedom. Sagittarius cats are adventurous and love to roam, so ensure they have the space to explore and perhaps even access to the outdoors.
- **Capricorn**: Establish structure and boundaries. Capricorn cats thrive with discipline and order, so set clear boundaries and maintain a structured routine.
- **Aquarius**: Embrace their quirks and independence. Aquarius cats are unique and may have unconventional habits, so allow them to express their individuality and don't be afraid to indulge their oddities.
- **Pisces**: Nurture their sensitivity and creativity. Pisces cats are dreamy and intuitive, so create a calm environment and consider introducing them to water-based toys or gentle music.

Conclusion

The Sun's position in your cat's astrological chart is a powerful determinant of their core personality, energy levels, and overall vitality. By understanding the influence of the Sun, you can better appreciate the unique qualities that make your cat who they are. Whether they are a bold Aries or a gentle Pisces, the Sun's energy shapes their identity and guides their interactions with the world.

As you continue through this book, you will discover how the Sun's influence interacts with other astrological elements, providing a comprehensive understanding of your cat's cosmic blueprint. By aligning your care and environment with your cat's Sun sign, you can foster a deeper bond and ensure they lead a happy, healthy life filled with love and vitality.

Chapter 2: The Moon and Your Cat

The Moon, the Earth's closest celestial neighbor, has long been associated with emotions, instincts, and the ebb and flow of life. In astrology, the Moon governs our inner world, reflecting how we process feelings, respond to our environment, and nurture ourselves and others. When it comes to cats, the Moon plays a significant role in shaping their moods, instincts, and emotional needs. Understanding the Moon's influence on your feline companion can help you cater to their emotional well-being and provide the care they need to thrive.

The Role of the Moon in Astrology

In astrology, the Moon represents the subconscious, our instincts, and how we react to the world on an emotional level. It is connected to the feminine, maternal energy and rules over the sign of Cancer. While the Sun reflects our outward personality and identity, the Moon governs the more hidden, internal aspects of who we are. It is deeply connected to our sense of security, our habits, and our innate responses to our surroundings.

For cats, the Moon's placement in their astrological chart reveals how they experience and express emotions, their instinctual behaviors, and what they need to feel safe and secure. The Moon influences how your cat reacts to changes in their environment, how they bond with others (both humans and animals), and how they handle stress.

How the Moon Influences Your Cat's Moods

The Moon is often referred to as the "ruler of moods," and its phases and position in the zodiac can have a noticeable impact on your cat's emotional state. Just as humans experience mood swings and emotional fluctuations, cats too are influenced by the waxing and waning of the Moon.

Cats are highly sensitive creatures, and their moods can shift with the changing phases of the Moon. During the Full Moon, for instance, you might notice your cat becoming more restless, energetic, or even anxious. The heightened energy of the Full Moon can lead to more active play or, conversely, increased irritability. On the other hand, during the New Moon, your cat might be more withdrawn, preferring solitude and quiet.

Each phase of the Moon brings its own energy, which can either amplify or diminish your cat's natural tendencies. For example, if your cat is already prone to being shy or reclusive, the New Moon might intensify this behavior, leading them to seek out dark, enclosed spaces. Conversely, if your cat is naturally playful and energetic, the Full Moon might lead to more pronounced displays of these behaviors.

The Moon and Feline Instincts

The Moon is also closely linked to instincts, which are particularly strong in cats. These instincts are primal behaviors that are often automatic and subconscious, driving your cat to hunt, groom, and protect themselves. The Moon's placement in your cat's chart can offer insights into how these instincts manifest and what triggers them.

For example, a cat with the Moon in a water sign, such as Cancer, Scorpio, or Pisces, might have highly developed nurturing instincts. These cats may be more likely to "mother" their toys, other pets, or even their human companions, displaying protective behaviors and a strong desire to care for those they love. They might also be more attuned to their surroundings, sensing changes in mood or atmosphere and responding instinctively.

Conversely, a cat with the Moon in a fire sign, such as Aries, Leo, or Sagittarius, might exhibit more aggressive or bold instincts. These cats could be more prone to hunting behaviors, chasing anything that moves, and asserting their dominance within their territory. Their instincts drive them to take charge, and they may be more reactive to perceived threats or challenges.

Understanding your cat's lunar instincts can help you create an environment that satisfies their primal needs. For instance, providing plenty of hunting-style toys and opportunities for exploration can fulfill the instincts of a fire Moon cat, while a water Moon cat might appreciate a calm, nurturing space where they feel safe and secure.

The Moon and Emotional Needs

Just as the Moon governs our deepest emotional needs, it also dictates what your cat requires to feel emotionally fulfilled and secure. Each cat has unique needs based on their Moon sign, and recognizing these can help you provide the right kind of support and care.

- **Cancer Moon Cats**: These cats are highly sensitive and emotionally attuned to their environment. They need a stable, nurturing home where they feel safe and loved. Routine and familiarity are important for them, and they may become anxious or withdrawn if their environment changes too much. These cats often form strong bonds with their human companions and may become clingy or needy if they feel insecure.

- **Leo Moon Cats**: Cats with the Moon in Leo crave attention and admiration. They need to feel like they are the center of the household and often thrive in environments where they are doted upon. These cats might demand more of your time and affection, and they enjoy being pampered with toys, treats, and cozy resting places. Their emotional well-being is closely tied to how much they feel appreciated and adored.
- **Virgo Moon Cats**: Virgo Moon cats are meticulous and detail-oriented. They require a clean, orderly environment to feel emotionally balanced. These cats may be particularly sensitive to disruptions in their routine and can become stressed if their surroundings are chaotic or unclean. They find comfort in routine and predictability, and their emotional needs are met through a sense of order and control.
- **Scorpio Moon Cats**: Cats with the Moon in Scorpio are intense and deeply emotional. They need privacy and a safe space where they can retreat when they feel overwhelmed. These cats often form deep, complex bonds with their owners, but they may be wary of strangers or other animals. They require an environment where their boundaries are respected, and they may need time alone to process their emotions.
- **Pisces Moon Cats**: Pisces Moon cats are dreamy and intuitive. They need a peaceful, tranquil environment where they can relax and feel at ease. These cats are often highly empathetic and may pick up on the emotions of those around them, so it's important to maintain a calm atmosphere in the home. They might enjoy soft, comfortable bedding, soothing music, or the gentle presence of a human companion who understands their need for emotional connection.

Recognizing your cat's emotional needs based on their Moon sign allows you to provide the care and support that helps them feel secure and content. Whether it's through creating a stable routine, offering plenty of affection, or giving them the space they need, understanding these needs is key to ensuring your cat's emotional well-being.

The Moon and Feline Bonding

The Moon also influences how your cat bonds with others, whether it's with their human family members, other pets, or even their favorite toys. The lunar placement in your cat's chart can reveal how they form attachments, how they express affection, and what they need in their relationships.

Cats with a strong Moon influence may be more likely to seek out close bonds and show affection in subtle ways, such as following you from room to room, gently nudging you with their head, or curling up on your lap. These cats may also be more sensitive to your moods, responding with comfort when you're feeling down or becoming more playful when you're in high spirits.

On the other hand, cats with a less dominant Moon influence might be more independent, preferring to spend time alone or interacting on their own terms. While they may still form strong bonds, they might express their affection in less obvious ways, such as through playful antics or by bringing you "gifts" like toys or small prey.

Understanding how your cat's Moon sign affects their bonding habits can help you strengthen your relationship with them. By being attuned to their needs and preferences, you can foster a deeper connection and provide the emotional support they require.

Moon Phases and Behavioral Patterns

The Moon goes through eight distinct phases during its cycle, and each phase brings a different energy that can influence your cat's behavior. By observing your cat during these phases, you can gain insights into how the lunar cycle affects their mood and instincts.

- **New Moon**: The New Moon marks the beginning of a new cycle and is often a time of introspection and rest. During this phase, your cat might be more withdrawn, preferring quiet and solitude. It's a good time to allow them to recharge and take a break from overly stimulating activities.
- **Waxing Crescent**: As the Moon begins to grow, your cat might become more curious and exploratory. This phase is associated with growth and new beginnings, so your cat may show increased interest in new toys, activities, or even new areas of your home.
- **First Quarter**: The First Quarter Moon is a time of action and challenges. Your cat might display more assertiveness or determination during this phase, whether it's insisting on a certain spot to sleep or demanding playtime. They may also be more likely to engage in territorial behaviors, such as marking their space or asserting dominance.
- **Waxing Gibbous**: As the Moon approaches fullness, your cat might become more focused and intent on completing tasks or perfecting their routine. This phase is associated with re-

finement and attention to detail, so your cat may spend more time grooming or organizing their favorite toys.

- **Full Moon**: The Full Moon is a time of heightened energy and emotions. Your cat might be more active, restless, or even anxious during this phase. They may display more pronounced behaviors, such as intense playfulness or increased vocalization. It's important to provide them with outlets for this energy, such as interactive play or opportunities to explore.
- **Waning Gibbous**: As the Moon begins to wane, your cat might become more reflective and introspective. This phase is associated with gratitude and giving back, so your cat may show more affection or seek comfort in familiar routines.
- **Last Quarter**: The Last Quarter Moon is a time of release and letting go. Your cat might be more relaxed and willing to let go of certain behaviors or habits that no longer serve them. It's a good time to introduce new routines or changes in their environment.
- **Waning Crescent**: The final phase of the Moon's cycle is associated with rest and recuperation. Your cat may be more subdued during this time, preferring to sleep more or spend time in quiet reflection. It's a period of closure and preparation for the next cycle, so allow your cat to rest and recharge.

By aligning your cat's activities and routines with the lunar phases, you can help them maintain a balanced emotional state and cater to their natural rhythms.

Conclusion

The Moon's influence on your cat is profound, shaping their moods, instincts, and emotional needs. Understanding the lunar aspects of your cat's astrological profile allows you to provide the care and environment that best supports their emotional well-being. Whether it's through recognizing their need for security, respecting their instinctual behaviors, or aligning their routines with the lunar cycle, honoring the Moon's impact can deepen your connection with your cat and help them lead a happy, fulfilled life.

As you continue to explore the astrological influences on your cat, remember that the Moon is just one piece of the puzzle. In the following chapters, we'll delve into the other planets and celestial bodies that contribute to the unique cosmic blueprint of your feline companion. Together, these insights will help you create a harmonious and nurturing environment that aligns with the cosmic forces shaping your cat's life.

Chapter 3: Mercury and Communication

Mercury, the planet closest to the Sun, is often regarded as the messenger of the gods in mythology and the ruler of communication, intellect, and curiosity in astrology. This swift-moving planet governs how we think, process information, and express ourselves. In the context of feline astrology, Mercury's influence extends to your cat's communication style, intelligence, and insatiable curiosity. Understanding Mercury's role in your cat's astrological profile can provide deep insights into how they interact with the world, how they solve problems, and how they convey their needs and desires to you.

The Role of Mercury in Astrology

Mercury, named after the Roman messenger god, is the planet that governs all forms of communication, thought processes, and mental agility. It is associated with the way we articulate our thoughts, the speed at which we process information, and our capacity for learning and adapting. In astrology, Mercury rules over the signs of Gemini and Virgo, both of which are known for their intellectual prowess, quick thinking, and communicative nature.

For cats, Mercury's position in their astrological chart reveals how they communicate with their environment, how they learn from their experiences, and the degree of their natural curiosity. Whether through vocalizations, body language, or behaviors, Mercury influences the ways in which your cat interacts with you and the world around them.

How Mercury Influences Your Cat's Communication Style

Cats have a wide range of communication methods, from vocalizations like meows, purrs, and hisses, to more subtle cues such as tail movements, ear positions, and eye contact. Mercury's placement in your cat's chart plays a significant role in shaping how they use these methods to express themselves.

- **Vocal Cats (Mercury in Air Signs)**: Cats with Mercury in air signs—Gemini, Libra, or Aquarius—are often more vocal and communicative. They tend to use a wide variety of sounds to convey their needs, desires, and emotions. A Gemini Mercury cat, for instance, might have a particularly diverse range of meows, each with its own specific meaning, from requesting food to seeking attention. These cats are also more likely to engage in conversations with their owners, responding to your voice with their own vocalizations.

- **Expressive Body Language (Mercury in Fire Signs)**: Cats with Mercury in fire signs—Aries, Leo, or Sagittarius—often use bold and expressive body language to communicate. These cats may be more likely to use dramatic tail movements, exaggerated ear positions, and direct eye contact to make their feelings known. A Leo Mercury cat, for example, might strut confidently with their tail held high when they're feeling proud or demand attention with a playful pounce or head-butt.

- **Subtle Communicators (Mercury in Earth Signs)**: Cats with Mercury in earth signs—Taurus, Virgo, or Capricorn—tend to be more subtle in their communication. They might rely on quieter signals, such as a gentle nudge, a slow blink, or a soft purr, to convey their needs. A Virgo Mercury cat might use specific routines or habits as a way to communicate, such as sitting by their food bowl at the same time each day or grooming themselves in a certain way to indicate contentment.

- **Intuitive Communicators (Mercury in Water Signs)**: Cats with Mercury in water signs—Cancer, Scorpio, or Pisces—are often highly intuitive in their communication. These cats may sense your emotions and respond accordingly, offering comfort when you're sad or giving you space when you're stressed. A Pisces Mercury cat, for instance, might be particularly sensitive to your tone of voice or body language, responding with empathetic behaviors like curling up next to you or softly meowing in response to your emotions.

Understanding your cat's communication style, as influenced by Mercury, allows you to better interpret their signals and respond to their needs. By paying attention to the nuances of their vocalizations, body language, and routines, you can develop a deeper connection and more effectively meet their emotional and physical needs.

Mercury and Feline Intelligence

Mercury is also the planet of the mind, governing how we think, learn, and solve problems. In cats, Mercury's influence can be seen in their intelligence and cognitive abilities, including how quickly they learn new skills, how they adapt to changes, and how they solve challenges in their environment.

- **Quick Learners (Mercury in Gemini or Virgo)**: Cats with Mercury in Gemini or Virgo are often exceptionally intelligent and quick learners. These cats might pick up on new commands, routines, or tricks faster than others. A Gemini Mercury cat, for example, might quickly figure out how to open doors or solve puzzle toys, while a Virgo Mercury cat may excel at understanding and following household routines, such as where and when they are fed.

- **Problem Solvers (Mercury in Capricorn or Aquarius)**: Cats with Mercury in Capricorn or Aquarius are natural problem solvers. They tend to approach challenges methodically, often finding clever solutions to obstacles in their environment. A Capricorn Mercury cat might methodically work out how to access a hidden toy or treat, while an Aquarius Mercury cat might find unique ways to entertain themselves, such as inventing games or exploring unusual parts of the house.

- **Curious Explorers (Mercury in Sagittarius or Aries)**: Cats with Mercury in Sagittarius or Aries are driven by a strong sense of curiosity. These cats are likely to explore every nook and cranny of their environment, often getting into places you might not expect. A Sagittarius Mercury cat might be particularly adventurous, seeking out new experiences and stimuli, while an Aries Mercury cat might show determination in figuring out how things work, such as how to open cabinets or operate simple mechanisms.

- **Emotional Intelligence (Mercury in Cancer or Pisces)**: Cats with Mercury in Cancer or Pisces often display a high level of emotional intelligence. They might be particularly attuned to the emotional atmosphere of their home, understanding and responding to your feelings in subtle ways. A Cancer Mercury cat might stay close to you when you're feeling down, offering comfort through their presence, while a Pisces Mercury cat might engage in behaviors that seem almost psychic, such as anticipating your movements or needs before you express them.

Recognizing your cat's intellectual strengths and tendencies can help you provide the right kind of stimulation and challenge for their mind. Interactive toys, puzzle feeders, and new environments to explore can all be excellent ways to engage a Mercury-influenced cat's intelligence and keep them mentally stimulated.

Mercury and Curiosity

Curiosity is a hallmark of Mercury's influence. This planet drives the desire to explore, learn, and understand the world. For cats, Mercury's position in their chart can indicate how curious they are, what piques their interest, and how they satisfy their innate need to explore.

- **Inquisitive Nature (Mercury in Air Signs)**: Cats with Mercury in air signs—Gemini, Libra, or Aquarius—are often highly inquisitive. These cats are likely to investigate anything new in their environment, from a new piece of furniture to a visitor's bag. They may also be more prone to getting into things, such as exploring cupboards, drawers, or even trying to escape to explore outside. These cats are driven by a desire to learn and understand everything around them.

- **Focused Curiosity (Mercury in Earth Signs)**: Cats with Mercury in earth signs—Taurus, Virgo, or Capricorn—tend to have a more focused and practical curiosity. They are interested in things that directly affect their comfort, such as new bedding, food, or toys. These cats might also be curious about changes in their environment but will approach new situations cautiously, evaluating whether it benefits them before fully engaging.

- **Adventurous Curiosity (Mercury in Fire Signs)**: Cats with Mercury in fire signs—Aries, Leo, or Sagittarius—are often bold and adventurous in their curiosity. These cats are likely to take risks in their exploration, such as climbing to high places, jumping into unknown spaces, or trying to interact with unfamiliar animals or people. They thrive on new experiences and are always looking for the next thrill.

- **Intuitive Curiosity (Mercury in Water Signs)**: Cats with Mercury in water signs—Cancer, Scorpio, or Pisces—tend to have a more intuitive and emotional curiosity. These cats might be particularly interested in investigating areas that carry strong emotional or sensory significance, such as a new person's scent or a spot where something significant happened. Their curiosity is often tied to their emotional state, and they may explore new things based on how they feel rather than pure intellectual interest.

Understanding your cat's level of curiosity can help you create an environment that satisfies their need to explore while keeping them safe. Providing safe areas for exploration, a variety of toys, and opportunities to engage with new stimuli can help channel their curiosity in positive ways.

Mercury Retrograde and Your Cat

Mercury retrograde is a well-known astrological event that occurs several times a year when Mercury appears to move backward in the sky. During this period, communication, travel, and technology often experience disruptions, and it's not uncommon for both humans and animals to feel the effects.

Cats, being sensitive creatures, can also be affected by Mercury retrograde. You might notice that your cat becomes more restless, confused, or anxious during this time. They may miscommunicate their needs, leading to misunderstandings between you and your cat, or they might become more accident-prone, knocking things over or getting into trouble more often than usual.

During Mercury retrograde, it's important to be patient with your cat and pay extra attention to their communication cues. Double-check that their needs are met, and try to maintain a stable and familiar routine to help them feel secure. If your cat seems particularly affected, providing extra comfort and reassurance can help them navigate the challenging energy of Mercury retrograde.

Conclusion

Mercury's influence on your cat is multifaceted, shaping their communication style, intelligence, and curiosity. By understanding how Mercury affects your cat, you can better interpret their signals, provide the mental stimulation they need, and create an environment that supports their natural inquisitiveness. Whether your cat is a quick-witted Gemini or a methodical Virgo, Mercury's energy plays a crucial role in how they interact with the world and express themselves.

As you continue to explore the astrological influences on your cat, remember that Mercury is just one part of their cosmic blueprint. In the following chapters, we'll delve into the other planets and celestial bodies that contribute to your cat's unique personality and behavior, providing a comprehensive understanding of how the cosmos shapes the life of your feline companion.

Chapter 4: Venus and Affection

Venus, the planet of love, beauty, and harmony, is often associated with all things related to affection, attraction, and pleasure. In astrology, Venus governs our approach to relationships, our aesthetic preferences, and the ways we express and receive love. For cats, Venus plays a significant role in shaping their affectionate nature, how they bond with humans and other pets, and even their preferences for certain textures, colors, and environments. Understanding the influence of Venus in your cat's astrological chart can provide deep insights into how they express love, what makes them feel comfortable, and how they form and maintain relationships.

The Role of Venus in Astrology

Venus, named after the Roman goddess of love and beauty, is the planet that governs everything related to affection, attraction, and harmony. It is associated with the way we form relationships, what we find beautiful, and how we seek comfort and pleasure in life. In astrology, Venus rules over the signs of Taurus and Libra, both of which are known for their love of beauty, peace, and relational harmony.

For cats, Venus's position in their astrological chart reveals how they express affection, what they find comforting and pleasurable, and how they interact with both their human companions and other animals. Whether through physical closeness, grooming behaviors, or the pursuit of comfort, Venus influences the ways in which your cat shows love and seeks out pleasurable experiences.

How Venus Influences Your Cat's Affectionate Nature

Venus is the planet of love, and its placement in your cat's chart can significantly affect how they express affection. Just as Venus influences human relationships, it also governs how cats form bonds and show love to those they care about.

- **Cuddly Cats (Venus in Taurus or Cancer)**: Cats with Venus in Taurus or Cancer are often exceptionally affectionate. These cats love physical closeness and will often seek out opportunities to cuddle with their human companions. A Taurus Venus cat, for example, may enjoy long periods of snuggling, preferring to sit on your lap or curl up next to you on the couch. These cats find comfort in physical touch and are likely to purr contentedly when they're close to you. Cancer Venus cats, on the other hand, might express their affection through nurturing behaviors, such as gently grooming you or other pets in the household.

- **Playful Affection (Venus in Leo or Sagittarius)**: Cats with Venus in Leo or Sagittarius often show their affection through playfulness. These cats may express love by engaging in interactive play, bringing you toys, or performing playful antics to get your attention. A Leo Venus cat might enjoy playing games where they can show off their agility and strength, such as chasing after toys or climbing to high perches, all while seeking your admiration. Sagittarius Venus cats, on the other hand, might express their affection through adventurous play, such as exploring new areas of the house with you or initiating playful chases.

- **Subtle Affection (Venus in Virgo or Capricorn)**: Cats with Venus in Virgo or Capricorn may express their affection in more subtle ways. These cats might not be as overtly cuddly as others, but they still show love through their actions and loyalty. A Virgo Venus cat, for example, might demonstrate affection by sticking to a routine that involves spending quiet time with you, such as sitting nearby while you work or gently nudging you when it's time for bed. Capricorn Venus cats might express love through protective behaviors, such as keeping a watchful eye on their territory and ensuring you're safe.

- **Social Affection (Venus in Libra or Aquarius)**: Cats with Venus in Libra or Aquarius are often highly social and enjoy forming bonds with multiple members of the household, including other pets. These cats might express their affection through social interactions, such as rubbing against you, giving gentle head butts, or even grooming other animals. A Libra Venus cat, for example, might be particularly charming, seeking to maintain harmony in the household by being affectionate with everyone. Aquarius Venus cats might show their love in more unconventional ways, such as bringing you gifts (like a toy or a found object) or engaging in unique social behaviors that make you smile.

- **Intuitive Affection (Venus in Pisces or Scorpio)**: Cats with Venus in Pisces or Scorpio often express their affection in deeply intuitive and emotional ways. These cats might be particularly sensitive to your moods and will seek to comfort you when you're feeling down. A Pisces Venus cat might curl up next to you and purr softly, offering quiet companionship during times of stress or sadness. Scorpio Venus cats might form intense bonds with their human companions, showing their love through loyalty and deep, meaningful eye contact.

Understanding how Venus influences your cat's affectionate nature allows you to recognize and reciprocate their expressions of love, strengthening the bond between you and your feline friend. By being attuned to the ways your cat shows affection, whether through cuddles, play, or subtle gestures, you can create an environment where they feel secure and loved.

Venus and Feline Relationships

Venus governs relationships, and its placement in your cat's chart can offer insights into how they interact with other animals and humans. Whether your cat is a social butterfly or prefers one-on-one interactions, Venus's influence plays a key role in their relational dynamics.

- **Bonding with Humans (Venus in Cancer or Libra)**: Cats with Venus in Cancer or Libra are often strongly bonded to their human companions. These cats may form close, loving relationships with the people they live with, seeking out their company and expressing affection regularly. A Cancer Venus cat might be particularly attached to a single person in the household, following them around and seeking comfort from them during times of stress. Libra Venus cats, on the other hand, might spread their affection evenly among all members of the household, enjoying social interactions and maintaining harmony within the group.
- **Relationships with Other Pets (Venus in Gemini or Sagittarius)**: Cats with Venus in Gemini or Sagittarius tend to be more social with other animals. These cats might enjoy the company of other pets, engaging in playful interactions and forming close bonds with their fellow furry friends. A Gemini Venus cat might be particularly communicative with other pets, using a variety of vocalizations and body language to express themselves. Sagittarius Venus cats, on the other hand, might enjoy playing with other animals, especially if it involves chasing, wrestling, or exploring together.
- **Selective Relationships (Venus in Scorpio or Capricorn)**: Cats with Venus in Scorpio or Capricorn may be more selective in their relationships, forming deep bonds with a few individuals rather than being broadly social. These cats might take their time to warm up to new people or animals, but once they do, the bond is often intense and enduring. A Scorpio Venus cat might be particularly loyal to one person or pet, showing affection through protective behaviors and deep connection. Capricorn Venus cats might prefer relationships based on trust and respect, showing their love through consistent, reliable behavior.

- **Independent Relationships (Venus in Aquarius or Aries)**: Cats with Venus in Aquarius or Aries might value their independence in relationships, enjoying social interactions on their own terms. These cats might be affectionate, but they also need their space and may not always seek out constant companionship. An Aquarius Venus cat might be more aloof, choosing to interact when they feel like it and retreating when they need alone time. Aries Venus cats might show affection in bursts of energy, enjoying playtime or cuddles but also needing time to themselves to recharge.

- **Nurturing Relationships (Venus in Taurus or Virgo)**: Cats with Venus in Taurus or Virgo might take on a nurturing role in their relationships, especially with other animals. These cats might be seen grooming other pets, taking care of younger animals, or even acting protectively towards those they love. A Taurus Venus cat might show their nurturing side by ensuring that everyone in the household is comfortable, often checking on their human and animal companions to make sure they're okay. Virgo Venus cats might be meticulous in their care, making sure that everyone's needs are met, from food and water to emotional comfort.

Understanding how Venus influences your cat's relationships can help you foster positive interactions between them and other pets or people. By recognizing your cat's social needs and preferences, you can create an environment that supports healthy, loving relationships, whether they prefer to bond closely with one individual or enjoy the company of many.

Venus and Aesthetic Preferences

Venus is not only the planet of love and relationships but also of beauty and aesthetics. It governs what we find pleasing to the eye and what brings us comfort and joy in our environment. For cats, Venus's placement in their chart can reveal their preferences for certain textures, colors, and overall surroundings.

- **Comfort and Luxury (Venus in Taurus or Libra)**: Cats with Venus in Taurus or Libra often have a strong preference for comfort and luxury. These cats might be drawn to soft, plush bedding, cozy blankets, and warm, inviting spaces. A Taurus Venus cat might prefer to nap in the softest spot in the house, whether it's a cushioned chair, a pile of blankets, or a sun-drenched windowsill. Libra Venus cats, on the other hand, might appreciate a well-balanced and aesthetically pleasing environment, enjoying spaces that are not only comfortable but also harmonious in color and design.

- **Simplicity and Cleanliness (Venus in Virgo or Capricorn)**: Cats with Venus in Virgo or Capricorn might prefer simpler, more orderly environments. These cats might be more sensitive to clutter or disarray, preferring spaces that are clean, organized, and functional. A Virgo Venus cat might gravitate towards neatly arranged bedding or prefer a space where they can keep an eye on their surroundings. Capricorn Venus cats might enjoy environments that are both practical and comfortable, perhaps favoring sturdy, well-made furniture or spaces where they can observe the household from a safe vantage point.

- **Bold and Bright (Venus in Leo or Sagittarius)**: Cats with Venus in Leo or Sagittarius might be attracted to bold, bright colors and dynamic environments. These cats might enjoy spaces that are vibrant and full of life, with plenty of stimuli to keep them engaged. A Leo Venus cat might appreciate a space that reflects their regal nature, perhaps enjoying a spot where they can be the center of attention or a perch with a commanding view. Sagittarius Venus cats might enjoy environments that offer opportunities for exploration, such as a window with a view of the outside world or a room filled with interesting textures and objects.

- **Unique and Unconventional (Venus in Aquarius or Pisces)**: Cats with Venus in Aquarius or Pisces might have more unconventional aesthetic preferences. These cats might be drawn to unusual textures, quirky objects, or spaces that offer a sense of mystery and intrigue. An Aquarius Venus cat might enjoy exploring odd nooks and crannies, finding comfort in spaces that are off the beaten path or filled with unique items. Pisces Venus cats might be drawn to soft, dreamy environments, perhaps enjoying a space filled with soft lighting, gentle music, or flowing fabrics.

- **Warm and Cozy (Venus in Cancer or Scorpio)**: Cats with Venus in Cancer or Scorpio might prefer warm, cozy environments that offer a sense of security and intimacy. These cats might be drawn to spaces that feel safe and comforting, such as a quiet corner of the house, a covered bed, or a space that offers privacy. A Cancer Venus cat might enjoy napping in a spot that feels like a "nest," surrounded by soft blankets or pillows. Scorpio Venus cats might prefer darker, more enclosed spaces where they can retreat and feel protected from the outside world.

Understanding your cat's aesthetic preferences can help you create a living space that aligns with their Venusian tendencies, making them feel more comfortable and content in their environment. Whether it's providing them with a cozy, plush bed, arranging their favorite toys in a neat and orderly fashion, or creating a space filled with interesting textures and colors, catering to your cat's aesthetic preferences can enhance their overall well-being.

Conclusion

Venus's influence on your cat is multifaceted, shaping their affectionate nature, relationships, and aesthetic preferences. By understanding how Venus affects your cat, you can better interpret their expressions of love, foster positive interactions with others, and create an environment that brings them comfort and joy. Whether your cat is a cuddly Taurus or a playful Leo, Venus's energy plays a crucial role in how they relate to the world and those around them.

As you continue to explore the astrological influences on your cat, remember that Venus is just one piece of the puzzle. In the following chapters, we'll delve into the other planets and celestial bodies that contribute to your cat's unique personality and behavior, providing a comprehensive understanding of how the cosmos shapes the life of your feline companion.

Chapter 5: Mars and Action

Mars, the fiery red planet named after the Roman god of war, is the celestial body that governs energy, drive, aggression, and action in astrology. Often associated with raw power and assertiveness, Mars is the force that propels us into action, fuels our ambitions, and sometimes sparks conflict. In the context of feline astrology, Mars's influence can be seen in your cat's activity levels, playfulness, aggression, and territorial instincts. Understanding Mars's role in your cat's astrological chart can offer valuable insights into their energetic needs, how they express anger or frustration, and their natural tendencies toward defending their space.

The Role of Mars in Astrology

In astrology, Mars represents our physical energy, desire for action, and the way we assert ourselves. It is associated with courage, competition, and the primal instincts that drive us to survive and thrive. Mars rules over the signs of Aries and Scorpio, both of which are known for their intensity, determination, and strong will.

For cats, Mars's placement in their astrological chart reveals how they express their energy, how they engage in play and exploration, and how they respond to perceived threats or challenges. Mars influences a cat's drive to hunt, their level of physical activity, and their propensity for aggressive behavior, whether in play or in defense of their territory.

How Mars Influences Your Cat's Activity Levels

Mars is the planet of action, and its placement in your cat's chart plays a significant role in determining their natural energy levels and activity preferences. Whether your cat is a high-energy dynamo or a more laid-back companion, Mars's influence is at the core of their physical behavior.

- **High-Energy Cats (Mars in Fire Signs)**: Cats with Mars in fire signs—Aries, Leo, or Sagittarius—are often bursting with energy. These cats are typically very active, enjoying lots of playtime, exploration, and physical exertion. A Mars in Aries cat, for instance, might be particularly enthusiastic about chasing toys, running around the house, or climbing to the highest point they can reach. They are driven by a need to constantly be in motion, and they thrive on activities that challenge their physical abilities. A Leo Mars cat might channel their energy into play that allows them to showcase their strength and agility, often engaging in activities that allow them to "perform" or take center stage. Sagittarius Mars cats might have a love for adventure, enjoying activities that allow them to explore new spaces or take on new challenges.

- **Moderately Active Cats (Mars in Air Signs)**: Cats with Mars in air signs—Gemini, Libra, or Aquarius—tend to have a balanced approach to activity. These cats are often energetic, but they also enjoy mental stimulation and social interaction. A Mars in Gemini cat might split their time between bursts of play and periods of curiosity-driven exploration, investigating every nook and cranny while still enjoying interactive games. Libra Mars cats may prefer play that involves social interaction, whether with humans or other animals, and may be more inclined to engage in play when it's part of a shared activity. Aquarius Mars cats might enjoy activities that are unique or unconventional, showing a preference for toys or games that are mentally stimulating as well as physically engaging.

- **Low to Moderate Activity Cats (Mars in Earth Signs)**: Cats with Mars in earth signs—Taurus, Virgo, or Capricorn—tend to have a more measured approach to activity. These cats are usually more grounded and may prefer structured or purposeful play. A Mars in Taurus cat might enjoy activities that involve comfort and routine, such as leisurely chasing a favorite toy or playing in a familiar environment. They may not be as hyperactive as their fire sign counterparts but will engage in play that feels rewarding or satisfying. Virgo Mars cats might enjoy play that is methodical and precise, such as carefully stalking a toy or engaging in activities that mimic hunting. Capricorn Mars cats might be more focused on achieving specific goals during play, showing persistence in catching their "prey" or completing a physical challenge.

- **Varied Activity Levels (Mars in Water Signs)**: Cats with Mars in water signs—Cancer, Scorpio, or Pisces—often have activity levels that are closely tied to their emotions. These cats may have bursts of energy that coincide with their mood, becoming very active during moments of excitement or stress. A Mars in Cancer cat might show increased activity when they feel particularly secure or when playing in an environment that feels like "home." Scorpio Mars cats might channel their energy into intense, focused play, often showing a deep concentration when stalking or chasing toys. Pisces Mars cats might have a more whimsical approach to play, enjoying activities that engage their imagination or mimic their fluid, dreamy nature.

Understanding your cat's natural energy levels as influenced by Mars can help you create an environment that meets their physical needs. Providing appropriate outlets for their energy, such as interactive toys, climbing structures, or safe outdoor spaces, can help keep them healthy and happy.

Mars and Feline Aggression

Mars is also the planet of aggression, governing how we express anger, frustration, and assertiveness. For cats, Mars's influence can be seen in their responses to perceived threats, their territorial behavior, and how they engage in aggressive play.

- **Assertive Cats (Mars in Aries or Scorpio)**: Cats with Mars in Aries or Scorpio are often very assertive and may display strong territorial instincts. These cats might be quick to defend their space, whether from other animals or unfamiliar humans. A Mars in Aries cat might not hesitate to assert their dominance through hissing, swatting, or chasing away intruders, showing little fear in confrontational situations. Scorpio Mars cats might display more calculated aggression, often responding to perceived threats with intense focus and determination. These cats may also be more prone to holding grudges, reacting aggressively if they feel their trust has been violated.
- **Playful Aggression (Mars in Leo or Sagittarius)**: Cats with Mars in Leo or Sagittarius may express aggression in a more playful manner. These cats might enjoy rough-and-tumble play, often pouncing on toys or engaging in mock battles with other animals. A Mars in Leo cat might channel their aggression into playful displays of strength, showing off their physical prowess while still maintaining a sense of fun. Sagittarius Mars cats might enjoy chasing games or activities that allow them to "hunt" in a playful, non-threatening way. While these cats can be aggressive during play, it's usually in good spirits and rarely crosses into genuine hostility.
- **Reserved Aggression (Mars in Taurus or Capricorn)**: Cats with Mars in Taurus or Capricorn might be more reserved in their aggression, showing their assertiveness only when absolutely necessary. These cats are typically more controlled and may only display aggression

when they feel their boundaries have been crossed. A Mars in Taurus cat might defend their territory or possessions with a calm but firm stance, using body language to signal their dominance without immediately resorting to physical confrontation. Capricorn Mars cats might approach aggression with a strategic mindset, carefully choosing when and how to assert themselves in a way that is calculated and efficient.

- **Emotional Aggression (Mars in Cancer or Pisces)**: Cats with Mars in Cancer or Pisces may express aggression that is closely tied to their emotional state. These cats might become aggressive when they feel threatened, stressed, or overwhelmed, often reacting in ways that are more emotional than calculated. A Mars in Cancer cat might lash out if they feel their home or loved ones are in danger, showing protectiveness that is driven by a deep emotional connection to their environment. Pisces Mars cats might display aggression in situations where they feel misunderstood or cornered, often reacting with a mix of fear and frustration. These cats may also be more prone to passive-aggressive behavior, such as sulking or withdrawing when upset.

Understanding how Mars influences your cat's aggression can help you manage and mitigate any problematic behaviors. By recognizing the triggers that lead to aggression and providing appropriate outlets for their assertive tendencies, you can help your cat maintain a healthy balance between assertiveness and harmony.

Mars and Playfulness

Playfulness is another aspect of Mars's influence, as this planet governs physical activity and the desire to engage in challenging or stimulating activities. For cats, play is often a way to express their natural hunting instincts, burn off excess energy, and explore their environment.

- **Energetic Play (Mars in Fire Signs)**: Cats with Mars in fire signs—Aries, Leo, or Sagittarius—are often highly playful and enjoy engaging in activities that allow them to expend their abundant energy. These cats might love chasing fast-moving toys, engaging in high-energy games like fetch, or exploring their environment with enthusiasm. A Mars in Aries cat might particularly enjoy toys that mimic the thrill of the chase, such as laser pointers or feather wands that dart around unpredictably. Leo Mars cats might prefer toys that allow them to "show off" their skills, such as climbing trees or catching airborne toys. Sagittarius Mars cats might enjoy activities that involve exploration, such as interactive puzzles or toys that require them to "hunt" for treats.

- **Interactive Play (Mars in Air Signs)**: Cats with Mars in air signs—Gemini, Libra, or Aquarius—often enjoy interactive play that involves both physical and mental stimulation. These cats might prefer games that engage their intellect as well as their bodies, such as puzzle feeders or toys that require problem-solving skills. A Mars in Gemini cat might enjoy a variety of different toys and activities, often switching between them to keep themselves entertained. Libra Mars cats might enjoy playing with other animals or people, engaging in games that foster social interaction and cooperation. Aquarius Mars cats might be drawn to unique or unconventional toys, enjoying play that challenges their curiosity and creativity.

- **Methodical Play (Mars in Earth Signs)**: Cats with Mars in earth signs—Taurus, Virgo, or Capricorn—might approach play in a more methodical and purposeful manner. These cats may prefer games that mimic real-life scenarios, such as hunting or stalking. A Mars in Taurus cat might enjoy slow, deliberate play, such as carefully stalking a toy mouse or methodically batting at a ball. Virgo Mars cats might enjoy activities that require precision and focus, such as playing with interactive toys that involve carefully timed movements. Capricorn Mars cats might approach play with a sense of purpose, engaging in activities that challenge their physical and mental abilities in a structured way.

- **Imaginative Play (Mars in Water Signs)**: Cats with Mars in water signs—Cancer, Scorpio, or Pisces—often engage in play that is imaginative and emotionally driven. These cats might enjoy activities that allow them to express their emotions or explore their inner world. A Mars in Cancer cat might enjoy play that involves nurturing or caring for toys, such as carrying a stuffed animal around or "cuddling" with a soft toy. Scorpio Mars cats might engage in intense, focused play, often showing a deep concentration when stalking or catching their "prey." Pisces Mars cats might enjoy dreamy, whimsical play, such as chasing light reflections or playing with soft, flowing fabrics.

Understanding your cat's play preferences as influenced by Mars can help you provide the right types of toys and activities to keep them engaged and satisfied. Whether your cat prefers high-energy games, interactive puzzles, or imaginative play, catering to their Mars-driven tendencies can enhance their overall well-being and happiness.

Mars and Territorial Behavior

Territorial behavior is another area where Mars's influence is strongly felt. As the planet of assertiveness and defense, Mars governs how your cat protects their space and responds to perceived intrusions.

- **Strong Territorial Instincts (Mars in Aries or Scorpio)**: Cats with Mars in Aries or Scorpio often have strong territorial instincts. These cats are likely to be very protective of their space, whether it's their favorite sleeping spot, food bowl, or the entire house. A Mars in Aries cat might be quick to assert their dominance, using body language or vocalizations to warn other animals or people to stay out of their territory. Scorpio Mars cats might be more strategic in their approach, carefully observing intruders before deciding how to react. These cats are likely to be very aware of their surroundings and may become anxious or aggressive if they feel their territory is being threatened.

- **Balanced Territoriality (Mars in Leo or Capricorn)**: Cats with Mars in Leo or Capricorn might display a more balanced approach to territorial behavior. These cats are likely to be protective of their space, but they may also be more discerning about what they consider a threat. A Mars in Leo cat might assert their territorial boundaries in a confident, commanding manner, often using their presence and posture to deter intruders. Capricorn Mars cats might take a more practical approach, defending their territory when necessary but otherwise maintaining a calm, controlled demeanor.

- **Social Territoriality (Mars in Libra or Aquarius)**: Cats with Mars in Libra or Aquarius might have a more social approach to territorial behavior. These cats are likely to be protective of their space, but they may also be more willing to share it with others, especially if they feel a strong bond with the other animals or people in their environment. A Mars in Libra cat might prefer to maintain harmony in their territory, using subtle cues to establish boundaries without resorting to aggression. Aquarius Mars cats might be more open to sharing their space, especially if they find the other animals or people interesting or stimulating.

- **Emotional Territoriality (Mars in Cancer or Pisces)**: Cats with Mars in Cancer or Pisces may display territorial behavior that is closely tied to their emotional state. These cats are likely to be protective of spaces that hold emotional significance for them, such as their sleeping area, favorite toys, or places where they feel safe and secure. A Mars in Cancer cat might become particularly defensive of their home and family, showing protectiveness towards the people or animals they care about. Pisces Mars cats might have a more fluid approach to territoriality, defending their space when they feel threatened but otherwise being more adaptable to changes in their environment.

Understanding your cat's territorial behavior as influenced by Mars can help you manage potential conflicts and create a peaceful, secure environment for them. By recognizing their need to assert their boundaries and providing them with safe, designated spaces, you can help your cat feel more confident and secure in their home.

Conclusion

Mars's influence on your cat is dynamic and multifaceted, shaping their activity levels, aggression, playfulness, and territorial behavior. By understanding how Mars affects your cat, you can better meet their physical and emotional needs, whether through providing the right types of play, managing their energy levels, or creating a secure environment that respects their territorial instincts. Whether your cat is an energetic Aries or a focused Scorpio, Mars's energy plays a crucial role in how they interact with the world and express their natural instincts.

As you continue to explore the astrological influences on your cat, remember that Mars is just one piece of the puzzle. In the following chapters, we'll delve into the other planets and celestial bodies that contribute to your cat's unique personality and behavior, providing a comprehensive understanding of how the cosmos shapes the life of your feline companion.

Chapter 6: Jupiter and Growth

Jupiter, the largest planet in our solar system, is often associated with expansion, growth, abundance, and good fortune in astrology. As the planet of wisdom and opportunity, Jupiter brings a sense of optimism, generosity, and exploration. For cats, Jupiter's influence is significant in shaping their overall growth—both physical and emotional—as well as their sense of luck and happiness. Understanding Jupiter's role in your cat's astrological chart can offer valuable insights into their development, their experiences of joy and fulfillment, and the ways in which they attract positive experiences and opportunities into their lives.

The Role of Jupiter in Astrology

In astrology, Jupiter is known as the planet of expansion and abundance. It governs growth, both in terms of personal development and the expansion of one's horizons. Jupiter is associated with wisdom, higher learning, and the pursuit of knowledge, as well as with luck, optimism, and the capacity for joy. It rules over the signs of Sagittarius and Pisces, both of which are known for their expansive, philosophical, and generous natures.

For cats, Jupiter's placement in their astrological chart reveals how they experience growth and development throughout their lives, how they express their natural curiosity and desire for exploration, and how they attract luck and positive experiences. Jupiter influences your cat's overall sense of happiness and well-being, shaping their outlook on life and their ability to embrace opportunities for growth and enrichment.

How Jupiter Influences Your Cat's Growth

Jupiter's influence on growth is expansive, affecting both the physical and emotional development of your cat. Whether it's their growth from kittenhood to adulthood or their emotional maturation over time, Jupiter plays a key role in guiding your cat's journey of growth and evolution.

- **Physical Growth (Jupiter in Earth Signs)**: Cats with Jupiter in earth signs—Taurus, Virgo, or Capricorn—often experience steady, reliable physical growth. These cats may develop a strong, sturdy physique, with a robust constitution that reflects Jupiter's expansive influence. A Jupiter in Taurus cat, for example, might grow to be particularly solid and muscular, with a strong appetite and a love for the comforts of life. Virgo Jupiter cats might have a more refined, lean build, with a focus on health and well-being that influences their growth patterns. Capricorn Jupiter cats might develop a well-proportioned, athletic physique, reflecting their disciplined approach to life and growth.

- **Emotional Growth (Jupiter in Water Signs)**: Cats with Jupiter in water signs—Cancer, Scorpio, or Pisces—may experience profound emotional growth throughout their lives. These cats are often deeply intuitive and sensitive, with a strong connection to their inner emotional world. A Jupiter in Cancer cat might show emotional growth through their deepening bonds with their human companions, becoming more nurturing and affectionate over time. Scorpio Jupiter cats might experience emotional growth through transformative experiences, developing resilience and inner strength as they navigate life's challenges. Pisces Jupiter cats might show growth in their empathy and compassion, becoming more attuned to the emotions of those around them and offering comfort and support when needed.

- **Intellectual Growth (Jupiter in Air Signs)**: Cats with Jupiter in air signs—Gemini, Libra, or Aquarius—often show significant intellectual growth, driven by their natural curiosity and desire for knowledge. These cats are likely to engage in behaviors that stimulate their minds, such as exploring new environments, solving puzzles, or learning new tricks. A Jupiter in Gemini cat might show intellectual growth through their ability to learn quickly, adapting to new situations with ease and curiosity. Libra Jupiter cats might develop a strong sense of fairness and balance, showing growth in their ability to navigate social interactions and relationships. Aquarius Jupiter cats might show growth through their innovative thinking, finding unique solutions to problems and exploring new ways of interacting with the world.

- **Spiritual Growth (Jupiter in Fire Signs)**: Cats with Jupiter in fire signs—Aries, Leo, or Sagittarius—often experience growth through adventure and exploration. These cats are likely to be driven by a sense of purpose and a desire to expand their horizons, whether through physical exploration or spiritual growth. A Jupiter in Aries cat might show growth through their courage and willingness to take on new challenges, becoming more confident and assertive as they mature. Leo Jupiter cats might experience growth through their creative expression and leadership, developing a strong sense of self and a desire to shine in all they do.

Sagittarius Jupiter cats might show growth through their love of adventure and exploration, constantly seeking out new experiences and opportunities for learning.

Understanding how Jupiter influences your cat's growth can help you support their development, whether through providing opportunities for exploration, fostering emotional connections, or encouraging intellectual stimulation. By recognizing the ways in which your cat is naturally inclined to grow, you can create an environment that nurtures their development and helps them reach their full potential.

Jupiter and Feline Luck

Jupiter is often referred to as the planet of luck, bringing opportunities and good fortune to those it touches. For cats, Jupiter's influence can manifest as a natural ability to attract positive experiences, whether it's finding the coziest spot in the house, making new friends, or stumbling upon hidden treasures.

- **Attracting Opportunities (Jupiter in Fire Signs)**: Cats with Jupiter in fire signs—Aries, Leo, or Sagittarius—are often naturally lucky, attracting opportunities for adventure, play, and excitement. These cats might seem to always find the best places to explore, the most engaging toys, or the most interesting new experiences. A Jupiter in Aries cat might have a knack for finding the most thrilling activities, often leading the charge in playtime or discovering new areas to explore. Leo Jupiter cats might attract attention and admiration wherever they go, often finding themselves in the spotlight and enjoying the affection and praise of those around them. Sagittarius Jupiter cats might be particularly fortunate in their adventures, often discovering new and exciting things that bring them joy and satisfaction.
- **Social Luck (Jupiter in Air Signs)**: Cats with Jupiter in air signs—Gemini, Libra, or Aquarius—often experience luck in their social interactions, attracting positive relationships and friendships with ease. These cats might be naturally charming and sociable, easily making friends with other animals or winning the affection of their human companions. A Jupiter in Gemini cat might be particularly skilled at communicating their needs, often attracting the attention and care they desire from others. Libra Jupiter cats might excel in creating harmony and balance in their relationships, often finding themselves surrounded by love and support.

Aquarius Jupiter cats might attract unique and interesting friendships, often forming bonds with animals or people who share their sense of curiosity and adventure.

- **Material Luck (Jupiter in Earth Signs)**: Cats with Jupiter in earth signs—Taurus, Virgo, or Capricorn—might experience luck in the form of material comforts and stability. These cats might be particularly good at finding the coziest spots in the house, the tastiest treats, or the most comfortable beds. A Jupiter in Taurus cat might seem to always find themselves in the most luxurious and comfortable surroundings, enjoying the finer things in life with ease. Virgo Jupiter cats might attract opportunities for health and well-being, often finding the best foods, supplements, or care routines that support their physical and emotional health. Capricorn Jupiter cats might be naturally lucky in achieving their goals, often finding themselves in positions of authority or success within their environment.
- **Emotional Luck (Jupiter in Water Signs)**: Cats with Jupiter in water signs—Cancer, Scorpio, or Pisces—might experience luck in the form of emotional fulfillment and deep connections. These cats might be particularly fortunate in forming strong bonds with their human companions, often attracting love, care, and emotional support. A Jupiter in Cancer cat might find themselves surrounded by a loving and nurturing environment, often attracting the affection and attention they crave. Scorpio Jupiter cats might attract transformative experiences that help them grow and evolve, often finding themselves in situations that lead to deep emotional fulfillment. Pisces Jupiter cats might be naturally lucky in finding comfort and peace, often attracting soothing and supportive environments that help them feel safe and secure.

Understanding how Jupiter influences your cat's luck can help you recognize and support the positive experiences they attract into their lives. Whether it's through fostering their natural curiosity, supporting their social interactions, or providing a comfortable and nurturing environment, you can help your cat make the most of Jupiter's influence and enjoy a life filled with opportunities and good fortune.

Jupiter and Feline Happiness

Jupiter is also the planet of joy and happiness, influencing your cat's overall sense of well-being and contentment. A cat with a strong Jupiter influence is likely to be optimistic, joyful, and generally happy with their life and surroundings.

- **Joyful Exploration (Jupiter in Fire Signs)**: Cats with Jupiter in fire signs—Aries, Leo, or Sagittarius—often find happiness in exploration and adventure. These cats are likely to be most content when they have the freedom to roam, play, and discover new things. A Jupiter in Aries cat might find joy in physical challenges, such as climbing, jumping, or engaging in high-energy play. Leo Jupiter cats might be happiest when they are the center of attention, enjoying the admiration and affection of their human companions. Sagittarius Jupiter cats might find their greatest happiness in exploration, whether it's exploring new areas of the house, engaging in outdoor adventures, or discovering new toys and activities.

- **Social Happiness (Jupiter in Air Signs)**: Cats with Jupiter in air signs—Gemini, Libra, or Aquarius—are likely to find happiness in social interactions and relationships. These cats are often happiest when they are surrounded by others, whether it's their human family members, other pets, or even new acquaintances. A Jupiter in Gemini cat might find joy in engaging in playful conversations, whether through vocalizations or body language, often seeking out interaction and communication. Libra Jupiter cats might be happiest in harmonious, balanced environments where they can enjoy the company of others without conflict. Aquarius Jupiter cats might find happiness in unique social interactions, enjoying relationships that are stimulating, interesting, and full of shared experiences.

- **Comfort and Contentment (Jupiter in Earth Signs)**: Cats with Jupiter in earth signs—Taurus, Virgo, or Capricorn—often find happiness in comfort, stability, and routine. These cats are likely to be most content when they have a comfortable, secure environment where they can relax and enjoy life's simple pleasures. A Jupiter in Taurus cat might find happiness in the comfort of a warm, soft bed, a tasty meal, or a gentle petting session. Virgo Jupiter cats might be happiest when they have a structured routine that supports their health and well-being, enjoying the predictability and order that comes with a well-maintained environment. Capricorn Jupiter cats might find happiness in achieving their goals, whether it's successfully catching a toy, maintaining their territory, or simply enjoying the fruits of their labor in a well-earned rest.

- **Emotional Fulfillment (Jupiter in Water Signs)**: Cats with Jupiter in water signs—Cancer, Scorpio, or Pisces—often find happiness in emotional connections and deep, meaningful experiences. These cats are likely to be most content when they feel loved, secure, and emotionally fulfilled. A Jupiter in Cancer cat might find happiness in the warmth and security of a loving home, often seeking out affection and comfort from their human companions. Scorpio Jupiter cats might be happiest when they are engaged in deep, transformative experiences, whether it's through intense play, exploration, or bonding with others. Pisces Jupiter cats might find happiness in dreamy, soothing environments, enjoying the peace and tranquility that comes from being in a safe, comforting space.

Understanding how Jupiter influences your cat's happiness can help you create an environment that supports their well-being and contentment. Whether it's through providing opportunities for exploration, fostering social interactions, or creating a comfortable, nurturing space, you can help your cat experience the joy and fulfillment that Jupiter brings.

Conclusion

Jupiter's influence on your cat is expansive and uplifting, shaping their growth, luck, and overall happiness. By understanding how Jupiter affects your cat, you can support their development, recognize the positive experiences they attract, and create an environment that nurtures their joy and well-being. Whether your cat is an adventurous Sagittarius or a nurturing Cancer, Jupiter's energy plays a crucial role in helping them live a life filled with growth, opportunity, and happiness.

As you continue to explore the astrological influences on your cat, remember that Jupiter is just one piece of the puzzle. In the following chapters, we'll delve into the other planets and celestial bodies that contribute to your cat's unique personality and behavior, providing a comprehensive understanding of how the cosmos shapes the life of your feline companion.

Chapter 7: Saturn and Discipline

Saturn, the great taskmaster of the zodiac, is a planet often associated with discipline, boundaries, responsibility, and structure. In astrology, Saturn's influence can be both challenging and rewarding, teaching us the importance of hard work, perseverance, and the necessity of limitations. For cats, Saturn's presence in their astrological chart plays a crucial role in shaping their sense of discipline, their understanding of boundaries, and their approach to responsibility. By exploring Saturn's impact on your cat, you can gain a deeper understanding of how they respond to rules, their behavior within the household, and how they manage their natural instincts within a structured environment.

The Role of Saturn in Astrology

Saturn, named after the Roman god of time and harvest, is a planet that governs the principles of order, discipline, and maturity. It is associated with the challenges and lessons that come from facing limitations and the rewards that come from meeting those challenges with patience and diligence. Saturn rules over the signs of Capricorn and traditionally Aquarius, both of which are known for their focus on structure, responsibility, and long-term planning.

For cats, Saturn's placement in their astrological chart reveals how they approach the concept of discipline, how they navigate the boundaries set by their environment, and how they fulfill their responsibilities—whether that means maintaining their territory, following household rules, or managing their natural instincts within the confines of domestic life. Saturn also influences a cat's ability to learn from experience and adapt to the expectations placed upon them.

Saturn's Influence on Your Cat's Sense of Discipline

Discipline, in the context of feline behavior, refers to a cat's ability to regulate their actions and adhere to established rules or routines. Saturn's influence is key in shaping how well your cat can manage their impulses, follow the boundaries set by their human companions, and develop a sense of self-control.

- **Structured Discipline (Saturn in Earth Signs)**: Cats with Saturn in earth signs—Taurus, Virgo, or Capricorn—are often naturally inclined towards discipline and structure. These cats may have a strong sense of routine and may be more willing to follow the rules set by their human companions. A Saturn in Taurus cat might be particularly disciplined in their daily habits, such as feeding times, grooming, and sleeping patterns. These cats may find comfort in a consistent routine and may be less likely to engage in disruptive behavior. Virgo Saturn cats might exhibit a meticulous approach to discipline, often showing a preference for cleanliness and order in their environment. They may be particularly adept at adhering to household rules, especially those related to maintaining a tidy space. Capricorn Saturn cats might embody the qualities of responsibility and self-control, often acting with a sense of duty towards their role within the household. These cats might be particularly disciplined when it comes to guarding their territory or maintaining their position within the social hierarchy.

- **Flexible Discipline (Saturn in Air Signs)**: Cats with Saturn in air signs—Gemini, Libra, or Aquarius—may approach discipline with a balance of structure and flexibility. These cats might be able to adapt to rules and routines while still maintaining a sense of independence. A Saturn in Gemini cat might be disciplined in their interactions, often showing restraint when it comes to playtime or social interactions. These cats might learn quickly from experience, adapting their behavior to fit within the boundaries set by their environment. Libra Saturn cats might exhibit a disciplined approach to maintaining harmony within the household, often following rules that promote peace and balance. These cats might be particularly good at managing their behavior in social situations, such as interacting with other pets or visitors. Aquarius Saturn cats might demonstrate a unique approach to discipline, often finding innovative ways to adhere to rules while still maintaining their individuality. These cats might be particularly skilled at balancing their need for freedom with the expectations placed upon them.

- **Emotional Discipline (Saturn in Water Signs)**: Cats with Saturn in water signs—Cancer, Scorpio, or Pisces—may exhibit discipline that is closely tied to their emotional state. These cats might approach discipline with sensitivity and a deep awareness of their environment. A Saturn in Cancer cat might show discipline in their caregiving behaviors, often adhering to routines that involve nurturing or protecting their loved ones. These cats might be particularly disciplined when it comes to managing their emotional needs, such as seeking comfort or maintaining a sense of security. Scorpio Saturn cats might exhibit a disciplined approach to their instincts, often showing a strong sense of control over their more intense emotions or behaviors. These cats might be particularly adept at managing their territorial instincts, often showing restraint in situations that might provoke aggression in others. Pisces Saturn cats might approach discipline with a sense of compassion, often adhering to rules that promote the well-being of others. These cats might be particularly disciplined in managing their emotional responses, often showing a calm and composed demeanor in stressful situations.

- **Energetic Discipline (Saturn in Fire Signs)**: Cats with Saturn in fire signs—Aries, Leo, or Sagittarius—may approach discipline with a focus on energy and action. These cats might channel their natural energy into disciplined behaviors, often showing a strong sense of purpose in their actions. A Saturn in Aries cat might be disciplined in their approach to physical activity, often showing a strong sense of determination in achieving their goals. These cats might be particularly disciplined when it comes to managing their energy levels, often engaging in focused play or exercise. Leo Saturn cats might exhibit discipline in their leadership roles, often showing a strong sense of responsibility towards maintaining order within their territory. These cats might be particularly disciplined when it comes to protecting their space or maintaining their position within the social hierarchy. Sagittarius Saturn cats might approach discipline with a focus on exploration and learning, often showing a disciplined approach to acquiring new knowledge or skills. These cats might be particularly disciplined when it comes to managing their curiosity, often showing restraint in situations that might lead to danger or disruption.

Understanding how Saturn influences your cat's sense of discipline can help you create a structured environment that supports their natural tendencies. By recognizing the ways in which your cat is naturally inclined to follow rules and routines, you can provide the guidance and structure they need to thrive.

Saturn and Feline Boundaries

Boundaries are an essential aspect of Saturn's influence, governing how your cat perceives and respects the limits set by their environment. Whether it's the boundaries of their territory, the rules of the household, or their interactions with other animals, Saturn plays a key role in shaping how your cat navigates these limitations.

- **Territorial Boundaries (Saturn in Earth Signs)**: Cats with Saturn in earth signs—Taurus, Virgo, or Capricorn—are likely to have a strong sense of territorial boundaries. These cats might be particularly protective of their space and may show a clear understanding of the limits of their territory. A Saturn in Taurus cat might be particularly focused on maintaining the physical boundaries of their space, often marking their territory through scent or other behaviors. These cats might be particularly sensitive to intrusions into their space and may take a firm stance in defending their boundaries. Virgo Saturn cats might exhibit a disciplined approach to maintaining the cleanliness and order of their territory, often showing a preference for well-defined spaces that are free from clutter or disruption. Capricorn Saturn cats might approach territorial boundaries with a sense of responsibility, often taking on the role of protector within the household. These cats might be particularly adept at managing the boundaries between different areas of their territory, ensuring that each space is used appropriately.
- **Social Boundaries (Saturn in Air Signs)**: Cats with Saturn in air signs—Gemini, Libra, or Aquarius—may approach boundaries with a focus on social interactions. These cats might be particularly aware of the boundaries between themselves and others, often showing a clear understanding of the limits of social interaction. A Saturn in Gemini cat might be particularly skilled at managing the boundaries of communication, often showing restraint in their vocalizations or interactions. These cats might be particularly good at reading social cues and adapting their behavior to fit within the boundaries of social interaction. Libra Saturn cats might exhibit a disciplined approach to maintaining social harmony, often showing a clear understanding of the boundaries of personal space and interaction. These cats might be particularly good at managing the dynamics of social interaction, ensuring that everyone within the household respects each other's boundaries. Aquarius Saturn cats might approach social boundaries with a sense of independence, often finding unique ways to interact with others while still maintaining their own space. These cats might be particularly skilled at balancing their need for social interaction with their desire for autonomy.
- **Emotional Boundaries (Saturn in Water Signs)**: Cats with Saturn in water signs—Cancer, Scorpio, or Pisces—may exhibit a strong sense of emotional boundaries. These cats might be particularly sensitive to the emotional atmosphere of their environment and may show a clear understanding of the limits of emotional interaction. A Saturn in Cancer cat might be

particularly focused on maintaining the emotional boundaries of their family, often taking on the role of caregiver or protector. These cats might be particularly sensitive to the emotional needs of others and may show a strong sense of responsibility in maintaining emotional harmony within the household. Scorpio Saturn cats might exhibit a disciplined approach to managing their emotional boundaries, often showing a strong sense of control over their more intense emotions. These cats might be particularly adept at maintaining their privacy and ensuring that their emotional boundaries are respected. Pisces Saturn cats might approach emotional boundaries with a sense of compassion, often showing a clear understanding of the limits of emotional interaction. These cats might be particularly sensitive to the emotional needs of others and may show a strong sense of responsibility in maintaining emotional harmony within the household.

- **Energetic Boundaries (Saturn in Fire Signs)**: Cats with Saturn in fire signs—Aries, Leo, or Sagittarius—may approach boundaries with a focus on energy and action. These cats might be particularly aware of the limits of their energy and may show a clear understanding of the boundaries of physical activity. A Saturn in Aries cat might be particularly focused on maintaining the boundaries of physical space, often showing a strong sense of determination in defending their territory. These cats might be particularly skilled at managing the boundaries of physical interaction, ensuring that their space is respected by others. Leo Saturn cats might exhibit a disciplined approach to maintaining the boundaries of leadership, often showing a clear understanding of the limits of their authority. These cats might be particularly good at managing the dynamics of power within the household, ensuring that everyone respects the boundaries of leadership. Sagittarius Saturn cats might approach boundaries with a sense of exploration, often showing a disciplined approach to expanding their territory while still respecting the limits of their environment. These cats might be particularly skilled at balancing their need for exploration with their understanding of the boundaries of their space.

Understanding how Saturn influences your cat's sense of boundaries can help you create a harmonious environment that respects their need for structure and limits. By recognizing the ways in which your cat naturally manages boundaries, you can provide the guidance and support they need to feel secure and confident within their environment.

Saturn and Feline Responsibility

Responsibility is another key aspect of Saturn's influence, governing how your cat perceives and fulfills their role within the household. Whether it's maintaining their territory, following household rules, or managing their natural instincts, Saturn plays a key role in shaping how your cat approaches their responsibilities.

- **Territorial Responsibility (Saturn in Earth Signs)**: Cats with Saturn in earth signs—Taurus, Virgo, or Capricorn—are likely to take their territorial responsibilities very seriously. These cats might be particularly focused on maintaining the physical boundaries of their space and may show a strong sense of duty in protecting their territory. A Saturn in Taurus cat might be particularly diligent in marking their territory, often using scent or other behaviors to ensure that their space is clearly defined. These cats might be particularly sensitive to any changes in their environment and may take a firm stance in defending their territory. Virgo Saturn cats might exhibit a meticulous approach to maintaining the cleanliness and order of their territory, often taking on the role of caretaker within the household. These cats might be particularly diligent in ensuring that their space is well-maintained and free from clutter or disruption. Capricorn Saturn cats might approach territorial responsibility with a sense of authority, often taking on the role of protector within the household. These cats might be particularly diligent in managing the boundaries between different areas of their territory, ensuring that each space is used appropriately.
- **Social Responsibility (Saturn in Air Signs)**: Cats with Saturn in air signs—Gemini, Libra, or Aquarius—may approach responsibility with a focus on social interaction. These cats might be particularly aware of their role within the social dynamics of the household and may show a strong sense of duty in maintaining harmony and balance. A Saturn in Gemini cat might be particularly diligent in managing communication within the household, often taking on the role of mediator or communicator. These cats might be particularly skilled at ensuring that everyone within the household is heard and understood. Libra Saturn cats might exhibit a strong sense of responsibility in maintaining social harmony, often taking on the role of peacemaker within the household. These cats might be particularly diligent in ensuring that everyone within the household respects each other's boundaries and maintains a sense of

balance. Aquarius Saturn cats might approach social responsibility with a sense of independence, often taking on the role of innovator or leader within the household. These cats might be particularly diligent in ensuring that the social dynamics of the household are fair and just.

- **Emotional Responsibility (Saturn in Water Signs)**: Cats with Saturn in water signs—Cancer, Scorpio, or Pisces—may exhibit a strong sense of emotional responsibility. These cats might be particularly sensitive to the emotional needs of others and may show a strong sense of duty in maintaining emotional harmony within the household. A Saturn in Cancer cat might be particularly diligent in caring for their family, often taking on the role of caregiver or protector. These cats might be particularly sensitive to the emotional needs of others and may show a strong sense of responsibility in maintaining emotional harmony within the household. Scorpio Saturn cats might exhibit a strong sense of responsibility in managing their own emotions, often taking on the role of protector within the household. These cats might be particularly diligent in ensuring that their emotional boundaries are respected and that their privacy is maintained. Pisces Saturn cats might approach emotional responsibility with a sense of compassion, often taking on the role of healer or caretaker within the household. These cats might be particularly sensitive to the emotional needs of others and may show a strong sense of duty in maintaining emotional harmony within the household.

- **Energetic Responsibility (Saturn in Fire Signs)**: Cats with Saturn in fire signs—Aries, Leo, or Sagittarius—may approach responsibility with a focus on energy and action. These cats might be particularly aware of their role in maintaining the physical dynamics of the household and may show a strong sense of duty in managing their energy and activity levels. A Saturn in Aries cat might be particularly diligent in maintaining their physical space, often taking on the role of protector within the household. These cats might be particularly skilled at managing the boundaries of physical interaction, ensuring that their space is respected by others. Leo Saturn cats might exhibit a strong sense of responsibility in maintaining the leadership dynamics of the household, often taking on the role of leader or protector. These cats might be particularly diligent in ensuring that everyone within the household respects the boundaries of leadership. Sagittarius Saturn cats might approach responsibility with a sense of exploration, often taking on the role of guide or mentor within the household. These cats might be particularly diligent in ensuring that their exploration is balanced with their understanding of the boundaries of their space.

Understanding how Saturn influences your cat's sense of responsibility can help you provide the support and structure they need to fulfill their role within the household. By recognizing the ways in which your cat naturally approaches responsibility, you can create an environment that encourages their growth and development in a way that is both nurturing and supportive.

Conclusion

Saturn's influence on your cat is profound, shaping their sense of discipline, boundaries, and responsibility. By understanding how Saturn affects your cat, you can better guide them in navigating the challenges and expectations of their environment, whether it's through maintaining a structured routine, respecting boundaries, or fulfilling their responsibilities within the household. Whether your cat is a disciplined Capricorn or a sensitive Cancer, Saturn's energy plays a crucial role in helping them develop the self-control and maturity they need to thrive.

As you continue to explore the astrological influences on your cat, remember that Saturn is just one piece of the puzzle. In the following chapters, we'll delve into the other planets and celestial bodies that contribute to your cat's unique personality and behavior, providing a comprehensive understanding of how the cosmos shapes the life of your feline companion.

Chapter 8: Uranus and Change

Uranus, the planet of innovation, rebellion, and sudden change, is a force of unpredictability and surprise in astrology. Often associated with revolution and the breaking of tradition, Uranus brings unexpected events, eccentricity, and a flair for the unconventional. For cats, Uranus's influence manifests in sudden behavioral shifts, quirky habits, and a tendency to embrace or even create chaos in their environment. Understanding Uranus's role in your cat's astrological chart can offer insights into their unpredictable nature, how they handle change, and the unique quirks that make them stand out.

The Role of Uranus in Astrology

Uranus, named after the ancient Greek sky god, is known as the planet of change, disruption, and originality. It governs all things unconventional and is associated with sudden breakthroughs, technological advances, and a desire to break free from limitations. Uranus rules the sign of Aquarius, a sign known for its innovative thinking, independence, and forward-looking vision.

For cats, Uranus's placement in their astrological chart reveals how they respond to change, how they express their individuality, and how they might disrupt the status quo in their environment. Uranus influences your cat's tendency towards eccentric behavior, their reactions to sudden events, and their ability to adapt (or resist) changes in their routine or surroundings.

How Uranus Influences Your Cat's Behavior

Uranus's influence on behavior is often marked by sudden, unexpected shifts and a flair for the unusual. Cats with strong Uranus influences might exhibit behaviors that are unpredictable, quirky, or completely out of the ordinary.

- **Sudden Behavioral Shifts (Uranus in Fire Signs)**: Cats with Uranus in fire signs—Aries, Leo, or Sagittarius—might experience sudden bursts of energy or dramatic changes in behavior. These cats are often highly spirited and may switch from calm and composed to hyperactive and excitable in a matter of moments. A Uranus in Aries cat might suddenly bolt around the house, leaping from furniture to furniture with seemingly boundless energy, only to settle down just as quickly as the mood strikes. Leo Uranus cats might display sudden demands for attention, going from aloof to intensely affectionate, or they might suddenly decide to perform for an audience, showing off their playful antics. Sagittarius Uranus cats might exhibit unpredictable behaviors related to exploration, such as suddenly deciding to escape outside or engage in a new, daring activity.

- **Quirky Habits (Uranus in Air Signs)**: Cats with Uranus in air signs—Gemini, Libra, or Aquarius—are likely to have a variety of quirky, unusual habits. These cats might engage in behaviors that are eccentric, unpredictable, and often amusing. A Uranus in Gemini cat might have a habit of suddenly "talking" to objects, chattering away at inanimate items like a favorite toy or even the television. They might also switch between different behaviors rapidly, keeping you guessing about what they'll do next. Libra Uranus cats might display odd preferences for specific spots or objects, such as only drinking water from a certain glass or insisting on sitting in one particular chair, no matter how inconvenient. Aquarius Uranus cats might engage in behaviors that are completely out of the norm, such as watching the world upside down from an unusual perch or developing a fascination with strange, unexpected items.

- **Unpredictable Reactions (Uranus in Water Signs)**: Cats with Uranus in water signs—Cancer, Scorpio, or Pisces—might have unpredictable emotional reactions and behaviors. These cats are often highly sensitive and may react in ways that are surprising or difficult to anticipate. A Uranus in Cancer cat might suddenly become unusually clingy or, conversely, suddenly withdraw and seek solitude without warning. These cats might also develop unexpected attachments to certain objects or places, showing a strong emotional response to things that others might overlook. Scorpio Uranus cats might display unpredictable bursts of intensity, such as suddenly pouncing on an unsuspecting toy with ferocity or deciding to guard a particular spot with unusual determination. Pisces Uranus cats might have reactions that seem almost otherworldly, such as suddenly staring intently at something invisible or engaging in behaviors that seem more like daydreaming than anything else.

- **Resistance to Change (Uranus in Earth Signs)**: Cats with Uranus in earth signs—Taurus, Virgo, or Capricorn—might exhibit behaviors that reflect a resistance to change or a desire to control their environment in unpredictable ways. These cats might be particularly sensitive to disruptions in their routine and may react in unexpected ways when their environment is altered. A Uranus in Taurus cat might suddenly refuse to eat their usual food if something about it has changed, such as the texture or even the brand of dish it's served in. They might also display sudden stubbornness in maintaining their territory or personal space. Virgo Uranus cats might develop peculiar habits related to cleanliness or order, such as only using the litter box if it's perfectly clean or arranging their toys in a specific way and becoming upset if anything is moved. Capricorn Uranus cats might display unpredictable behavior when it comes to their role within the household, suddenly deciding to take on a new "job" or responsibility, such as guarding a specific area or overseeing the household's comings and goings.

Understanding how Uranus influences your cat's behavior can help you better navigate their unpredictable tendencies and appreciate the unique quirks that make them who they are. By recognizing the ways in which your cat expresses their individuality, you can create an environment that accommodates their need for both stability and spontaneity.

Uranus and Feline Adaptability

Uranus's influence on adaptability is significant, as this planet governs how well (or poorly) your cat responds to changes in their environment. While some cats may embrace change with curiosity and enthusiasm, others might resist it, showing signs of stress or discomfort.

- **Embracing Change (Uranus in Fire Signs)**: Cats with Uranus in fire signs—Aries, Leo, or Sagittarius—are often more willing to embrace change, especially if it offers new opportunities for excitement or exploration. These cats might show a positive response to changes in their environment, such as the introduction of new toys, the rearrangement of furniture, or even a move to a new home. A Uranus in Aries cat might quickly adapt to a new routine, often finding ways to make the most of their new surroundings. Leo Uranus cats might view change as an opportunity to assert their presence and leadership, quickly taking charge of new spaces or situations. Sagittarius Uranus cats might actively seek out change, often displaying enthusiasm for new experiences, whether it's exploring a new part of the house or meeting new people or pets.

- **Cautious Adaptation (Uranus in Earth Signs)**: Cats with Uranus in earth signs—Taurus, Virgo, or Capricorn—might be more cautious in their approach to change, often requiring time to adjust to new situations. These cats might be more resistant to sudden changes in their environment and may show signs of stress or discomfort if their routine is disrupted. A Uranus in Taurus cat might take longer to adapt to changes in their surroundings, often needing reassurance and familiarity before they feel comfortable in a new space. Virgo Uranus cats might approach change with caution, often analyzing their new environment before deciding how to proceed. These cats might be particularly sensitive to changes in their routine or the cleanliness of their space. Capricorn Uranus cats might approach change with a sense of responsibility, often taking on the role of maintaining order and stability in the face of new challenges.

- **Emotional Adaptation (Uranus in Water Signs)**: Cats with Uranus in water signs—Cancer, Scorpio, or Pisces—might experience changes on a deeply emotional level, often responding with a mix of curiosity and caution. These cats might be particularly sensitive to the emotional atmosphere of their environment and may require time to adjust to new situations. A Uranus in Cancer cat might show a strong attachment to their home and family, often needing reassurance and comfort when faced with change. Scorpio Uranus cats might approach change with intensity, often showing a mix of curiosity and suspicion as they explore new environments. These cats might be particularly adept at navigating emotional changes, often using their intuition to guide them. Pisces Uranus cats might adapt to change in a more fluid, dreamy manner, often going with the flow and finding comfort in their inner world rather than their external environment.

- **Intellectual Adaptation (Uranus in Air Signs)**: Cats with Uranus in air signs—Gemini, Libra, or Aquarius—are likely to adapt to change in a more intellectual, analytical manner. These cats might approach new situations with curiosity and a desire to understand the changes around them. A Uranus in Gemini cat might be particularly inquisitive when faced with change, often exploring new environments with enthusiasm and a desire to learn. Libra Uranus cats might approach change with a focus on maintaining balance and harmony, often seeking to create a sense of order in their new surroundings. These cats might be particularly skilled at navigating social changes, often adapting quickly to new relationships or social dynamics. Aquarius Uranus cats might embrace change as an opportunity for innovation, often finding new ways to interact with their environment or solve problems in the face of new challenges.

Understanding how Uranus influences your cat's adaptability can help you support them during times of change, whether it's a move to a new home, the introduction of a new pet, or changes in their daily routine. By recognizing the ways in which your cat processes and responds to change, you can provide the reassurance and support they need to navigate new situations with confidence.

Uranus and Feline Quirks

One of the most delightful aspects of Uranus's influence is the development of quirky, eccentric behaviors that make your cat truly unique. These quirks might manifest in a variety of ways, from unusual habits to surprising preferences.

- **Unique Habits (Uranus in Air Signs)**: Cats with Uranus in air signs—Gemini, Libra, or Aquarius—are likely to develop a range of unique habits that reflect their intellectual curiosity and desire for stimulation. A Uranus in Gemini cat might have a habit of "talking" to themselves or to inanimate objects, often vocalizing in a way that seems almost conversational. These cats might also enjoy engaging in unusual activities, such as playing with unconventional toys or exploring strange, out-of-the-way places. Libra Uranus cats might develop habits that reflect their love of balance and beauty, such as arranging their toys in a particular way or showing a preference for specific colors or textures. Aquarius Uranus cats might display truly eccentric habits, such as sleeping in the most unexpected places or developing a fascination with things that other cats might ignore, like watching the movement of shadows or investigating electronic devices.

- **Unexpected Preferences (Uranus in Earth Signs)**: Cats with Uranus in earth signs—Taurus, Virgo, or Capricorn—might develop unexpected preferences related to their physical environment or routines. A Uranus in Taurus cat might show a strong preference for certain types of bedding, refusing to sleep anywhere but on a particular blanket or pillow. These cats might also develop a taste for unusual foods or treats, showing a surprising preference for certain flavors or textures. Virgo Uranus cats might have peculiar habits related to cleanliness or order, such as only drinking water from a specific bowl or insisting on a particular routine before eating. Capricorn Uranus cats might develop a preference for specific activities or "jobs," such as guarding a particular area of the house or taking on the role of overseeing certain household activities.

- **Emotional Quirks (Uranus in Water Signs)**: Cats with Uranus in water signs—Cancer, Scorpio, or Pisces—might display emotional quirks that reflect their deep sensitivity and intuition. A Uranus in Cancer cat might develop an attachment to a specific object, such as a toy or blanket, that they carry with them everywhere as a source of comfort. These cats might also display unusual behaviors related to their emotional connections, such as insisting on sleeping with a particular person or reacting strongly to certain sounds or smells. Scorpio Uranus cats might exhibit intense, focused behaviors that seem almost ritualistic, such as repeatedly returning to the same spot or engaging in specific actions before settling down. Pisces Uranus cats might display dreamy, whimsical behaviors, such as staring off into space or engaging in activities that seem more like play-acting than anything else.
- **Playful Quirks (Uranus in Fire Signs)**: Cats with Uranus in fire signs—Aries, Leo, or Sagittarius—are likely to have playful quirks that reflect their energetic, adventurous nature. A Uranus in Aries cat might develop a habit of suddenly launching into play at the most unexpected moments, often pouncing on invisible prey or chasing after imaginary objects. These cats might also enjoy games that involve a lot of movement and excitement, often inventing their own rules or engaging in play that seems completely spontaneous. Leo Uranus cats might have a flair for the dramatic, often engaging in playful behaviors that draw attention to themselves, such as performing tricks or "showing off" their skills. Sagittarius Uranus cats might display playful quirks related to exploration, such as constantly seeking out new places to investigate or engaging in games that mimic hunting or adventuring.

Understanding and appreciating the quirky behaviors that Uranus brings to your cat's personality can help you celebrate their individuality and create an environment that allows them to express their unique traits. By recognizing the special quirks that make your cat who they are, you can deepen your bond with them and enjoy the surprises and delights that come with living with a Uranus-influenced feline.

Uranus and Disruption

Uranus is also known as the planet of disruption, and its influence can sometimes bring chaos and upheaval to your cat's life. These disruptions might manifest as sudden changes in behavior, unexpected reactions to new situations, or a tendency to create chaos in their environment.

- **Creating Chaos (Uranus in Fire Signs)**: Cats with Uranus in fire signs—Aries, Leo, or Sagittarius—might have a tendency to create chaos in their environment, often through their energetic and unpredictable actions. A Uranus in Aries cat might suddenly decide to knock over objects, disrupt a peaceful moment with a burst of energy, or engage in behavior that seems designed to stir things up. These cats might enjoy the thrill of creating chaos, often viewing it as a form of play or excitement. Leo Uranus cats might create chaos by demanding attention in dramatic ways, such as knocking over items to get your focus or interrupting other pets' activities to assert their dominance. Sagittarius Uranus cats might create chaos through their adventurous spirit, often getting into places they shouldn't or engaging in activities that lead to messes or disruptions.

- **Disrupting Routines (Uranus in Earth Signs)**: Cats with Uranus in earth signs—Taurus, Virgo, or Capricorn—might disrupt routines or create upheaval in their environment, often as a reaction to changes or perceived challenges. A Uranus in Taurus cat might suddenly refuse to follow their usual routine, such as rejecting their usual food or choosing a new favorite spot to sleep that's inconvenient or unusual. These cats might also disrupt their environment by moving objects or rearranging their space in ways that suit their new preferences. Virgo Uranus cats might disrupt routines related to cleanliness or order, such as refusing to use the litter box if something about it has changed or insisting on a new cleaning routine. Capricorn Uranus cats might create disruption by taking on new "responsibilities" within the household, such as deciding to guard a different area or changing their behavior in ways that affect the entire household.

- **Emotional Upheaval (Uranus in Water Signs)**: Cats with Uranus in water signs—Cancer, Scorpio, or Pisces—might experience or create emotional upheaval, often as a reaction to changes in their environment or relationships. A Uranus in Cancer cat might suddenly become emotionally distant or unusually clingy, reacting strongly to perceived threats to their sense of security. These cats might also create emotional upheaval by reacting unpredictably to changes in their home or routine, often requiring extra reassurance and comfort. Scorpio Uranus cats might create emotional turmoil through intense, unpredictable behaviors, such as suddenly becoming possessive of a particular person or object or reacting aggressively to perceived threats. Pisces Uranus cats might experience emotional upheaval in more subtle ways, such as withdrawing into themselves or displaying behaviors that reflect their internal emotional state.

- **Social Disruption (Uranus in Air Signs)**: Cats with Uranus in air signs—Gemini, Libra, or Aquarius—might create social disruption, often through their unpredictable interactions with others. A Uranus in Gemini cat might suddenly change their social behavior, such as becoming unusually talkative or, conversely, going silent without warning. These cats might also disrupt social dynamics by engaging in unexpected or confusing behaviors that affect their relationships with other pets or people. Libra Uranus cats might create social upheaval by disrupting the balance of the household, such as favoring one person or pet over another in ways that cause tension. Aquarius Uranus cats might disrupt social interactions by engaging in eccentric or unusual behaviors that others find difficult to understand or adapt to.

Understanding how Uranus influences your cat's tendency towards disruption can help you manage their more chaotic behaviors and provide the stability they need to navigate changes in their environment. By recognizing the ways in which your cat might create or react to upheaval, you can provide the support and guidance they need to maintain balance and harmony in their life.

Conclusion

Uranus's influence on your cat is powerful and unpredictable, bringing sudden changes, quirky behaviors, and a touch of chaos to their life. By understanding how Uranus affects your cat, you can better appreciate their unique traits, support them through times of change, and celebrate the quirks that make them who they are. Whether your cat is an adventurous Sagittarius or an eccentric Aquarius, Uranus's energy plays a crucial role in shaping their behavior and adding a sense of spontaneity and excitement to their life.

As you continue to explore the astrological influences on your cat, remember that Uranus is just one piece of the puzzle. In the following chapters, we'll delve into the other planets and celestial bodies that contribute to your cat's unique personality and behavior, providing a comprehensive understanding of how the cosmos shapes the life of your feline companion.

Chapter 9: Neptune and Mysticism

Neptune, the planet of dreams, intuition, and mysticism, holds a deep and enigmatic influence in astrology. Often associated with the unseen, the spiritual, and the subconscious, Neptune governs everything from dreams and illusions to creativity and psychic sensitivity. For cats, Neptune's presence in their astrological chart manifests in behaviors that are often mysterious, intuitive, and dreamlike. Understanding Neptune's role in your cat's life can offer insights into their dreaming habits, their uncanny sense of intuition, and the subtle, often mystical ways they interact with the world around them.

The Role of Neptune in Astrology

Neptune, named after the Roman god of the sea, is the planet that governs the realm of dreams, illusions, spirituality, and the subconscious. It is associated with the dissolution of boundaries, the merging of the physical and spiritual, and the exploration of the unknown. Neptune rules the sign of Pisces, a sign known for its deep empathy, creativity, and connection to the mystical and spiritual realms.

For cats, Neptune's placement in their astrological chart reveals how they experience and express their dreams, how they tap into their intuitive senses, and how they engage with the mysterious or unseen aspects of their environment. Neptune influences your cat's capacity for empathy, their connection to the spiritual or mystical, and their tendency to engage in behaviors that are elusive, enigmatic, or difficult to explain.

Neptune's Influence on Your Cat's Dreams

Dreaming is one of the most direct ways Neptune's influence manifests in your cat's life. Cats spend a significant portion of their lives sleeping, and during this time, Neptune's energy guides them through a rich and complex inner world filled with dreams and subconscious experiences.

- **Vivid Dreaming (Neptune in Water Signs):** Cats with Neptune in water signs—Cancer, Scorpio, or Pisces—are likely to experience particularly vivid and emotionally charged dreams. These cats may twitch, purr, or even vocalize in their sleep, giving you glimpses into the dreamscapes they inhabit. A Neptune in Cancer cat might have dreams that revolve around their sense of home and family, perhaps dreaming of their interactions with you or other animals in the household. These dreams might be deeply emotional, reflecting the strong bonds they share with those they love. Scorpio Neptune cats might experience intense, sometimes mysterious dreams that involve themes of power, transformation, or hidden secrets. These cats might appear restless or deeply focused in their sleep, as if they are working through complex emotions or scenarios. Pisces Neptune cats, being naturally attuned to the dream world, might experience dreams that are whimsical, fantastical, or deeply spiritual. These cats might seem to drift peacefully through their sleep, occasionally twitching or making soft sounds that suggest they are exploring a world beyond the physical.

- **Symbolic Dreaming (Neptune in Earth Signs)**: Cats with Neptune in earth signs—Taurus, Virgo, or Capricorn—might have dreams that are more grounded and symbolic, often reflecting their connection to the physical world. These cats might dream of activities that mirror their waking life, such as hunting, exploring, or interacting with their environment. A Neptune in Taurus cat might dream of comforting, pleasurable experiences, such as enjoying a meal, basking in the sun, or lounging in a favorite spot. These dreams might reflect their deep connection to physical comfort and their appreciation for the sensory pleasures of life. Virgo Neptune cats might have dreams that involve organization, routine, or problem-solving, perhaps reflecting their natural inclination towards order and precision. These cats might appear to be working through tasks or scenarios in their sleep, as if they are rehearsing or refining their skills. Capricorn Neptune cats might experience dreams that involve themes of responsibility, structure, or ambition, perhaps reflecting their role within the household or their sense of duty. These cats might appear determined or focused in their sleep, as if they are pursuing a goal or managing a task.

- **Creative Dreaming (Neptune in Air Signs)**: Cats with Neptune in air signs—Gemini, Libra, or Aquarius—might experience dreams that are highly imaginative, creative, and filled with intellectual stimulation. These cats might dream of exploring new ideas, engaging in social interactions, or solving puzzles. A Neptune in Gemini cat might have dreams that involve communication, exploration, or curiosity, perhaps reflecting their natural inquisitiveness and desire for mental stimulation. These cats might appear particularly active in their sleep, as if they are engaged in lively, dynamic scenarios. Libra Neptune cats might dream of harmony, beauty, or social interaction, perhaps reflecting their appreciation for balance and their desire to connect with others. These cats might appear serene or content in their sleep, as if they are enjoying peaceful, pleasant experiences. Aquarius Neptune cats might have dreams that involve innovation, independence, or unconventional ideas, perhaps reflecting their unique perspective on the world. These cats might appear thoughtful or introspective in their sleep, as if they are exploring new concepts or envisioning alternative realities.

- **Mystical Dreaming (Neptune in Fire Signs)**: Cats with Neptune in fire signs—Aries, Leo, or Sagittarius—might experience dreams that are filled with energy, adventure, and a sense of the mystical or otherworldly. These cats might dream of exploring unknown territories, embarking on epic quests, or encountering beings or scenarios that are beyond the ordinary. A Neptune in Aries cat might have dreams that involve action, competition, or challenge, perhaps reflecting their natural drive and adventurous spirit. These cats might appear restless or animated in their sleep, as if they are actively engaging in daring or thrilling experiences. Leo Neptune cats might dream of leadership, creativity, or performance, perhaps reflecting their desire to shine and be admired. These cats might appear regal or confident in their sleep, as if they are commanding attention or leading a grand adventure. Sagittarius Neptune cats might have dreams that involve exploration, discovery, or spiritual journeying, perhaps reflecting their love of adventure and their quest for knowledge. These cats might appear deeply absorbed in their sleep, as if they are traveling through vast, uncharted realms or seeking out profound truths.

Understanding how Neptune influences your cat's dreams can help you appreciate the richness of their inner world and the role that dreaming plays in their overall well-being. By observing your cat's behavior during sleep, you can gain insights into the themes and experiences that resonate most deeply with them, whether it's the comfort of home, the thrill of adventure, or the pursuit of spiritual enlightenment.

Neptune and Feline Intuition

Neptune is also the planet of intuition, governing the subtle, often subconscious ways in which we perceive and understand the world around us. For cats, Neptune's influence enhances their natural instincts, making them highly sensitive to the emotions, energies, and unseen forces in their environment.

- **Heightened Sensitivity (Neptune in Water Signs)**: Cats with Neptune in water signs—Cancer, Scorpio, or Pisces—are likely to have a heightened sensitivity to the emotions and energies around them. These cats might be particularly attuned to your moods, often sensing when you're happy, sad, or stressed, and responding in ways that reflect their deep empathy. A Neptune in Cancer cat might be especially nurturing, often staying close to you when you're feeling down or offering comfort through gentle purring or physical closeness. These cats might also be sensitive to changes in the home environment, such as the arrival of new people or animals, and may react with either caution or curiosity. Scorpio Neptune cats might exhibit a strong, almost psychic intuition, often knowing things without being shown or told. These cats might seem to understand your thoughts or intentions before you express them, and they may have a knack for discovering hidden or secretive things. Pisces Neptune cats, being naturally connected to the spiritual and mystical, might display an uncanny ability to sense the unseen, whether it's perceiving subtle changes in energy, detecting the presence of something unknown, or simply "knowing" when something is about to happen.
- **Practical Intuition (Neptune in Earth Signs)**: Cats with Neptune in earth signs—Taurus, Virgo, or Capricorn—might have a more grounded, practical form of intuition, often using their instincts to navigate the physical world with ease. These cats might be particularly good at finding hidden objects, sensing changes in the environment, or predicting natural events. A Neptune in Taurus cat might have a strong sense of where to find the most comfortable spots, the best places to hide, or the ideal moments to seek out affection or food. These cats might also be sensitive to the physical needs of others, often knowing when you need comfort, warmth, or a moment of peace. Virgo Neptune cats might exhibit a keen intuition when it comes to health and well-being, often sensing when something is amiss, whether it's a change in their diet, a shift in routine, or a subtle sign of illness in themselves or others. These cats might also be particularly adept at navigating complex environments, using their intuition to avoid dangers or solve problems. Capricorn Neptune cats might have an intuitive understanding of structure and responsibility, often sensing when it's time to take action or when something requires attention or care. These cats might also be particularly good at managing their energy and resources, intuitively knowing when to conserve their strength or when to take advantage of an opportunity.

- **Social Intuition (Neptune in Air Signs)**: Cats with Neptune in air signs—Gemini, Libra, or Aquarius—might exhibit a form of intuition that is closely tied to social interaction and communication. These cats might be particularly good at reading social cues, understanding body language, or sensing the dynamics of relationships. A Neptune in Gemini cat might have an intuitive understanding of communication, often knowing just the right moment to meow, purr, or nudge you for attention. These cats might also be particularly skilled at sensing changes in the social atmosphere, such as shifts in mood or tension between people. Libra Neptune cats might exhibit a strong intuition when it comes to maintaining harmony and balance in their relationships, often sensing when something is off and taking steps to restore peace. These cats might also be particularly good at mediating conflicts or creating a sense of calm in tense situations. Aquarius Neptune cats might have an intuitive sense of individuality and freedom, often knowing when to assert their independence or when to step back and give others space. These cats might also be particularly attuned to the unique dynamics of their social environment, often sensing when something unusual or unexpected is about to happen.

- **Spiritual Intuition (Neptune in Fire Signs)**: Cats with Neptune in fire signs—Aries, Leo, or Sagittarius—might exhibit a form of intuition that is deeply connected to their spiritual or mystical side. These cats might be particularly sensitive to the unseen forces in their environment, often displaying behaviors that suggest a connection to something beyond the physical world. A Neptune in Aries cat might have an intuitive understanding of action and timing, often sensing the perfect moment to strike, pounce, or engage in play. These cats might also exhibit a strong sense of purpose, often acting with a conviction that seems to be guided by something greater than themselves. Leo Neptune cats might have a deep connection to their inner power and creativity, often sensing the right moment to express themselves or take the lead. These cats might also display a strong intuition when it comes to recognizing their own potential, often sensing when they are capable of achieving something extraordinary. Sagittarius Neptune cats might have an intuitive sense of exploration and discovery, often sensing when it's time to embark on a new adventure or when there is something more to learn or experience. These cats might also display a strong connection to the spiritual or mystical, often engaging in behaviors that suggest a deeper understanding of the world around them.

Understanding how Neptune influences your cat's intuition can help you appreciate their ability to perceive and respond to the subtle, often unseen aspects of their environment. By recognizing the ways in which your cat uses their intuition, you can create an environment that supports their natural instincts and enhances their sense of connection to the world around them.

Neptune and Feline Mysticism

Neptune is also the planet of mysticism, governing the ways in which we connect to the spiritual, the mystical, and the unseen. For cats, Neptune's influence can manifest in behaviors that are deeply mysterious, enigmatic, or connected to something beyond the ordinary.

- **Mysterious Behavior (Neptune in Water Signs)**: Cats with Neptune in water signs—Cancer, Scorpio, or Pisces—are likely to exhibit behaviors that are deeply mysterious and often difficult to explain. These cats might engage in activities that seem to have no clear purpose or that suggest a connection to something unseen. A Neptune in Cancer cat might have a habit of staring intently at seemingly empty spaces, as if they are seeing something beyond the physical. These cats might also display a deep connection to certain objects or places, often returning to them repeatedly as if they hold some special significance. Scorpio Neptune cats might engage in behaviors that are secretive or hidden, often disappearing for long periods or engaging in activities that are difficult to observe or understand. These cats might also have a strong connection to the occult or the mysterious, often displaying an interest in things that are dark, hidden, or unknown. Pisces Neptune cats, being naturally attuned to the mystical, might engage in behaviors that are dreamlike, ethereal, or otherworldly. These cats might seem to drift between the physical and spiritual realms, often displaying a sense of being in two worlds at once.

- **Spiritual Connection (Neptune in Earth Signs)**: Cats with Neptune in earth signs—Taurus, Virgo, or Capricorn—might display a spiritual connection that is grounded in the physical world. These cats might engage in behaviors that suggest a deep connection to nature, the earth, or the physical environment. A Neptune in Taurus cat might have a strong connection to the natural world, often displaying behaviors that suggest a deep appreciation for the earth's beauty and bounty. These cats might be particularly drawn to natural materials, such as wood, stone, or plants, and may engage in rituals that connect them to the earth. Virgo

Neptune cats might exhibit a spiritual connection that is focused on health, well-being, or the physical body. These cats might engage in behaviors that suggest a deep understanding of the body's needs, often sensing when something is out of balance or when healing is needed. Capricorn Neptune cats might display a spiritual connection that is focused on responsibility, duty, or the structure of life. These cats might engage in behaviors that suggest a deep understanding of the cycles of life, often displaying a sense of purpose or destiny in their actions.

- **Mystical Exploration (Neptune in Air Signs)**: Cats with Neptune in air signs—Gemini, Libra, or Aquarius—might engage in behaviors that reflect a mystical exploration of ideas, concepts, or the unknown. These cats might display a deep curiosity about the mysteries of life, often engaging in activities that suggest a desire to understand the unseen. A Neptune in Gemini cat might engage in behaviors that are exploratory and inquisitive, often seeking to uncover the mysteries of their environment. These cats might display a fascination with symbols, signs, or patterns, often engaging in activities that suggest a deep connection to the intellectual mysteries of life. Libra Neptune cats might exhibit a mystical connection to beauty, harmony, or balance, often engaging in activities that suggest a deep appreciation for the aesthetic or spiritual aspects of life. These cats might be particularly drawn to objects or environments that are harmonious, beautiful, or filled with a sense of peace. Aquarius Neptune cats might engage in behaviors that reflect a deep connection to the unconventional or the visionary, often displaying a fascination with the future, technology, or the unknown. These cats might be particularly drawn to activities that challenge the boundaries of the ordinary, often exploring the mysteries of life in ways that are innovative, unique, or ahead of their time.

- **Spiritual Leadership (Neptune in Fire Signs)**: Cats with Neptune in fire signs—Aries, Leo, or Sagittarius—might display a sense of spiritual leadership, often engaging in behaviors that suggest a connection to a higher purpose or calling. These cats might exhibit a deep sense of mission, often acting as if they are guided by something greater than themselves. A Neptune in Aries cat might display a strong sense of purpose, often engaging in behaviors that suggest a desire to lead, protect, or guide others. These cats might also exhibit a deep connection to the spiritual aspects of courage, bravery, or action, often acting as if they are driven by a higher calling. Leo Neptune cats might display a sense of spiritual leadership that is focused on creativity, expression, or the sharing of light. These cats might engage in behaviors that suggest a deep connection to the divine aspects of creativity, often acting as if they are channels for something greater than themselves. Sagittarius Neptune cats might exhibit a spiritual connection that is focused on exploration, discovery, or the quest for knowledge. These cats might engage in behaviors that suggest a deep connection to the spiritual aspects of adventure, often acting as if they are on a journey to uncover the mysteries of life.

Understanding how Neptune influences your cat's connection to mysticism can help you appreciate the deeper, often mysterious aspects of their behavior. By recognizing the ways in which your cat engages with the spiritual or mystical, you can create an environment that supports their connection to the unseen and enhances their sense of wonder and exploration.

Conclusion

Neptune's influence on your cat is profound and mysterious, shaping their dreams, intuition, and connection to the mystical aspects of life. By understanding how Neptune affects your cat, you can better appreciate the richness of their inner world, the depth of their intuitive abilities, and the subtle, often enigmatic ways they interact with their environment. Whether your cat is a dreamy Pisces or an intuitive Cancer, Neptune's energy plays a crucial role in helping them navigate the mysteries of life and connect with the unseen forces that shape their existence.

As you continue to explore the astrological influences on your cat, remember that Neptune is just one piece of the puzzle. In the following chapters, we'll delve into the other planets and celestial bodies that contribute to your cat's unique personality and behavior, providing a comprehensive understanding of how the cosmos shapes the life of your feline companion.

Chapter 10: Pluto and Transformation

Pluto, the planet of transformation, power, and rebirth, holds a deep and intense influence in astrology. Often associated with profound change, the cycles of life and death, and the process of re-generation, Pluto governs the forces that drive us to confront our deepest fears, embrace change, and emerge stronger on the other side. For cats, Pluto's presence in their astrological chart is reflected in their capacity for resilience, their experiences of transformation, and the ways in which they navigate life's most challenging and intense moments. Understanding Pluto's role in your cat's life can offer insights into their ability to adapt to change, their emotional depth, and their capacity for renewal and growth through difficult experiences.

The Role of Pluto in Astrology

Pluto, named after the Roman god of the underworld, is the planet that governs transformation, power, and the hidden forces that shape our lives. It is associated with the process of death and re-birth, the uncovering of deep truths, and the destruction of the old to make way for the new. Pluto rules the sign of Scorpio, a sign known for its intensity, depth, and connection to the cycles of trans-formation and renewal.

For cats, Pluto's placement in their astrological chart reveals how they experience and navigate transformative experiences, how they tap into their inner power and resilience, and how they engage with the darker or more challenging aspects of life. Pluto influences your cat's capacity for emotional depth, their ability to face and overcome adversity, and their natural tendencies towards renewal and regeneration.

Pluto's Influence on Transformative Experiences

Transformation is the core theme of Pluto's influence, and for cats, this can manifest in a variety of ways throughout their lives. Whether it's through physical changes, emotional growth, or life-al-tering events, Pluto's energy drives your cat to confront challenges and emerge stronger.

- **Physical Transformation (Pluto in Earth Signs)**: Cats with Pluto in earth signs—Taurus, Virgo, or Capricorn—might experience transformation primarily through physical changes. These cats may undergo significant shifts in their physical appearance, health, or environment that require them to adapt and grow. A Pluto in Taurus cat might experience physical trans-formations related to their body, such as changes in weight, coat condition, or overall health.

These cats might face challenges that force them to reassess their physical needs and habits, leading to a deeper understanding of their body and how to care for it. Virgo Pluto cats might experience transformations related to their health and well-being, often going through periods of illness or recovery that require them to adopt new routines or habits. These cats might emerge from these experiences with a renewed sense of vitality and a greater appreciation for the importance of self-care. Capricorn Pluto cats might experience transformations related to their role within the household or their environment, often facing changes that challenge their sense of structure or stability. These cats might learn to adapt to new responsibilities or environments, developing a stronger sense of resilience and determination as a result.

- **Emotional Transformation (Pluto in Water Signs)**: Cats with Pluto in water signs—Cancer, Scorpio, or Pisces—are likely to experience transformation primarily on an emotional level. These cats might undergo deep emotional changes that alter the way they connect with others and process their feelings. A Pluto in Cancer cat might experience transformations related to their sense of security, family, or home life. These cats might face emotional challenges that require them to confront their fears of abandonment, loss, or change, leading to a deeper understanding of their emotional needs and a stronger connection to those they love. Scorpio Pluto cats, being naturally attuned to the energy of transformation, might experience intense emotional upheavals that force them to confront their deepest fears and desires. These cats might undergo significant emotional growth as they learn to embrace the cycles of life and death, emerging with a greater sense of inner power and self-awareness. Pisces Pluto cats might experience transformations related to their spiritual or intuitive life, often going through periods of deep introspection or spiritual awakening. These cats might emerge from these experiences with a renewed sense of purpose and a stronger connection to the mystical or unseen aspects of life.

- **Intellectual Transformation (Pluto in Air Signs)**: Cats with Pluto in air signs—Gemini, Libra, or Aquarius—might experience transformation primarily on an intellectual or social level. These cats might undergo changes in the way they think, communicate, or interact with others, leading to a deeper understanding of themselves and their place in the world. A Pluto in Gemini cat might experience transformations related to their communication style or intellectual interests. These cats might face challenges that force them to rethink their approach to learning, interacting with others, or expressing themselves, leading to a greater sense of intellectual depth and curiosity. Libra Pluto cats might experience transformations related to their relationships or social dynamics, often going through periods of intense connection or conflict that challenge their sense of balance and harmony. These cats might emerge from these experiences with a stronger sense of fairness and a deeper understanding of the complexities of relationships. Aquarius Pluto cats might experience transformations related to their sense of individuality or their role within larger social groups. These cats might face challenges that force them to confront issues of independence, freedom, or social justice, leading to a greater sense of purpose and a deeper connection to their ideals.

- **Spiritual Transformation (Pluto in Fire Signs)**: Cats with Pluto in fire signs—Aries, Leo, or Sagittarius—might experience transformation primarily on a spiritual or existential level. These cats might undergo changes that challenge their sense of identity, purpose, or connection to the larger forces at work in their lives. A Pluto in Aries cat might experience transformations related to their sense of self or personal power. These cats might face challenges that force them to confront their fears of failure, loss, or vulnerability, leading to a greater sense of courage and determination. Leo Pluto cats might experience transformations related to their sense of creativity, leadership, or self-expression, often going through periods of intense self-reflection or personal growth. These cats might emerge from these experiences with a renewed sense of confidence and a deeper understanding of their unique gifts and talents. Sagittarius Pluto cats might experience transformations related to their beliefs, values, or sense of purpose, often going through periods of spiritual exploration or existential questioning. These cats might emerge from these experiences with a greater sense of wisdom and a deeper connection to the larger forces that shape their lives.

Understanding how Pluto influences your cat's transformative experiences can help you support them through periods of change and growth. By recognizing the ways in which your cat is naturally inclined to experience transformation, you can provide the guidance and care they need to navigate these challenging moments and emerge stronger on the other side.

Pluto and Feline Resilience

Resilience is another key aspect of Pluto's influence, governing your cat's ability to recover from adversity, bounce back from challenges, and continue to thrive despite difficulties. Pluto's energy imbues your cat with the strength and determination to overcome obstacles and grow from their experiences.

- **Physical Resilience (Pluto in Earth Signs)**: Cats with Pluto in earth signs—Taurus, Virgo, or Capricorn—might exhibit strong physical resilience, often recovering quickly from injuries, illnesses, or other physical challenges. These cats might have a natural ability to endure physical hardships and emerge stronger and healthier as a result. A Pluto in Taurus cat might display a remarkable ability to recover from physical setbacks, often showing a strong will to survive and thrive. These cats might also exhibit a deep connection to their body, using their resilience to maintain their physical well-being even in the face of challenges. Virgo Pluto cats might exhibit resilience in their approach to health and wellness, often adopting new routines or habits that help them recover from illness or injury. These cats might also be particularly diligent in maintaining their physical health, using their resilience to prevent future setbacks. Capricorn Pluto cats might exhibit resilience in their ability to endure physical hardships, often using their strength and determination to overcome obstacles and achieve their goals. These cats might also be particularly disciplined in their approach to physical challenges, using their resilience to build strength and endurance over time.
- **Emotional Resilience (Pluto in Water Signs)**: Cats with Pluto in water signs—Cancer, Scorpio, or Pisces—might exhibit strong emotional resilience, often recovering quickly from emotional setbacks, trauma, or loss. These cats might have a natural ability to process and release emotions, allowing them to heal and grow from their experiences. A Pluto in Cancer cat might display remarkable emotional resilience, often bouncing back from emotional challenges with a renewed sense of security and connection. These cats might also be particularly adept at nurturing themselves and others, using their resilience to maintain strong emotional bonds even in difficult times. Scorpio Pluto cats, being naturally attuned to the energy of transformation, might exhibit resilience in their ability to face and overcome intense

emotional challenges. These cats might have a natural ability to confront their deepest fears, process their emotions, and emerge stronger and more self-aware as a result. Pisces Pluto cats might exhibit resilience in their ability to navigate the complexities of their emotional and spiritual life, often using their deep empathy and intuition to heal and grow from their experiences. These cats might also be particularly skilled at using their resilience to maintain their sense of inner peace and spiritual connection, even in the face of emotional turmoil.

- **Intellectual Resilience (Pluto in Air Signs)**: Cats with Pluto in air signs—Gemini, Libra, or Aquarius—might exhibit strong intellectual resilience, often recovering quickly from mental challenges, setbacks, or changes in their environment. These cats might have a natural ability to adapt to new situations, solve problems, and continue to learn and grow even in difficult circumstances. A Pluto in Gemini cat might display remarkable intellectual resilience, often bouncing back from challenges to their communication or learning with a renewed sense of curiosity and engagement. These cats might also be particularly adept at using their mental agility to navigate complex situations, using their resilience to maintain their intellectual sharpness and adaptability. Libra Pluto cats might exhibit resilience in their ability to maintain balance and harmony in their relationships, often using their diplomatic skills to navigate social challenges and maintain their sense of fairness and justice. These cats might also be particularly skilled at using their resilience to build and maintain strong, supportive relationships, even in the face of conflict or change. Aquarius Pluto cats might exhibit resilience in their ability to think independently and challenge the status quo, often using their innovative thinking to overcome obstacles and drive positive change. These cats might also be particularly skilled at using their resilience to maintain their sense of individuality and purpose, even in the face of societal pressures or challenges.

- **Spiritual Resilience (Pluto in Fire Signs)**: Cats with Pluto in fire signs—Aries, Leo, or Sagittarius—might exhibit strong spiritual resilience, often recovering quickly from existential challenges, crises of faith, or periods of doubt. These cats might have a natural ability to reconnect with their sense of purpose and passion, using their resilience to continue pursuing their goals and dreams even in the face of adversity. A Pluto in Aries cat might display remarkable spiritual resilience, often bouncing back from challenges to their sense of self or personal power with a renewed sense of determination and courage. These cats might also be particularly adept at using their inner strength to overcome obstacles and continue to grow and evolve on their spiritual journey. Leo Pluto cats might exhibit resilience in their ability to maintain their creative expression and leadership, often using their confidence and charisma to navigate challenges and inspire others. These cats might also be particularly skilled at using their resilience to maintain their sense of self-worth and pride, even in the face of criticism or setbacks. Sagittarius Pluto cats might exhibit resilience in their ability to continue exploring and expanding their horizons, often using their adventurous spirit and love of learning to overcome obstacles and continue pursuing their quest for knowledge and truth. These cats might also be particularly skilled at using their resilience to maintain their sense of optimism and hope, even in the face of uncertainty or adversity.

Understanding how Pluto influences your cat's resilience can help you support them through challenging times and help them harness their inner strength to overcome obstacles and continue to thrive. By recognizing the ways in which your cat naturally expresses resilience, you can provide the guidance and care they need to navigate life's challenges with grace and strength.

Pluto and Feline Power

Power is another key aspect of Pluto's influence, governing your cat's ability to tap into their inner strength, assert their will, and navigate the complexities of life with a sense of purpose and determination. Pluto's energy imbues your cat with a deep sense of power and the ability to transform themselves and their environment.

- **Physical Power (Pluto in Earth Signs)**: Cats with Pluto in earth signs—Taurus, Virgo, or Capricorn—might exhibit strong physical power, often using their strength and determination to achieve their goals and assert their will. These cats might have a natural ability to harness their physical energy and use it to overcome obstacles and challenges. A Pluto in Taurus cat might display remarkable physical power, often using their strength and endurance to protect their territory, defend their resources, or achieve their goals. These cats might also be particularly adept at using their physical power to maintain their sense of security and stability, even in the face of challenges. Virgo Pluto cats might exhibit power in their ability to maintain their health and well-being, often using their discipline and attention to detail to keep their body in peak condition. These cats might also be particularly skilled at using their physical power to achieve their goals, whether it's through agility, speed, or strength. Capricorn Pluto cats might exhibit power in their ability to endure physical challenges and achieve their long-term goals, often using their discipline and determination to overcome obstacles and continue moving forward. These cats might also be particularly adept at using their physical power to build and maintain their sense of authority and control within their environment.

- **Emotional Power (Pluto in Water Signs)**: Cats with Pluto in water signs—Cancer, Scorpio, or Pisces—might exhibit strong emotional power, often using their depth of feeling and empathy to navigate the complexities of life and relationships. These cats might have a natural ability to tap into their emotional strength and use it to overcome challenges and achieve their goals. A Pluto in Cancer cat might display remarkable emotional power, often using their deep connection to their loved ones to protect and nurture those they care about. These cats might also be particularly adept at using their emotional power to maintain their sense of security and stability, even in the face of emotional challenges. Scorpio Pluto cats, being naturally attuned to the energy of power and transformation, might exhibit power in their ability to confront and overcome intense emotional challenges. These cats might have a natural ability to tap into their inner strength and use it to navigate the darkest and most difficult aspects of life, emerging stronger and more self-aware as a result. Pisces Pluto cats might exhibit power in their ability to navigate the complexities of their emotional and spiritual life, often using their deep empathy and intuition to heal and grow from their experiences. These cats might also be particularly skilled at using their emotional power to maintain their sense of inner peace and spiritual connection, even in the face of emotional turmoil.

- **Intellectual Power (Pluto in Air Signs)**: Cats with Pluto in air signs—Gemini, Libra, or Aquarius—might exhibit strong intellectual power, often using their mental agility and creativity to overcome challenges and achieve their goals. These cats might have a natural ability to harness their intellectual energy and use it to navigate the complexities of life and relationships. A Pluto in Gemini cat might display remarkable intellectual power, often using their mental agility and curiosity to solve problems, learn new things, and adapt to new situations. These cats might also be particularly adept at using their intellectual power to communicate their needs and desires, even in challenging situations. Libra Pluto cats might exhibit power in their ability to maintain balance and harmony in their relationships, often using their diplomatic skills and sense of fairness to navigate social challenges and maintain strong, supportive relationships. These cats might also be particularly skilled at using their intellectual power to build and maintain their sense of justice and fairness, even in the face of conflict or change. Aquarius Pluto cats might exhibit power in their ability to think independently and challenge the status quo, often using their innovative thinking to overcome obstacles and drive positive change. These cats might also be particularly skilled at using their intellectual power to maintain their sense of individuality and purpose, even in the face of societal pressures or challenges.

- **Spiritual Power (Pluto in Fire Signs)**: Cats with Pluto in fire signs—Aries, Leo, or Sagittarius—might exhibit strong spiritual power, often using their sense of purpose and passion to overcome challenges and achieve their goals. These cats might have a natural ability to harness their spiritual energy and use it to navigate the complexities of life and relationships. A Pluto in Aries cat might display remarkable spiritual power, often using their sense of purpose and determination to overcome obstacles and achieve their goals. These cats might also be particularly adept at using their spiritual power to maintain their sense of self-worth and confidence, even in the face of challenges or setbacks. Leo Pluto cats might exhibit power in their ability to express their creativity and leadership, often using their charisma and confidence to inspire others and achieve their goals. These cats might also be particularly skilled at using their spiritual power to maintain their sense of self-worth and pride, even in the face of criticism or challenges. Sagittarius Pluto cats might exhibit power in their ability to continue exploring and expanding their horizons, often using their adventurous spirit and love of learning to overcome obstacles and continue pursuing their quest for knowledge and truth. These cats might also be particularly skilled at using their spiritual power to maintain their sense of optimism and hope, even in the face of uncertainty or adversity.

Understanding how Pluto influences your cat's sense of power can help you support them in harnessing their inner strength and using it to overcome challenges and achieve their goals. By recognizing the ways in which your cat naturally expresses power, you can provide the guidance and care they need to navigate life's challenges with confidence and purpose.

Conclusion

Pluto's influence on your cat is deep and transformative, shaping their experiences of change, resilience, and power. By understanding how Pluto affects your cat, you can better support them through periods of transformation and help them harness their inner strength to overcome obstacles and continue to thrive. Whether your cat is a resilient Scorpio or a determined Capricorn, Pluto's energy plays a crucial role in helping them navigate the complexities of life and emerge stronger, wiser, and more self-aware.

As you continue to explore the astrological influences on your cat, remember that Pluto is just one piece of the puzzle. In the following chapters, we'll delve into the other planets and celestial bodies that contribute to your cat's unique personality and behavior, providing a comprehensive understanding of how the cosmos shapes the life of your feline companion.

Part II: Zodiac Signs and Feline Traits

Chapter 11: Aries Cat: Traits, Behavior, and Needs of Cats Born Under the Sign of Aries

Aries, the first sign of the zodiac, is ruled by the fiery and assertive planet Mars. Known for their boldness, energy, and pioneering spirit, Aries cats embody the qualities of this cardinal fire sign. They are often the leaders of the pack, the first to explore new territories, and the most daring of all the zodiac signs. Understanding the unique traits, behavior, and needs of an Aries cat can help you provide the right environment and care to nurture their adventurous and spirited nature.

Aries Cat Traits

Aries cats are born between March 21 and April 19, under the influence of Mars, the planet of action, energy, and aggression. These cats are typically characterized by their boldness, confidence, and high energy levels. They are natural leaders, always ready to take charge and assert their dominance in any situation.

- **Bold and Confident**: Aries cats are not shy. They are the type to walk into a room with their heads held high, ready to explore every corner and meet every new face. They exude confidence and are often fearless, taking on challenges that might intimidate other cats.
- **Energetic and Active**: As a fire sign, Aries is synonymous with energy. Aries cats are often full of life, always on the move, and rarely seen sitting still. They have a high level of physical energy and need plenty of outlets to burn off their excess vitality. Whether it's chasing after toys, climbing to the highest perch, or running around the house at full speed, Aries cats thrive on activity.
- **Independent and Adventurous**: Aries cats are highly independent. They enjoy exploring their surroundings and are often the first to venture into new territories. Their adventurous spirit drives them to seek out new experiences, whether it's exploring the great outdoors or investigating every nook and cranny of your home.
- **Assertive and Competitive**: Aries cats are natural leaders and can be quite assertive. They are not afraid to demand what they want, whether it's food, attention, or a prime spot on the bed. They can also be competitive, especially when it comes to playing with other pets or asserting their dominance.

- **Impulsive and Headstrong**: With their ruling planet Mars, Aries cats can be impulsive and headstrong. They tend to act first and think later, which can sometimes lead them into trouble. Their impulsive nature means they might jump into situations without fully considering the consequences, whether it's chasing after something dangerous or getting into places they shouldn't be.
- **Affectionate but on Their Terms**: While Aries cats are affectionate, they like to be in control of when and how they receive attention. They may not be the type to sit on your lap for long periods, but they will show their love through quick, enthusiastic head bumps, playful pounces, or by simply being in your presence when they choose to be.

Aries Cat Behavior

The behavior of an Aries cat is often a direct reflection of their fiery, energetic, and adventurous nature. Understanding these behaviors can help you better interact with your Aries feline and create a harmonious environment that caters to their unique personality.

- **Playful and Engaging**: Aries cats are incredibly playful. They love engaging in games that challenge their agility and strength. Toys that mimic prey, such as feather wands or laser pointers, are particularly appealing to them. They also enjoy interactive play with their human companions, often initiating games by bringing you a toy or pouncing at your feet.
- **Explorative and Curious**: The curiosity of an Aries cat knows no bounds. They are the explorers of the zodiac, always eager to investigate new areas of their environment. Whether it's a new box, a recently opened door, or a high shelf they haven't conquered yet, an Aries cat will be the first to check it out.
- **Dominant and Territorial**: Aries cats can be quite territorial. They often establish dominance over their territory and may be assertive towards other pets in the household. This behavior can manifest in various ways, such as claiming the best sleeping spots, being the first to eat, or engaging in playful but dominant interactions with other animals.
- **Vocal and Expressive**: Aries cats are not shy about expressing themselves. They tend to be vocal, using a range of meows, purrs, and other sounds to communicate their needs and de-

sires. Whether they are hungry, want to play, or are just demanding attention, an Aries cat will let you know exactly what they want.

- **Brave but Sometimes Reckless**: The boldness of an Aries cat can sometimes lead to reckless behavior. They are brave and often fearless, which can be a double-edged sword. While their courage is admirable, it can sometimes lead them into risky situations. Whether it's leaping from high places, chasing after dangerous prey, or getting into tight spots, an Aries cat's adventurous spirit sometimes needs to be tempered with a bit of caution.
- **Quick to Anger, Quick to Forgive**: Aries cats have a fiery temperament, which means they can be quick to anger. However, they are also quick to forgive and forget. If they feel slighted or frustrated, they might hiss or swat, but their anger usually passes just as quickly as it flares up.

Needs of an Aries Cat

To keep an Aries cat happy, healthy, and fulfilled, it's essential to cater to their specific needs. These needs are primarily driven by their high energy levels, independent nature, and desire for adventure.

- **Plenty of Physical Activity**: Aries cats need plenty of physical activity to burn off their abundant energy. Regular play sessions are a must, and it's important to provide them with toys that stimulate their hunting instincts and keep them engaged. Climbing trees, scratching posts, and interactive toys are all excellent ways to keep an Aries cat active and satisfied.
- **Opportunities for Exploration**: Given their adventurous nature, Aries cats need opportunities to explore. If it's safe, allowing them some supervised outdoor time can be very beneficial. If keeping them indoors, ensure they have plenty of space to roam and explore within the home. New toys, boxes, and hiding spots will keep them entertained and mentally stimulated.
- **Clear Boundaries and Rules**: While Aries cats are independent and assertive, they also need clear boundaries and rules. Consistency is key when dealing with an Aries cat. They need to know what is acceptable and what is not, and it's essential to enforce these rules consistently to help them understand their limits.

- **Mental Stimulation**: In addition to physical activity, Aries cats also need mental stimulation. Puzzle toys, interactive feeders, and games that challenge their problem-solving abilities can help keep their sharp minds engaged. Boredom can lead to destructive behavior in an Aries cat, so keeping them mentally stimulated is crucial.
- **Affection and Attention on Their Terms**: While Aries cats are affectionate, they prefer to receive attention on their terms. It's important to respect their independence and not force affection upon them. They will come to you when they want attention, and when they do, they expect you to be ready to reciprocate.
- **Patience and Understanding**: Given their impulsive nature, Aries cats can sometimes be a handful. Patience and understanding are key when dealing with an Aries cat, especially when they get themselves into trouble. Positive reinforcement, rather than punishment, is the best approach to managing their behavior.
- **A Balanced Diet**: With their high energy levels, Aries cats need a balanced diet that provides them with the necessary nutrients to support their active lifestyle. High-quality cat food that is rich in protein will help maintain their muscle mass and keep them in top physical condition.
- **Regular Health Check-Ups**: Given their tendency to be adventurous and sometimes reckless, regular health check-ups are important for an Aries cat. Regular vet visits will help catch any potential health issues early, ensuring that your Aries cat remains in peak condition.

Conclusion

Aries cats are bold, energetic, and full of life. They bring a sense of adventure and excitement to any household, and their confident, independent nature makes them both challenging and rewarding companions. By understanding their unique traits, behavior, and needs, you can create an environment that supports their spirited personality and allows them to thrive.

Whether it's providing them with plenty of opportunities for physical activity, respecting their independence, or offering mental stimulation, catering to the needs of an Aries cat will help ensure that they remain happy, healthy, and fulfilled. As you continue to explore the astrological influences on your cat, remember that each Aries cat is unique, and their individual personality may vary depending on other factors in their astrological chart. However, the fiery and assertive spirit of Aries will always shine through, making your Aries cat a dynamic and unforgettable member of your family.

Chapter 12: Taurus Cat: Understanding the Steadfast, Comfort-Loving Nature of Taurus Cats

Taurus, the second sign of the zodiac, is ruled by Venus, the planet of love, beauty, and pleasure. Taurus cats, born between April 20 and May 20, embody the grounded, reliable, and comfort-loving qualities of this fixed earth sign. These cats are known for their steadfast nature, love of routine, and deep appreciation for the finer things in life. Understanding the unique traits, behavior, and needs of a Taurus cat can help you create a harmonious and nurturing environment that caters to their love of comfort and stability.

Taurus Cat Traits

Taurus cats are characterized by their steady, patient, and affectionate nature. They are typically more laid-back than other signs, preferring the comfort of a familiar routine and the security of a stable environment. These cats thrive in a peaceful, loving atmosphere where they can enjoy life's simple pleasures.

- **Steadfast and Reliable**: Taurus cats are known for their dependable and steady nature. They are creatures of habit, enjoying a consistent routine and the comfort of familiar surroundings. Once they find a routine that suits them, they are unlikely to deviate from it, which makes them easy to predict and a reliable presence in your life.
- **Loving and Affectionate**: Ruled by Venus, the planet of love, Taurus cats are naturally affectionate. They enjoy being close to their human companions and often seek out physical touch as a way to show their love. Whether it's curling up on your lap, nuzzling against you, or purring contentedly at your side, a Taurus cat loves to express their affection through touch.
- **Comfort-Loving**: Taurus cats have a deep appreciation for comfort and luxury. They enjoy soft, cozy places to sleep, the best food, and the most comfortable spots in the house. These cats are connoisseurs of comfort, and they will seek out the coziest corners, the warmest sunspots, and the most luxurious bedding.
- **Patient and Persistent**: Patience is a hallmark of Taurus cats. They are not easily ruffled and are content to wait for what they want. This patience also translates into persistence; once

a Taurus cat has set their sights on something, they are unlikely to give up until they get it, whether it's a treat, a particular spot, or your attention.

- **Stubborn and Tenacious**: While their persistence is admirable, Taurus cats can also be quite stubborn. Once they have made up their mind about something, it can be difficult to change it. They like things to be done their way and may resist attempts to alter their routine or environment.
- **Sensual and Indulgent**: With Venus as their ruling planet, Taurus cats have a strong connection to the senses. They enjoy indulging in life's pleasures, whether it's savoring a delicious meal, luxuriating in a soft bed, or enjoying a gentle petting session. They are often drawn to things that appeal to their senses, such as soft textures, pleasant smells, and soothing sounds.

Taurus Cat Behavior

The behavior of a Taurus cat is a direct reflection of their earthy, comfort-loving, and steadfast nature. Understanding these behaviors can help you better interact with your Taurus feline and create an environment that caters to their need for stability and comfort.

- **Routine-Oriented**: Taurus cats thrive on routine. They prefer a predictable daily schedule, and any disruption to their routine can cause them stress. They like to eat at the same time every day, sleep in the same spots, and follow a set pattern of behavior. Maintaining a consistent routine is key to keeping a Taurus cat happy and content.
- **Affectionate but Selective**: While Taurus cats are affectionate, they are also selective about when and how they receive attention. They prefer to be the ones to initiate contact and may be less receptive to affection when it's not on their terms. When they do seek out attention, it's often for extended periods, as they love to luxuriate in the comfort of your touch.
- **Territorial and Possessive**: Taurus cats can be quite territorial. They form strong attachments to their favorite spots and belongings, and they may not appreciate others intruding on their space. This territorial nature can extend to their human companions as well, leading them to be possessive of their favorite people.
- **Food-Loving**: Taurus cats are known for their love of food. They often have hearty appetites and enjoy savoring their meals. They may develop a preference for certain foods or treats and

can become quite insistent when it's time to eat. Their love of food means that it's important to monitor their diet to prevent overeating and weight gain.

- **Calm and Laid-Back**: Taurus cats are generally calm and laid-back, preferring a peaceful and quiet environment. They are not easily startled or agitated and tend to handle stress better than more high-strung signs. Their calm demeanor makes them a soothing presence in the household.
- **Stubborn and Resistant to Change**: One of the more challenging aspects of a Taurus cat's behavior is their stubbornness. They are resistant to change and may have difficulty adjusting to new environments, routines, or changes in the household. This stubbornness can also manifest in their refusal to try new foods, toys, or activities.

Needs of a Taurus Cat

To keep a Taurus cat happy, healthy, and fulfilled, it's essential to cater to their specific needs. These needs are primarily driven by their love of comfort, routine, and stability.

- **A Consistent Routine**: Consistency is crucial for a Taurus cat. They thrive on routine and feel most secure when their daily schedule is predictable. Feeding times, play sessions, and bedtime should all follow a regular pattern. Sudden changes to their routine can cause stress, so it's important to introduce any changes gradually.
- **Comfortable Sleeping Arrangements**: Taurus cats are comfort seekers, and they need a cozy, comfortable place to sleep. Providing them with soft bedding, warm blankets, and a quiet, peaceful sleeping area will ensure they get the rest they need. They may also appreciate having multiple sleeping spots throughout the house, so they can choose the most comfortable one depending on their mood.
- **High-Quality Food**: Given their love of food, it's important to provide a Taurus cat with high-quality meals that meet their nutritional needs. They appreciate flavorful, nutritious food, and they may have a preference for certain flavors or textures. It's important to monitor their food intake to prevent overeating and ensure they maintain a healthy weight.
- **Plenty of Affection**: While Taurus cats are independent, they also crave affection and attention from their human companions. They enjoy being petted, stroked, and cuddled, but it's

important to let them initiate these interactions. They are not the type to demand attention, but they will seek it out when they are in the mood for some affection.

- **A Stable Environment**: Stability is key to a Taurus cat's happiness. They prefer a peaceful, quiet home where they can feel safe and secure. They are not fond of sudden changes or disruptions, so it's important to maintain a stable environment for them. If changes are necessary, such as moving to a new home or introducing a new pet, it's important to do so gradually to give your Taurus cat time to adjust.
- **Opportunities for Sensory Indulgence**: Taurus cats have a strong connection to their senses, and they appreciate opportunities to indulge in sensory pleasures. Providing them with soft blankets, fragrant catnip, soothing music, or even a gentle massage can help satisfy their need for sensory stimulation. They also enjoy basking in the sun, so providing them with access to a sunny window or outdoor space can be very beneficial.
- **Patience and Understanding**: Taurus cats can be stubborn and resistant to change, so it's important to approach them with patience and understanding. They may take longer to adjust to new situations or routines, and it's important to give them the time they need to feel comfortable. Positive reinforcement and gentle encouragement are the best ways to guide a Taurus cat through any necessary changes.
- **Gentle Exercise**: While Taurus cats are generally laid-back, they still need regular exercise to maintain their health and prevent weight gain. Gentle, low-impact activities such as playing with feather wands, laser pointers, or interactive toys can help keep them active. They may also enjoy short bursts of play followed by relaxation, in line with their love of comfort and ease.

Conclusion

Taurus cats are the epitome of comfort, stability, and affection. They bring a sense of calm and serenity to any household, and their love of routine and consistency makes them easy companions. By understanding their unique traits, behavior, and needs, you can create an environment that supports their comfort-loving nature and allows them to thrive.

Whether it's providing them with a cozy sleeping spot, maintaining a consistent routine, or indulging their love of good food, catering to the needs of a Taurus cat will help ensure that they remain happy, healthy, and fulfilled. As you continue to explore the astrological influences on your cat, remember that each Taurus cat is unique, and their individual personality may vary depending on other factors in their astrological chart. However, the grounded, steadfast, and comfort-loving spirit of Taurus will always be a defining characteristic, making your Taurus cat a loyal and loving member of your family.

Chapter 13: Gemini Cat: The Curious, Playful, and Sociable Characteristics of Gemini Cats

Gemini, the third sign of the zodiac, is ruled by Mercury, the planet of communication, intellect, and adaptability. Gemini cats, born between May 21 and June 20, are known for their lively, inquisitive, and sociable nature. These cats are natural explorers, quick learners, and enjoy being in the middle of the action. Understanding the unique traits, behavior, and needs of a Gemini cat can help you create an environment that fosters their curious and playful spirit, while also catering to their need for mental stimulation and social interaction.

Gemini Cat Traits

Gemini cats are characterized by their lively and dualistic nature. They are quick-witted, adaptable, and love to engage with their environment and those around them. Their ever-curious minds are always on the lookout for something new and exciting to explore.

- **Curious and Inquisitive**: Gemini cats are inherently curious. They have a deep need to explore their surroundings and learn about everything in their environment. This curiosity often drives them to investigate every nook and cranny, whether it's a new toy, a freshly opened box, or a space they've never ventured into before. Their inquisitive nature means they are always on the lookout for new experiences, and they thrive in environments that offer plenty of variety and stimulation.
- **Playful and Energetic**: Play is a central part of a Gemini cat's life. They are energetic and love to engage in activities that challenge their agility, speed, and intellect. Gemini cats are often found darting around the house, chasing after toys, or engaging in playful interactions with their human companions or other pets. Their playfulness is infectious, and they have a knack for bringing joy and excitement to any situation.
- **Sociable and Communicative**: Gemini cats are natural communicators. They love to interact with their human companions, other animals, and even objects in their environment. These cats are often quite vocal, using a variety of sounds—meows, chirps, purrs—to express themselves. They also have a way of using body language and facial expressions to communicate their needs and desires. Gemini cats enjoy being part of the social dynamics in a household and often seek out interaction and attention.

- **Intelligent and Quick-Learning**: Ruled by Mercury, the planet of intellect, Gemini cats are highly intelligent and quick learners. They enjoy mental challenges and are often the first to figure out how to open doors, access treats, or solve puzzles. Their intelligence makes them adept at learning new tricks or behaviors, and they thrive when given tasks that engage their minds.
- **Adaptable and Versatile**: One of the defining traits of a Gemini cat is their adaptability. They can easily adjust to new environments, routines, and experiences. This versatility means that they are usually comfortable in a variety of settings, whether it's a bustling household or a quieter, more solitary environment. Gemini cats are also known for their dual nature, which means they can quickly switch between different moods and behaviors depending on the situation.
- **Restless and Easily Bored**: While their curiosity and intelligence are strengths, they can also lead to restlessness and boredom if not properly engaged. Gemini cats need constant stimulation, and if they don't receive it, they can become bored and may resort to destructive behavior as a way to entertain themselves.

Gemini Cat Behavior

The behavior of a Gemini cat reflects their lively, curious, and sociable nature. Understanding these behaviors can help you better interact with your Gemini feline and create an environment that meets their needs for stimulation and social engagement.

- **Explorative and Adventurous**: Gemini cats are natural explorers. They are always on the move, looking for new places to investigate and new experiences to enjoy. Whether it's climbing to the highest point in the room, crawling into a small space, or investigating a new object, a Gemini cat is always curious and eager to explore. This behavior is driven by their need to understand their environment and satisfy their curiosity.
- **Interactive and Engaging**: Gemini cats love to interact with their human companions and other pets. They enjoy engaging in play, conversation, and other forms of interaction. These cats are often at their happiest when they are in the middle of the action, whether it's playing a game with you, chasing after a toy, or simply following you around the house to see what

you're up to. Their sociable nature means they often seek out attention and enjoy being the center of activity.

- **Vocal and Expressive**: Communication is key for Gemini cats. They are often quite vocal and use a variety of sounds to express themselves. Whether they are meowing for attention, chirping in excitement, or purring contentedly, Gemini cats have a way of making their presence known. They also use body language, such as tail flicks, ear movements, and facial expressions, to convey their feelings and intentions.

- **Playful and Mischievous**: Play is a major part of a Gemini cat's behavior. They are playful by nature and enjoy engaging in activities that challenge their minds and bodies. This playfulness can sometimes lead to mischievous behavior, as they may get into things they shouldn't or create chaos in their quest for entertainment. However, their antics are usually more amusing than troublesome, and they have a way of winning you over with their charm.

- **Intellectual and Problem-Solving**: Gemini cats are highly intelligent and enjoy mental challenges. They are often quick to figure out puzzles, learn new tricks, or solve problems. Whether it's figuring out how to open a door, accessing a hidden treat, or learning a new behavior, Gemini cats excel at tasks that require thinking and problem-solving. They enjoy being mentally stimulated and thrive in environments that provide them with opportunities to use their intellect.

- **Restless and Impatient**: While Gemini cats are adaptable, they can also be restless and impatient. They have a hard time sitting still and may become bored or frustrated if they don't have enough to do. This restlessness can sometimes lead to fidgety behavior, such as pacing, scratching, or even vocalizing their displeasure. It's important to provide them with plenty of activities and stimulation to keep their minds and bodies engaged.

Needs of a Gemini Cat

To keep a Gemini cat happy, healthy, and fulfilled, it's essential to cater to their specific needs. These needs are primarily driven by their curiosity, intelligence, and sociable nature.

- **Mental Stimulation**: Gemini cats need plenty of mental stimulation to keep their sharp minds engaged. Puzzle toys, interactive feeders, and games that challenge their problem-solving abilities are ideal for keeping them entertained. Teaching them new tricks or introducing them to new activities can also help satisfy their need for intellectual engagement.

- **Variety and Change**: Given their adaptable nature, Gemini cats thrive on variety and change. They enjoy new experiences, whether it's a new toy, a different play area, or a novel routine. Regularly rotating their toys, changing their environment, or introducing new challenges can help keep them stimulated and prevent boredom.

- **Social Interaction**: Gemini cats are highly social and need regular interaction with their human companions and other pets. They enjoy being part of the social dynamics in a household and often seek out attention and engagement. Spending time playing with them, talking to them, or simply being in their presence can help meet their social needs.

- **Physical Activity**: In addition to mental stimulation, Gemini cats need regular physical activity to burn off their energy. They enjoy playing games that challenge their agility, such as chasing after toys, climbing, or jumping. Providing them with climbing trees, scratching posts, and plenty of space to run around can help keep them physically fit and mentally engaged.

- **Communication and Engagement**: Communication is key for a Gemini cat, so it's important to engage with them regularly. Talking to them, responding to their vocalizations, and engaging in interactive play can help meet their need for communication and connection. Gemini cats enjoy being heard and understood, so taking the time to engage with them on their terms is essential.

- **A Stimulating Environment**: Gemini cats need an environment that provides them with plenty of opportunities for exploration and discovery. This can include a variety of toys, interactive play spaces, and access to different areas of the home. Creating an environment that offers both physical and mental stimulation can help keep a Gemini cat happy and content.

- **Patience and Understanding**: Given their restless and sometimes mischievous nature, it's important to approach a Gemini cat with patience and understanding. They may get into trouble or become impatient if they don't have enough to do, so providing them with plenty of outlets for their energy and curiosity is key. Positive reinforcement and gentle guidance can help manage their behavior and encourage them to use their energy in constructive ways.

- **Regular Interaction**: Gemini cats thrive on social interaction, so it's important to spend regular time with them. Whether it's playing a game, having a conversation, or simply being in the same room, regular interaction helps keep them engaged and prevents them from feeling lonely or bored.

Conclusion

Gemini cats are lively, curious, and full of energy. They bring a sense of excitement and playfulness to any household, and their sociable, communicative nature makes them delightful companions. By understanding their unique traits, behavior, and needs, you can create an environment that supports their inquisitive and playful personality, allowing them to thrive.

Whether it's providing them with plenty of mental stimulation, engaging in regular social interaction, or creating a dynamic environment that offers variety and change, catering to the needs of a Gemini cat will help ensure that they remain happy, healthy, and fulfilled. As you continue to explore the astrological influences on your cat, remember that each Gemini cat is unique, and their individual personality may vary depending on other factors in their astrological chart. However, the curious, playful, and sociable spirit of Gemini will always be a defining characteristic, making your Gemini cat a lively and engaging member of your family.

Chapter 14: Cancer Cat: The Nurturing, Sensitive, and Home-Loving Nature of Cancer Cats

Cancer, the fourth sign of the zodiac, is ruled by the Moon, which governs emotions, instincts, and the home. Cancer cats, born between June 21 and July 22, embody the nurturing, sensitive, and home-loving qualities of this cardinal water sign. These cats are deeply connected to their families, have a strong sense of security and comfort, and are often the emotional center of their households. Understanding the unique traits, behavior, and needs of a Cancer cat can help you create a safe, loving, and stable environment that allows them to thrive.

Cancer Cat Traits

Cancer cats are characterized by their strong emotional sensitivity, loyalty, and deep attachment to their home and family. They are intuitive, caring, and often act as the protectors and nurturers within their household.

- **Nurturing and Caring**: Cancer cats are natural nurturers. They are often seen taking care of other animals in the household or showing affection towards their human companions. Their caring nature extends to all aspects of their life, whether it's gently grooming a fellow pet, offering comfort when you're feeling down, or simply being by your side when you need them.
- **Emotionally Sensitive**: Ruled by the Moon, Cancer cats are highly attuned to emotions. They can sense when something is off and often mirror the moods of those around them. If you're feeling sad or stressed, your Cancer cat will likely pick up on it and try to offer comfort in their own way. This emotional sensitivity makes them incredibly empathetic and deeply connected to their human companions.
- **Loyal and Protective**: Loyalty is a hallmark of Cancer cats. Once they form a bond with you, they are incredibly devoted and protective. They are the type of cat that will follow you around the house, always keeping an eye on you to make sure you're safe. This protective nature can also extend to their territory, making them highly alert to any changes or potential threats in their environment.

- **Home-Loving**: Cancer cats are true homebodies. They thrive in a stable, secure environment and are happiest when surrounded by familiar comforts. They form strong attachments to their home and may become anxious or stressed if their environment changes too much. A cozy, comforting space where they feel safe and secure is essential for a Cancer cat's well-being.

- **Intuitive and Instinctive**: Cancer cats have strong instincts and are often guided by their intuition. They seem to "just know" things, whether it's sensing when something is about to happen or understanding what you need without you having to say a word. This intuitive nature makes them highly responsive to the needs of their human companions and other pets in the household.

- **Moody and Reserved**: Like the phases of the Moon, Cancer cats can be moody and may go through periods of withdrawal. They might retreat to a quiet, safe space when they feel overwhelmed or need time to themselves. While they are generally affectionate, there will be times when they prefer solitude, and it's important to respect their need for personal space.

Cancer Cat Behavior

The behavior of a Cancer cat reflects their nurturing, sensitive, and home-loving nature. Understanding these behaviors can help you better interact with your Cancer feline and create an environment that meets their emotional and physical needs.

- **Affectionate and Clingy**: Cancer cats are deeply affectionate and often form strong attachments to their human companions. They enjoy being close to you, whether it's sitting on your lap, sleeping next to you, or following you from room to room. This affection can sometimes manifest as clinginess, with your Cancer cat wanting to be near you at all times. They thrive on physical touch and emotional closeness, and they may become anxious or stressed if they feel neglected or if you are away for long periods.

- **Protective and Alert**: Cancer cats are natural protectors. They are often highly alert to any changes in their environment and will quickly notice if something is amiss. This protective nature means they may be wary of strangers or new animals in the household, often taking some time to warm up to them. They are also likely to position themselves in a way that allows them to keep an eye on everything, ensuring that their home and family are safe.

- **Cautious and Introverted**: Cancer cats are generally cautious and may take their time when approaching new situations or people. They prefer to observe from a distance before fully engaging, and they may retreat to a safe space if they feel overwhelmed. This introverted nature means that they are more comfortable in familiar surroundings and may need extra reassurance when faced with changes or new experiences.
- **Comfort-Seeking**: Cancer cats have a deep love for comfort and will seek out the coziest spots in the house. They enjoy soft blankets, warm beds, and sunny windowsills where they can relax and feel secure. They are likely to have a favorite spot that they return to time and time again, where they feel safe and at peace.
- **Moody and Withdrawn**: Just as the Moon has phases, so too do Cancer cats experience mood swings. They may go through periods where they are more withdrawn and prefer to be alone. During these times, they may retreat to a quiet, secluded spot where they can be undisturbed. It's important to respect their need for solitude and give them the space they need to recharge emotionally.
- **Empathetic and Intuitive**: Cancer cats are highly empathetic and often mirror the emotions of those around them. They are quick to pick up on your moods and will often respond in kind, offering comfort when you're sad or being playful when you're happy. Their intuitive nature makes them highly attuned to your needs, and they often seem to know what you need before you do.

Needs of a Cancer Cat

To keep a Cancer cat happy, healthy, and fulfilled, it's essential to cater to their specific needs. These needs are primarily driven by their love of comfort, emotional sensitivity, and strong attachment to their home and family.

- **A Stable and Secure Environment**: Stability is key for a Cancer cat. They thrive in a consistent, secure environment where they feel safe and protected. Sudden changes to their routine, environment, or household can cause them significant stress, so it's important to maintain a stable and predictable atmosphere. If changes are necessary, such as moving to a new home or introducing a new pet, it's important to do so gradually and provide plenty of reassurance.

- **Comfortable and Cozy Spaces**: Cancer cats need a cozy, comfortable space where they can retreat and feel secure. Soft bedding, warm blankets, and quiet, secluded spots are essential for their well-being. They are likely to have a favorite spot in the house where they feel most at ease, and it's important to make this area as comfortable as possible.
- **Affection and Emotional Support**: Cancer cats are highly affectionate and need plenty of love and attention from their human companions. They thrive on physical touch, such as petting, cuddling, and being close to you. Regular interaction and emotional support are crucial for their happiness. They need to feel loved and valued, and they will often seek out your attention and affection to reinforce this bond.
- **Respect for Their Need for Solitude**: While Cancer cats are affectionate, they also need time alone to recharge emotionally. It's important to respect their need for solitude and provide them with a quiet, undisturbed space where they can retreat when they need a break. Pushing them to interact when they are not in the mood can lead to stress and anxiety, so it's best to let them come to you when they are ready.
- **A Strong Connection to Home**: Cancer cats have a deep connection to their home and need to feel secure in their surroundings. Providing them with a consistent environment that they can rely on is crucial for their well-being. They may also appreciate having access to familiar objects, such as a favorite blanket or toy, that provide them with comfort and a sense of continuity.
- **Gentle and Patient Handling**: Given their sensitive nature, Cancer cats need to be handled with care and patience. They may be more easily startled or upset than other cats, so it's important to approach them gently and avoid sudden movements or loud noises. Positive reinforcement and gentle encouragement are the best ways to build trust and help them feel secure.
- **Opportunities for Emotional Bonding**: Cancer cats thrive on emotional connections and need regular opportunities to bond with their human companions. Spending time with them, talking to them, and engaging in activities that they enjoy can help strengthen this bond. Whether it's a quiet cuddle session, a gentle grooming session, or simply sitting together in a peaceful environment, these moments of connection are essential for a Cancer cat's happiness.

Conclusion

Cancer cats are nurturing, sensitive, and deeply connected to their home and family. They bring a sense of warmth, love, and security to any household, and their caring, empathetic nature makes them deeply devoted companions. By understanding their unique traits, behavior, and needs, you can create an environment that supports their emotional and physical well-being, allowing them to thrive.

Whether it's providing them with a cozy, stable environment, offering plenty of affection and emotional support, or respecting their need for solitude, catering to the needs of a Cancer cat will help ensure that they remain happy, healthy, and fulfilled. As you continue to explore the astrological influences on your cat, remember that each Cancer cat is unique, and their individual personality may vary depending on other factors in their astrological chart. However, the nurturing, sensitive, and home-loving spirit of Cancer will always be a defining characteristic, making your Cancer cat a cherished and beloved member of your family.

Chapter 15: Leo Cat: The Regal, Proud, and Attention-Seeking Traits of Leo Cats

Leo, the fifth sign of the zodiac, is ruled by the Sun, the celestial body that represents life, energy, and self-expression. Leo cats, born between July 23 and August 22, embody the regal, proud, and attention-seeking qualities of this fixed fire sign. These cats are natural leaders, confident, and thrive in the spotlight. Understanding the unique traits, behavior, and needs of a Leo cat can help you create an environment that honors their majestic nature while providing them with the admiration and attention they crave.

Leo Cat Traits

Leo cats are characterized by their strong sense of self, charisma, and need for recognition. They are often the center of attention in any household, and their confident, commanding presence is impossible to ignore.

- **Regal and Majestic**: Leo cats carry themselves with a sense of majesty and pride. They have a natural grace and poise that makes them stand out from the crowd. Whether it's the way they walk, the way they sit, or the way they interact with others, there's an unmistakable air of royalty about them. They expect to be treated with respect and often act as though they are the rulers of their domain.
- **Confident and Self-Assured**: Confidence is a hallmark of Leo cats. They are rarely shy or uncertain and often approach the world with a bold, fearless attitude. This self-assuredness makes them natural leaders, and they are often the ones who take charge in group dynamics, whether it's with other pets or within their interactions with humans.
- **Attention-Seeking and Social**: Leo cats love being the center of attention. They thrive on admiration and enjoy being in the spotlight. Whether it's through playful antics, showing off their skills, or simply demanding affection, Leo cats are always looking for ways to draw attention to themselves. They are highly social and enjoy interacting with their human companions and other pets, often seeking out the limelight in any situation.
- **Proud and Dignified**: Pride is a key trait of Leo cats. They have a strong sense of dignity and self-worth, and they expect to be treated accordingly. They take pride in their appearance and often enjoy grooming themselves or being groomed. They are also proud of their abilities and

achievements, whether it's catching a toy, finding the best spot to lounge, or receiving praise from their humans.

- **Affectionate and Loyal**: Despite their regal demeanor, Leo cats are incredibly affectionate and loyal. They form strong bonds with their human companions and are devoted to those they love. They enjoy giving and receiving affection and often express their love through physical touch, such as cuddling, head-butting, or purring contentedly in your lap.
- **Dramatic and Expressive**: Leo cats have a flair for the dramatic. They are highly expressive and often use their body language, vocalizations, and actions to convey their emotions. Whether they are happy, displeased, or excited, a Leo cat will make sure you know exactly how they feel. Their dramatic nature can be both endearing and amusing, as they often put on a show to get what they want.

Leo Cat Behavior

The behavior of a Leo cat reflects their regal, confident, and attention-seeking nature. Understanding these behaviors can help you better interact with your Leo feline and create an environment that caters to their need for recognition and social interaction.

- **Commanding Attention**: Leo cats have a natural ability to command attention. They are not shy about making their presence known and will often go out of their way to ensure they are noticed. Whether it's through playful antics, vocal demands for attention, or simply positioning themselves in the center of the room, Leo cats are always looking for ways to be in the spotlight. They enjoy being admired and often seek out opportunities to show off their skills or charm their human companions.
- **Playful and Energetic**: Play is an important part of a Leo cat's life. They are energetic and enjoy engaging in activities that challenge their agility, strength, and intelligence. Leo cats often prefer games that allow them to show off, such as catching a toy mid-air or performing tricks. They also enjoy interactive play with their human companions, and they are likely to initiate games by bringing you a toy or engaging in playful behavior to grab your attention.
- **Social and Affectionate**: Leo cats are highly social and thrive on interaction with others. They enjoy being around their human companions and other pets, and they often seek out

attention and affection. They are known for their loyalty and will often follow their favorite humans from room to room, ensuring they are always close by. Leo cats enjoy being petted, cuddled, and groomed, and they often express their affection through purring, head-butting, and other forms of physical touch.

- **Dramatic and Vocal**: Drama is a significant part of a Leo cat's behavior. They are highly expressive and often use their vocalizations and body language to convey their emotions. A Leo cat will not hesitate to let you know when they are displeased, excited, or seeking attention. Their vocalizations can range from loud meows to chirps and purrs, and they often accompany these sounds with expressive body language, such as tail flicks, ear movements, and exaggerated gestures.

- **Territorial and Protective**: Leo cats have a strong sense of territory and often take on a protective role within their household. They are highly alert to any changes in their environment and will quickly notice if something is amiss. This territorial nature means they may be wary of strangers or new animals in the household, and they may take some time to warm up to them. Once they have established their territory, they are likely to defend it fiercely, ensuring that their domain remains secure.

- **Proud and Independent**: While Leo cats are affectionate and social, they also have a strong sense of independence. They take pride in their abilities and often prefer to do things on their own terms. This independence can sometimes make them appear aloof, but it is simply a reflection of their self-assured nature. They enjoy being admired and appreciated but do not like to be fussed over excessively.

Needs of a Leo Cat

To keep a Leo cat happy, healthy, and fulfilled, it's essential to cater to their specific needs. These needs are primarily driven by their love of attention, social interaction, and the desire to be recognized and appreciated.

- **Plenty of Attention and Recognition**: Leo cats thrive on attention and recognition. They enjoy being the center of attention and need regular interaction with their human companions. Spending time playing with them, grooming them, and praising them for their achievements can help meet their need for admiration. They appreciate being acknowledged and will often go out of their way to earn your approval.

- **Opportunities to Show Off**: Given their love of the spotlight, Leo cats need opportunities to show off their skills and abilities. Providing them with toys that allow them to demonstrate their agility and strength, such as feather wands, laser pointers, or climbing trees, can help satisfy their need to impress. Teaching them tricks or engaging in games that challenge their intelligence can also help keep them mentally stimulated and entertained.
- **A Comfortable and Luxurious Environment**: Leo cats have a natural affinity for comfort and luxury. They enjoy lounging in the best spots in the house, whether it's a sunny windowsill, a plush bed, or a cozy blanket. Providing them with a comfortable and luxurious environment, including soft bedding, warm spaces, and plenty of cozy spots to relax, will help keep them content and happy.
- **Social Interaction and Affection**: Leo cats are highly social and need regular interaction with their human companions and other pets. They enjoy being around others and often seek out affection and attention. Spending time with them, talking to them, and engaging in activities that they enjoy can help strengthen your bond and meet their social needs. They also appreciate being groomed and petted, as it reinforces their sense of connection and affection.
- **Respect for Their Independence**: While Leo cats enjoy attention, they also have a strong sense of independence. It's important to respect their need for autonomy and allow them to do things on their own terms. Pushing them to interact when they are not in the mood can lead to frustration, so it's best to let them come to you when they are ready. Providing them with space and allowing them to retreat to a quiet area when they need a break is essential for their well-being.
- **A Safe and Secure Territory**: Leo cats are territorial and need to feel secure in their environment. Providing them with a defined territory where they can feel safe and in control is crucial for their happiness. They may also appreciate having access to high perches or quiet spots where they can observe their surroundings and ensure their territory is secure.
- **Opportunities for Physical and Mental Stimulation**: Leo cats need regular physical and mental stimulation to keep them engaged and happy. Providing them with toys that challenge their agility, strength, and intelligence can help keep them entertained. They also enjoy inter-

active play with their human companions, so regular play sessions are essential. Engaging in activities that allow them to demonstrate their abilities and receive praise will help satisfy their need for recognition and mental stimulation.

Conclusion

Leo cats are regal, proud, and full of life. They bring a sense of grandeur and excitement to any household, and their confident, attention-seeking nature makes them unforgettable companions. By understanding their unique traits, behavior, and needs, you can create an environment that honors their majestic personality and allows them to thrive.

Whether it's providing them with plenty of attention and recognition, creating a luxurious and comfortable environment, or respecting their independence and territorial nature, catering to the needs of a Leo cat will help ensure that they remain happy, healthy, and fulfilled. As you continue to explore the astrological influences on your cat, remember that each Leo cat is unique, and their individual personality may vary depending on other factors in their astrological chart. However, the regal, proud, and attention-seeking spirit of Leo will always be a defining characteristic, making your Leo cat a charismatic and beloved member of your family.

Chapter 16: Virgo Cat: The Meticulous, Intelligent, and Health-Conscious Virgo Cats

Virgo, the sixth sign of the zodiac, is ruled by Mercury, the planet of communication, intellect, and analysis. Virgo cats, born between August 23 and September 22, embody the meticulous, intelligent, and health-conscious qualities of this mutable earth sign. These cats are often known for their precise behavior, keen intellect, and strong preference for cleanliness and routine. Understanding the unique traits, behavior, and needs of a Virgo cat can help you create an environment that caters to their desire for order, mental stimulation, and well-being.

Virgo Cat Traits

Virgo cats are characterized by their attention to detail, analytical nature, and a strong sense of duty towards their own health and well-being. They are often the perfectionists of the feline world, preferring things to be just right and taking a meticulous approach to everything they do.

- **Meticulous and Clean**: Virgo cats are highly meticulous, especially when it comes to cleanliness. They are often fastidious groomers, spending a significant amount of time ensuring their coat is spotless and well-maintained. They are likely to have a strong preference for a clean living environment, including a tidy litter box and well-organized spaces. They may even have specific preferences for where they eat, sleep, and play, preferring areas that are clean and orderly.
- **Intelligent and Analytical**: Ruled by Mercury, Virgo cats possess sharp intellect and an analytical mind. They are quick learners and enjoy tasks that challenge their problem-solving abilities. Whether it's figuring out how to open a door, solving a puzzle toy, or observing and understanding the routines of their human companions, Virgo cats approach the world with a methodical and thoughtful mindset.
- **Health-Conscious and Hygienic**: Virgo cats have a strong awareness of their health and well-being. They are likely to be particular about their diet, preferring foods that are fresh and nutritious. Their attention to detail extends to their hygiene, making them particular about their grooming habits and their environment. They may even display behaviors that suggest a preference for a healthy lifestyle, such as being more active, avoiding certain foods, or preferring natural, clean spaces.

- **Reserved and Modest**: Virgo cats tend to be more reserved and modest compared to more outgoing signs. They are not usually attention-seekers and may prefer to observe from the sidelines rather than being the center of attention. They can be somewhat shy or cautious around new people or environments, preferring to take their time to assess situations before fully engaging.
- **Dependable and Routine-Oriented**: Virgo cats thrive on routine and predictability. They are creatures of habit and feel most comfortable when their daily schedule is consistent. Whether it's feeding times, play sessions, or bedtime, Virgo cats appreciate knowing what to expect and may become unsettled if their routine is disrupted.
- **Perfectionistic and Picky**: The perfectionist tendencies of Virgo cats mean they can be quite particular about their preferences. Whether it's the type of food they eat, the texture of their bedding, or the cleanliness of their litter box, they know what they like and may be quick to show displeasure if something doesn't meet their standards. Their picky nature can extend to their interactions with others, as they may prefer the company of those who respect their need for order and cleanliness.

Virgo Cat Behavior

The behavior of a Virgo cat reflects their meticulous, intelligent, and health-conscious nature. Understanding these behaviors can help you better interact with your Virgo feline and create an environment that meets their need for order, mental stimulation, and well-being.

- **Grooming and Cleanliness**: Virgo cats are often fastidious about grooming. They spend a considerable amount of time cleaning themselves and ensuring their coat is free of dirt, debris, and tangles. This behavior is not just about hygiene but also reflects their desire for order and precision. A Virgo cat may also be particular about the cleanliness of their environment, preferring a tidy space with clean bedding, toys, and litter box. They may show signs of distress if their surroundings become too messy or disorganized.
- **Observant and Analytical**: Virgo cats are highly observant and often take a thoughtful approach to their environment. They are likely to spend time watching and analyzing the behaviors of their human companions, other pets, and the world around them. This analytical

nature makes them quick learners, and they often figure out patterns, routines, and even how to manipulate objects to get what they want. They enjoy mentally stimulating activities that allow them to use their intelligence, such as puzzle toys, interactive feeders, or games that challenge their problem-solving skills.

- **Routine-Oriented and Predictable**: Virgo cats thrive on routine and predictability. They prefer a consistent daily schedule and may become stressed or anxious if their routine is disrupted. Whether it's feeding times, play sessions, or bedtime, Virgo cats appreciate knowing what to expect and when. They are likely to remind you if you forget something important, such as their meal or regular grooming time.

- **Health-Conscious and Selective**: Virgo cats are often selective about what they eat and may prefer foods that are fresh, natural, and of high quality. They may turn up their noses at food that doesn't meet their standards, especially if it's not to their usual taste or freshness. Their health-conscious nature extends to their overall well-being, and they may exhibit behaviors that suggest a preference for a healthy lifestyle, such as staying active, choosing clean and comfortable spots to rest, or avoiding areas that they perceive as dirty or unsafe.

- **Reserved and Cautious**: Virgo cats are typically more reserved and cautious than other signs. They may be shy around new people or in unfamiliar environments, preferring to observe from a safe distance before fully engaging. They appreciate a quiet, peaceful atmosphere and may retreat to a safe, secluded spot if they feel overwhelmed or stressed. Their reserved nature means they are less likely to seek out attention or demand affection, but they are deeply loyal and affectionate with those they trust.

- **Picky and Perfectionistic**: Virgo cats can be quite particular about their preferences and may be quick to show displeasure if something doesn't meet their standards. Whether it's the type of food they eat, the cleanliness of their litter box, or the arrangement of their favorite toys, they know what they like and expect things to be just right. This perfectionist nature means they may be more sensitive to changes in their environment and may require extra attention to detail to keep them happy and content.

Needs of a Virgo Cat

To keep a Virgo cat happy, healthy, and fulfilled, it's essential to cater to their specific needs. These needs are primarily driven by their desire for cleanliness, mental stimulation, and a consistent routine.

- **A Clean and Organized Environment**: Cleanliness is crucial for a Virgo cat's well-being. They thrive in a clean, organized environment and may become stressed or anxious if their surroundings are messy or disorganized. Regular cleaning of their litter box, bedding, and living spaces is essential to keep them happy. Providing them with a tidy, comfortable space to rest and play will help them feel secure and content.
- **Regular Grooming**: Virgo cats are meticulous groomers, but they also appreciate a little help from their human companions. Regular grooming sessions, such as brushing their coat, trimming their nails, and cleaning their ears, will help keep them looking and feeling their best. These grooming sessions can also serve as a bonding experience, as Virgo cats enjoy the attention and care that comes with being groomed.
- **High-Quality, Nutritious Food**: Virgo cats are often selective about their diet and prefer foods that are fresh, natural, and nutritious. Providing them with high-quality cat food that meets their dietary needs is essential for their health and well-being. They may also appreciate a consistent feeding schedule, as they thrive on routine and predictability. Be mindful of their preferences and avoid feeding them food that is stale or unappetizing, as they are likely to reject it.
- **Mental Stimulation and Problem-Solving**: Virgo cats are intelligent and enjoy activities that challenge their minds. Providing them with puzzle toys, interactive feeders, and games that require problem-solving skills will help keep them mentally stimulated and engaged. Teaching them new tricks or introducing them to new activities can also help satisfy their need for intellectual engagement. They enjoy learning and figuring things out, so offering them challenges that require thought and analysis will keep them entertained and happy.

- **A Consistent Routine**: Routine is vital for a Virgo cat's sense of security and well-being. They thrive on a consistent daily schedule, whether it's feeding times, play sessions, or grooming rituals. Maintaining a predictable routine will help them feel secure and reduce stress. If changes are necessary, such as a shift in feeding times or the introduction of a new activity, it's essential to introduce them gradually and with care.
- **Respect for Their Preferences**: Virgo cats can be quite particular about their preferences, so it's important to respect their likes and dislikes. Whether it's the type of food they eat, the cleanliness of their litter box, or the arrangement of their favorite toys, paying attention to their preferences will help keep them happy and content. Being mindful of their need for order and cleanliness, and making adjustments to accommodate their preferences, will go a long way in ensuring their well-being.
- **Gentle and Patient Handling**: Given their reserved and cautious nature, Virgo cats need to be handled with care and patience. They may be more sensitive to changes or disruptions in their environment, so it's important to approach them gently and avoid sudden movements or loud noises. Positive reinforcement and gentle encouragement are the best ways to build trust and help them feel secure.

Conclusion

Virgo cats are meticulous, intelligent, and health-conscious, bringing a sense of order and precision to any household. They are attentive to detail, enjoy a clean and organized environment, and thrive on mental stimulation and routine. By understanding their unique traits, behavior, and needs, you can create an environment that supports their desire for order, cleanliness, and well-being, allowing them to thrive.

Whether it's providing them with a clean and comfortable living space, offering high-quality food, or engaging them in mentally stimulating activities, catering to the needs of a Virgo cat will help ensure that they remain happy, healthy, and fulfilled. As you continue to explore the astrological influences on your cat, remember that each Virgo cat is unique, and their individual personality may vary depending on other factors in their astrological chart. However, the meticulous, intelligent, and health-conscious spirit of Virgo will always be a defining characteristic, making your Virgo cat a refined and beloved member of your family.

Chapter 17: Libra Cat: The Sociable, Balanced, and Harmony-Seeking Libra Cats

Libra, the seventh sign of the zodiac, is ruled by Venus, the planet of love, beauty, and harmony. Libra cats, born between September 23 and October 22, embody the sociable, balanced, and harmony-seeking qualities of this cardinal air sign. These cats are natural diplomats, known for their love of social interaction, their desire for peace and balance in their environment, and their appreciation for beauty and comfort. Understanding the unique traits, behavior, and needs of a Libra cat can help you create an environment that fosters their love of companionship, their need for balance, and their desire for a harmonious, aesthetically pleasing space.

Libra Cat Traits

Libra cats are characterized by their sociable nature, love of balance, and deep appreciation for harmony in all aspects of their life. They are friendly, charming, and often play the role of the peacemaker in their household.

- **Sociable and Friendly**: Libra cats are highly social and enjoy the company of others, whether it's their human companions, other pets, or even strangers. They are the type of cat that will greet visitors at the door, eager to make new friends and be part of the social dynamics of the household. Their friendly and approachable nature makes them popular among people and pets alike.
- **Harmony-Seeking and Diplomatic**: Ruled by Venus, Libra cats have a natural inclination towards harmony and balance. They thrive in peaceful environments and are often the ones to mediate conflicts between other pets or even among their human family members. They dislike tension and will go out of their way to restore harmony in their surroundings. Their diplomatic nature makes them excellent at smoothing over disputes and ensuring that everyone gets along.
- **Charming and Affectionate**: Libra cats have a natural charm that is hard to resist. They are affectionate and enjoy being close to their human companions, often seeking out attention and affection in a gentle, non-demanding way. Their charm and grace make them delightful companions, and they are likely to win the hearts of everyone they meet.
- **Balanced and Fair-Minded**: Libra cats have a strong sense of balance and fairness. They prefer an environment where everything is in equilibrium, whether it's the amount of attention

they receive, the distribution of resources, or the overall atmosphere of the home. They are unlikely to be overly demanding or aggressive, preferring instead to maintain a calm and balanced demeanor.

- **Aesthetic and Beauty-Loving**: With Venus as their ruling planet, Libra cats have a deep appreciation for beauty and comfort. They are drawn to aesthetically pleasing environments and enjoy being surrounded by beautiful things, whether it's a cozy bed, a soft blanket, or a well-decorated space. They may even show a preference for certain colors, textures, or objects that appeal to their sense of beauty.
- **Indecisive and Contemplative**: One of the more challenging aspects of a Libra cat's personality is their tendency towards indecisiveness. They may take their time when making decisions, whether it's choosing a spot to sleep, deciding when to eat, or selecting a toy to play with. This contemplative nature means they often weigh their options carefully, seeking the perfect balance before taking action.

Libra Cat Behavior

The behavior of a Libra cat reflects their sociable, balanced, and harmony-seeking nature. Understanding these behaviors can help you better interact with your Libra feline and create an environment that meets their need for social interaction, balance, and beauty.

- **Social and Interactive**: Libra cats thrive on social interaction. They enjoy being around others and are likely to seek out the company of their human companions, other pets, or even visitors. They are often the first to greet new people or pets, eager to make friends and be part of the social dynamics of the household. Libra cats enjoy engaging in activities that involve others, whether it's playing with a toy alongside another pet or simply lounging in the same room as their human companions.
- **Peacemaking and Diplomatic**: Libra cats are natural peacemakers. They have a strong aversion to conflict and will often step in to mediate disputes between other pets or even between their human family members. If there is tension in the household, a Libra cat is likely to sense it and will go out of their way to restore harmony. This may involve physically placing them-

selves between the parties involved, offering affection to soothe tempers, or simply providing a calming presence.

- **Affectionate and Gentle**: Libra cats are affectionate but in a gentle, non-demanding way. They enjoy being close to their human companions and often seek out attention in a subtle, charming manner. They are likely to nuzzle against you, purr contentedly when petted, or quietly sit beside you to show their affection. Their gentle nature makes them easy to love, and they often form strong bonds with those they care about.

- **Balanced and Fair**: Balance is key for a Libra cat. They prefer environments where there is a sense of fairness and equality, whether it's in the distribution of attention, the availability of resources, or the overall atmosphere of the home. They are unlikely to be overly demanding or aggressive, instead preferring to maintain a calm and balanced demeanor. If they sense that something is out of balance, they may become uneasy and will seek to restore harmony.

- **Aesthetic Preferences**: Libra cats have a keen sense of aesthetics and may show a preference for certain colors, textures, or objects in their environment. They are drawn to beautiful and comfortable spaces and may choose to spend time in areas that are particularly well-decorated or pleasing to the eye. Whether it's a cozy bed with a soft blanket or a sunny spot with a view, Libra cats appreciate the finer things in life and will gravitate towards spaces that reflect their love of beauty.

- **Indecisiveness and Contemplation**: Libra cats can be indecisive, often taking their time to make decisions. This may manifest in behaviors such as pacing back and forth before choosing a spot to sleep, taking a long time to select a toy, or hesitating before deciding when to eat. Their contemplative nature means they often weigh their options carefully, seeking the perfect balance before taking action. This indecisiveness can sometimes be frustrating, but it's simply a reflection of their desire for harmony and perfection.

Needs of a Libra Cat

To keep a Libra cat happy, healthy, and fulfilled, it's essential to cater to their specific needs. These needs are primarily driven by their love of social interaction, their desire for balance and harmony, and their appreciation for beauty and comfort.

- **Regular Social Interaction**: Libra cats thrive on social interaction and need regular engagement with their human companions and other pets. They enjoy being part of the social dynamics of the household and often seek out opportunities to interact with others. Spending time playing with them, talking to them, or simply being in the same room with them can help meet their need for companionship. They also appreciate having visitors and may enjoy meeting new people and making new friends.

- **A Peaceful and Harmonious Environment**: Balance and harmony are crucial for a Libra cat's well-being. They thrive in environments that are peaceful, calm, and free from conflict. Creating a harmonious atmosphere in your home, where there is a sense of fairness and equality, will help keep a Libra cat content. They may become stressed or anxious if there is tension or discord in the household, so it's important to address any issues promptly and ensure that everyone gets along.

- **Comfortable and Aesthetically Pleasing Spaces**: Libra cats have a deep appreciation for beauty and comfort. They enjoy being surrounded by aesthetically pleasing and comfortable spaces, so it's important to provide them with cozy, well-decorated areas to relax and sleep. Whether it's a soft bed with a luxurious blanket, a sunny windowsill with a view, or a quiet corner with tasteful decor, creating beautiful spaces for your Libra cat will help them feel at ease and happy.

- **Fair and Balanced Attention**: Libra cats prefer a balanced approach to attention and affection. They appreciate being noticed and loved, but they are not overly demanding. It's important to provide them with a fair share of attention, ensuring that they feel valued and included without overwhelming them. Regularly engaging with them through petting, grooming, or simply spending time together will help them feel secure and appreciated.

- **Gentle Handling and Patience**: Given their gentle and diplomatic nature, Libra cats need to be handled with care and patience. They are sensitive to harsh or aggressive behavior and may become upset if they feel threatened or treated unfairly. Approaching them with kindness, offering gentle encouragement, and respecting their need for balance will help build trust and strengthen your bond with them.

- **Opportunities for Aesthetic Enjoyment**: Libra cats enjoy environments that appeal to their sense of beauty and aesthetics. Providing them with spaces that are well-decorated, comfortable, and pleasing to the eye will enhance their well-being. They may also enjoy exploring new, visually appealing spaces or interacting with objects that are beautiful or interesting to them.

- **Respect for Their Decision-Making Process**: Libra cats can be indecisive, so it's important to respect their decision-making process. If they take their time choosing a spot to sleep, deciding when to eat, or selecting a toy, it's important to be patient and allow them to make their choice at their own pace. Rushing them or trying to force a decision may cause them stress, so it's best to let them take their time and find their own balance.

Conclusion

Libra cats are sociable, balanced, and harmony-seeking, bringing a sense of peace, beauty, and charm to any household. They are affectionate, friendly, and deeply connected to the social dynamics of their environment. By understanding their unique traits, behavior, and needs, you can create an environment that supports their love of companionship, their desire for balance, and their appreciation for beauty and harmony, allowing them to thrive.

Whether it's providing them with regular social interaction, creating a peaceful and harmonious home, or offering them aesthetically pleasing spaces to enjoy, catering to the needs of a Libra cat will help ensure that they remain happy, healthy, and fulfilled. As you continue to explore the astrological influences on your cat, remember that each Libra cat is unique, and their individual personality may vary depending on other factors in their astrological chart. However, the sociable, balanced, and harmony-seeking spirit of Libra will always be a defining characteristic, making your Libra cat a delightful and beloved member of your family.

Chapter 18: Scorpio Cat: The Intense, Mysterious, and Loyal Scorpio Cats

Scorpio, the eighth sign of the zodiac, is ruled by Pluto, the planet of transformation, power, and mystery, as well as Mars, the planet of action and desire. Scorpio cats, born between October 23 and November 21, embody the intense, mysterious, and fiercely loyal qualities of this fixed water sign. These cats are known for their deep emotional depth, strong will, and enigmatic presence. Understanding the unique traits, behavior, and needs of a Scorpio cat can help you create an environment that respects their complexity, honors their loyalty, and provides the space they need to thrive.

Scorpio Cat Traits

Scorpio cats are characterized by their intense emotions, mysterious demeanor, and unyielding loyalty. They are deeply connected to their environment and the people in it, often forming strong, almost unbreakable bonds with their human companions.

- **Intense and Passionate**: Scorpio cats are intense in everything they do. Whether it's playtime, hunting, or showing affection, they approach life with a level of passion and focus that is unmatched by other signs. Their emotions run deep, and they often experience the world in a way that is both powerful and profound. This intensity makes them incredibly driven and purposeful in their actions.
- **Mysterious and Enigmatic**: Ruled by Pluto, Scorpio cats have an air of mystery about them. They are often difficult to read, keeping their true thoughts and feelings hidden beneath the surface. Their enigmatic nature can make them seem aloof or distant, but this is simply their way of protecting themselves and maintaining control over their environment. They enjoy their privacy and may retreat to quiet, secluded spaces when they need time to themselves.
- **Loyal and Devoted**: Loyalty is a hallmark of Scorpio cats. Once they form a bond with someone, they are fiercely loyal and protective. They take their relationships seriously and expect the same level of commitment in return. This loyalty extends to their territory as well; they are highly protective of their home and may be wary of strangers or new animals in their environment.
- **Strong-Willed and Determined**: Scorpio cats are known for their strong will and determination. They are not easily swayed or deterred once they set their mind on something.

Whether it's catching a toy, asserting their dominance, or seeking out affection, Scorpio cats are relentless in their pursuits. Their determination can sometimes come across as stubbornness, but it is simply a reflection of their focused nature.

- **Secretive and Private**: Privacy is important to Scorpio cats. They value their alone time and may be secretive about their activities or whereabouts. They are unlikely to reveal their full personality to just anyone, preferring instead to keep their true selves hidden from view. This secretive nature makes them intriguing companions, but it also means they require a level of trust and respect from those around them.
- **Emotionally Complex**: Scorpio cats have a deep emotional complexity that sets them apart from other signs. They feel things deeply and are often highly intuitive, sensing the emotions of those around them. This emotional depth can make them sensitive and reactive, but it also allows them to form profound connections with their human companions.

Scorpio Cat Behavior

The behavior of a Scorpio cat reflects their intense, mysterious, and loyal nature. Understanding these behaviors can help you better interact with your Scorpio feline and create an environment that respects their need for privacy, emotional depth, and loyalty.

- **Focused and Purposeful**: Scorpio cats are highly focused and purposeful in their actions. They approach tasks with determination and are unlikely to give up until they achieve their goal. Whether it's hunting, playing, or exploring, Scorpio cats are fully engaged in whatever they are doing. This focused behavior makes them excellent hunters and problem-solvers, as they are willing to put in the time and effort needed to succeed.
- **Mysterious and Observant**: Scorpio cats are often quiet observers, taking in their surroundings with a keen eye. They may watch from a distance, carefully assessing the situation before making a move. This mysterious behavior makes them seem aloof or distant at times, but it is simply their way of gathering information and maintaining control over their environment. They are unlikely to reveal their true intentions or emotions easily, preferring to keep others guessing.

- **Protective and Territorial**: Scorpio cats are highly protective of their territory and the people they care about. They may be wary of strangers or new animals in the household and are likely to assert their dominance if they feel threatened. This protective behavior extends to their human companions as well; Scorpio cats will go to great lengths to ensure the safety and well-being of those they love. They are fiercely loyal and will defend their territory and loved ones with determination.
- **Emotionally Intuitive and Sensitive**: Scorpio cats are highly intuitive and often pick up on the emotions of those around them. They may sense when you are feeling sad, stressed, or happy, and they will respond accordingly. Their emotional sensitivity makes them excellent companions during difficult times, as they are capable of providing comfort and support when needed. However, this sensitivity also means they can be reactive, especially if they sense tension or conflict in their environment.
- **Secretive and Independent**: Scorpio cats value their privacy and may be secretive about their activities. They are unlikely to share their full personality with just anyone, preferring to keep certain aspects of themselves hidden from view. This secretive nature can make them seem mysterious or unpredictable, but it is simply their way of maintaining control over their environment. They enjoy their independence and may seek out quiet, secluded spaces where they can be alone with their thoughts.
- **Affectionate but on Their Terms**: While Scorpio cats are deeply loyal and affectionate, they prefer to show their love on their own terms. They may not be as outwardly affectionate as other signs, but when they do show affection, it is sincere and meaningful. They enjoy physical touch and may seek out petting, cuddling, or grooming, but only when they are in the mood. Their affection is not given lightly, and they expect the same level of loyalty and commitment in return.

Needs of a Scorpio Cat

To keep a Scorpio cat happy, healthy, and fulfilled, it's essential to cater to their specific needs. These needs are primarily driven by their intense emotions, desire for privacy, and deep loyalty.

- **A Secure and Private Environment**: Scorpio cats need a secure and private environment where they can feel safe and in control. Providing them with quiet, secluded spaces where they can retreat when they need time alone is essential. These spaces should be comfortable and free from distractions, allowing them to relax and recharge. They may also appreciate having high perches or hiding spots where they can observe their surroundings without being seen.

- **Respect for Their Privacy**: Privacy is crucial for a Scorpio cat's well-being. They value their alone time and may become stressed or agitated if they feel their privacy is being invaded. It's important to respect their need for solitude and avoid forcing them into situations where they feel uncomfortable or exposed. Allowing them to come to you when they are ready will help build trust and strengthen your bond.

- **Emotional Support and Stability**: Scorpio cats are emotionally complex and need a stable, supportive environment where they can feel secure. They are sensitive to changes in their environment and may react strongly to tension or conflict. Providing them with a calm, peaceful atmosphere will help them feel at ease. It's also important to be mindful of their emotional needs, offering comfort and reassurance when they are feeling vulnerable or stressed.

- **Mental and Physical Stimulation**: Given their intense focus and determination, Scorpio cats need regular mental and physical stimulation to keep them engaged. Providing them with challenging toys, puzzle feeders, and interactive play sessions will help satisfy their need for stimulation. They also enjoy activities that allow them to use their hunting instincts, such as chasing toys or exploring new environments.

- **Strong Bonds and Loyalty**: Scorpio cats form deep, lasting bonds with their human companions and expect loyalty in return. Building trust with a Scorpio cat requires patience, consistency, and respect. Once they trust you, they will be fiercely loyal and devoted. It's important to honor this loyalty by being attentive to their needs and showing them the same level of commitment and affection.

- **Opportunities for Exploration and Discovery**: Scorpio cats are naturally curious and enjoy exploring their environment. Providing them with opportunities to discover new spaces, objects, or toys will keep them mentally stimulated and satisfied. They may appreciate access to outdoor spaces, such as a secure garden or balcony, where they can explore safely. If outdoor access is not possible, creating an indoor environment with plenty of hiding spots, climbing structures, and interactive toys will help satisfy their curiosity.

- **Respect for Their Independent Nature**: Scorpio cats value their independence and prefer to do things on their own terms. It's important to respect their need for autonomy and allow them the freedom to make their own choices. Forcing them into situations or activities they are not comfortable with can lead to stress and frustration. Instead, offer them options and let them decide when and how they want to engage.

Conclusion

Scorpio cats are intense, mysterious, and deeply loyal, bringing a sense of depth, intrigue, and devotion to any household. They are emotionally complex, highly intuitive, and fiercely protective of their loved ones and their territory. By understanding their unique traits, behavior, and needs, you can create an environment that respects their need for privacy, honors their loyalty, and provides the space they need to thrive.

Whether it's providing them with a secure and private environment, offering emotional support and stability, or respecting their independent nature, catering to the needs of a Scorpio cat will help ensure that they remain happy, healthy, and fulfilled. As you continue to explore the astrological influences on your cat, remember that each Scorpio cat is unique, and their individual personality may vary depending on other factors in their astrological chart. However, the intense, mysterious, and loyal spirit of Scorpio will always be a defining characteristic, making your Scorpio cat a powerful and cherished member of your family.

Chapter 19: Sagittarius Cat: The Adventurous, Freedom-Loving, and Optimistic Sagittarius Cats

Sagittarius, the ninth sign of the zodiac, is ruled by Jupiter, the planet of expansion, adventure, and optimism. Sagittarius cats, born between November 22 and December 21, embody the adventurous, freedom-loving, and optimistic qualities of this mutable fire sign. These cats are natural explorers, driven by a desire to discover new places, meet new people, and experience all that life has to offer. Understanding the unique traits, behavior, and needs of a Sagittarius cat can help you create an environment that supports their love of freedom, adventure, and their inherently positive outlook on life.

Sagittarius Cat Traits

Sagittarius cats are characterized by their boundless energy, curious nature, and love of freedom. They are often the most adventurous of all the zodiac signs, always eager to explore the world around them and seek out new experiences.

- **Adventurous and Curious**: Sagittarius cats are born explorers. They have an insatiable curiosity and are always on the lookout for new adventures. Whether it's climbing to the highest point in the house, investigating a new toy, or trying to escape outside to explore the world beyond, Sagittarius cats are driven by a desire to discover and experience new things. This adventurous spirit makes them fearless and bold, often willing to take risks in pursuit of their next great adventure.

- **Freedom-Loving and Independent**: Ruled by Jupiter, the planet of expansion and freedom, Sagittarius cats value their independence above all else. They dislike feeling confined or restricted and prefer to have the freedom to roam and explore at will. This independent nature means they may resist being held or confined for long periods, preferring instead to go where their curiosity leads them. They thrive in environments that allow them to exercise their freedom and independence.

- **Optimistic and Joyful**: Sagittarius cats have a naturally optimistic outlook on life. They are cheerful, playful, and always seem to have a positive attitude, even in challenging situations. Their joyful nature is contagious, and they often bring a sense of fun and excitement to any household. Sagittarius cats approach life with a sense of wonder and enthusiasm, making them delightful companions.

- **Energetic and Playful**: Sagittarius cats are full of energy and love to play. They are often on the move, darting from one activity to the next with boundless enthusiasm. They enjoy games that challenge their agility, speed, and intelligence, and they are always up for a game of chase, fetch, or hide-and-seek. Their high energy levels mean they need plenty of physical activity to stay happy and healthy.

- **Inquisitive and Intelligent**: Sagittarius cats are highly intelligent and enjoy solving puzzles and figuring out new challenges. Their inquisitive nature means they are always learning, whether it's figuring out how to open doors, exploring new environments, or observing the behaviors of those around them. They are quick learners and enjoy mental stimulation, making them eager to engage in activities that challenge their intellect.

- **Social and Friendly**: Sagittarius cats are sociable and enjoy the company of others, whether it's their human companions, other pets, or even strangers. They are friendly and approachable, often seeking out interaction and making new friends with ease. Their sociable nature means they are usually at the center of household activities, and they enjoy being part of the action.

Sagittarius Cat Behavior

The behavior of a Sagittarius cat reflects their adventurous, freedom-loving, and optimistic nature. Understanding these behaviors can help you better interact with your Sagittarius feline and create an environment that supports their need for exploration, social interaction, and mental and physical stimulation.

- **Explorative and Adventurous**: Sagittarius cats are natural explorers. They are always on the move, looking for new places to investigate and new experiences to enjoy. Whether it's climbing to the highest shelf, crawling into small spaces, or attempting to escape outside, Sagittarius cats are driven by their curiosity and love of adventure. This behavior is often accompanied by a fearless attitude, as they are willing to take risks in pursuit of their next great discovery.

- **Playful and Energetic**: Play is a central part of a Sagittarius cat's life. They are full of energy and love engaging in activities that challenge their physical abilities and intellect. Sagittarius cats enjoy games that involve running, jumping, and chasing, and they often initiate play with their human companions or other pets. Their high energy levels mean they need regular play sessions to burn off excess energy and stay happy and healthy.

- **Social and Friendly**: Sagittarius cats are highly social and enjoy interacting with others. They are often the first to greet new people or animals in the household and are eager to make new friends. Their friendly and approachable nature makes them popular among both humans and pets. They enjoy being part of social activities and are likely to position themselves in the middle of the action, whether it's during playtime, mealtime, or simply lounging with their family.

- **Inquisitive and Intelligent**: Sagittarius cats are curious and intelligent, always seeking out new challenges to keep their minds engaged. They enjoy activities that require problem-solving and mental stimulation, such as puzzle toys, interactive feeders, or learning new tricks. Their inquisitive nature means they are quick to figure out new situations and are often the first to explore unfamiliar environments or objects.

- **Independent and Freedom-Loving**: Independence is key for a Sagittarius cat. They dislike feeling confined or restricted and prefer to have the freedom to explore at will. This independent nature means they may resist being held or confined for long periods, preferring instead to go where their curiosity leads them. They thrive in environments that allow them to exercise their independence and are happiest when they have the freedom to come and go as they please.

- **Optimistic and Resilient**: Sagittarius cats have a naturally optimistic outlook on life. They are cheerful, playful, and always seem to bounce back quickly from setbacks. Their positive attitude is contagious, and they often bring a sense of fun and excitement to any household. Even when faced with challenges, Sagittarius cats maintain their sense of joy and enthusiasm, making them resilient and adaptable companions.

Needs of a Sagittarius Cat

To keep a Sagittarius cat happy, healthy, and fulfilled, it's essential to cater to their specific needs. These needs are primarily driven by their love of freedom, adventure, and their naturally optimistic outlook on life.

- **Opportunities for Exploration and Adventure**: Sagittarius cats need plenty of opportunities to explore and satisfy their adventurous spirit. Providing them with access to a secure outdoor space, such as a garden or balcony, will allow them to explore safely. If outdoor access is not possible, creating an indoor environment with plenty of hiding spots, climbing structures, and interactive toys will help satisfy their curiosity and need for adventure. Regularly rotating their toys or introducing new challenges can keep them engaged and prevent boredom.

- **Physical Activity and Play**: Given their high energy levels, Sagittarius cats need regular physical activity to stay happy and healthy. Engaging them in play sessions that involve running, jumping, and chasing will help burn off excess energy and keep them physically fit. Toys that mimic prey, such as feather wands, laser pointers, and balls, are particularly appealing to Sagittarius cats. They also enjoy games that challenge their agility and speed, so providing them with plenty of space to run and play is essential.

- **Mental Stimulation and Learning**: Sagittarius cats are highly intelligent and enjoy activities that challenge their minds. Providing them with puzzle toys, interactive feeders, and games that require problem-solving skills will help keep their minds engaged. Teaching them new tricks or introducing them to new activities can also help satisfy their need for intellectual stimulation. They enjoy learning and figuring things out, so offering them challenges that require thought and analysis will keep them entertained and happy.

- **Social Interaction and Companionship**: Sagittarius cats thrive on social interaction and need regular engagement with their human companions and other pets. They enjoy being part of social activities and often seek out the company of others. Spending time playing with them, talking to them, or simply being in the same room with them can help meet their need for companionship. They also appreciate having visitors and may enjoy meeting new people and making new friends.

- **Freedom and Independence**: Independence is crucial for a Sagittarius cat's well-being. They need the freedom to explore and make their own choices. It's important to respect their need for autonomy and avoid confining them for long periods. Providing them with opportunities to explore and exercise their independence will help keep them happy and fulfilled. Allowing them to come and go as they please, whether it's through access to a secure outdoor space or the freedom to roam within the home, is essential for their happiness.
- **A Positive and Supportive Environment**: Sagittarius cats have a naturally optimistic outlook on life and thrive in environments that are positive and supportive. Creating a cheerful, happy atmosphere in your home will help reinforce their positive attitude and keep them in good spirits. They are sensitive to the mood of their environment, so maintaining a joyful and upbeat atmosphere will help them feel secure and content.
- **Respect for Their Adventurous Spirit**: Sagittarius cats are born adventurers, so it's important to respect and support their need for exploration and discovery. Encouraging their adventurous spirit by providing them with new experiences, challenges, and opportunities to explore will help keep them engaged and satisfied. Offering them a variety of toys, activities, and environments to explore will help satisfy their curiosity and prevent boredom.

Conclusion

Sagittarius cats are adventurous, freedom-loving, and optimistic, bringing a sense of excitement, joy, and exploration to any household. They are curious, intelligent, and always eager to discover new experiences and meet new people. By understanding their unique traits, behavior, and needs, you can create an environment that supports their love of freedom, adventure, and their inherently positive outlook on life, allowing them to thrive.

Whether it's providing them with plenty of opportunities for exploration and play, offering mental stimulation and learning, or respecting their need for independence and social interaction, catering to the needs of a Sagittarius cat will help ensure that they remain happy, healthy, and fulfilled. As you continue to explore the astrological influences on your cat, remember that each Sagittarius cat is unique, and their individual personality may vary depending on other factors in their astrological chart. However, the adventurous, freedom-loving, and optimistic spirit of Sagittarius will always be a defining characteristic, making your Sagittarius cat a joyful and cherished member of your family.

Chapter 20: Capricorn Cat: The Disciplined, Ambitious, and Practical Capricorn Cats

Capricorn, the tenth sign of the zodiac, is ruled by Saturn, the planet of discipline, responsibility, and structure. Capricorn cats, born between December 22 and January 19, embody the disciplined, ambitious, and practical qualities of this cardinal earth sign. These cats are often seen as the "old souls" of the feline world, displaying a level of seriousness, determination, and focus that is unique among their peers. Understanding the unique traits, behavior, and needs of a Capricorn cat can help you create an environment that supports their need for order, achievement, and stability.

Capricorn Cat Traits

Capricorn cats are characterized by their strong sense of discipline, ambition, and practicality. They are often driven by a desire to achieve their goals and are willing to put in the necessary work to get there. These cats value structure, consistency, and a well-organized environment.

- **Disciplined and Responsible**: Capricorn cats are naturally disciplined and responsible. They are not the type to engage in frivolous or reckless behavior; instead, they approach life with a sense of duty and purpose. Whether it's maintaining a clean and orderly environment or adhering to a routine, Capricorn cats take their responsibilities seriously. This disciplined nature often makes them reliable and predictable, as they are likely to stick to established habits and routines.

- **Ambitious and Goal-Oriented**: Ambition is a key trait of Capricorn cats. They are driven by a desire to achieve and often set goals for themselves, whether it's mastering a new skill, asserting dominance in their territory, or simply earning the affection of their human companions. Capricorn cats are not easily deterred and will persistently pursue their objectives until they succeed. This ambition is often coupled with a strong work ethic, as they are willing to put in the effort needed to achieve their goals.

- **Practical and Realistic**: Ruled by Saturn, the planet of structure and reality, Capricorn cats have a practical and realistic outlook on life. They are not prone to daydreaming or fanciful thinking; instead, they focus on what is tangible and achievable. This practical nature makes them excellent problem-solvers, as they approach challenges with logic and a clear sense of what needs to be done. Capricorn cats are also likely to be resourceful, finding practical solutions to everyday problems.

- **Serious and Reserved**: Capricorn cats tend to be more serious and reserved than other signs. They are not as playful or carefree as some of their feline counterparts, preferring instead to observe and analyze their environment. This reserved nature means they may be more selective about their interactions, preferring to engage with those they trust and respect. While they may not be as outwardly affectionate, Capricorn cats form deep, lasting bonds with those they care about.
- **Loyal and Dependable**: Loyalty is a hallmark of Capricorn cats. Once they form a bond with their human companions, they are deeply committed and will go to great lengths to protect and support those they love. Their dependable nature means they are always there when you need them, providing a steady, reassuring presence in your life. Capricorn cats are also likely to be protective of their territory and may be cautious or wary of strangers.
- **Patient and Persistent**: Patience is a defining trait of Capricorn cats. They are willing to wait for what they want and are not easily discouraged by setbacks or delays. This patience is coupled with persistence, as Capricorn cats are determined to achieve their goals no matter how long it takes. Their ability to stay focused and remain patient in the face of challenges makes them resilient and successful in their endeavors.

Capricorn Cat Behavior

The behavior of a Capricorn cat reflects their disciplined, ambitious, and practical nature. Understanding these behaviors can help you better interact with your Capricorn feline and create an environment that supports their need for structure, achievement, and stability.

- **Structured and Routine-Oriented**: Capricorn cats thrive on structure and routine. They prefer a predictable daily schedule and are likely to stick to established habits. Whether it's feeding times, play sessions, or bedtime, Capricorn cats appreciate knowing what to expect and when. They may become stressed or anxious if their routine is disrupted, so it's important to maintain consistency in their daily life.

- **Serious and Observant**: Capricorn cats tend to be more serious and observant than other signs. They are likely to spend time watching and analyzing their environment, carefully assessing situations before taking action. This observant behavior makes them excellent problem-solvers, as they are able to anticipate challenges and plan their next move accordingly. Capricorn cats are also likely to be more reserved in their interactions, preferring to observe from a distance before engaging.

- **Goal-Oriented and Determined**: Capricorn cats are highly goal-oriented and determined in their pursuits. Whether it's mastering a new skill, securing a comfortable spot in the house, or earning the attention of their human companions, Capricorn cats approach their goals with focus and persistence. They are not easily deterred by obstacles and will work tirelessly to achieve their objectives. This determination often makes them successful in whatever they set out to do.

- **Practical and Resourceful**: Capricorn cats are practical and resourceful, often finding simple, effective solutions to everyday problems. They are unlikely to engage in unnecessary or frivolous behavior, preferring instead to focus on what needs to be done. This practical nature makes them efficient and reliable, as they are always looking for the most effective way to achieve their goals. Capricorn cats are also likely to be resourceful in their use of toys, space, and other resources, finding creative ways to meet their needs.

- **Loyal and Protective**: Loyalty is a key characteristic of Capricorn cats. They are deeply committed to their human companions and will go to great lengths to protect those they care about. This loyalty extends to their territory as well, as Capricorn cats are likely to be protective of their home and may be cautious or wary of strangers. Their protective nature means they may be quick to assert their dominance if they feel their territory is threatened.

- **Reserved and Selective**: Capricorn cats are more reserved and selective in their interactions. They may be cautious around new people or environments, preferring to observe and assess before fully engaging. This reserved nature means they are unlikely to seek out attention or affection unless they feel comfortable and secure. However, once they form a bond with someone, Capricorn cats are deeply loyal and committed, often showing their affection in subtle, meaningful ways.

Needs of a Capricorn Cat

To keep a Capricorn cat happy, healthy, and fulfilled, it's essential to cater to their specific needs. These needs are primarily driven by their desire for structure, achievement, and a well-organized environment.

- **A Structured and Predictable Environment**: Structure is crucial for a Capricorn cat's well-being. They thrive on routine and predictability, so it's important to maintain a consistent daily schedule. Feeding times, play sessions, and grooming rituals should all follow a regular pattern to help them feel secure and at ease. Disruptions to their routine can cause stress, so it's important to introduce any changes gradually and with care.
- **Opportunities for Achievement and Success**: Capricorn cats are driven by a desire to achieve, so it's important to provide them with opportunities to succeed. Engaging them in activities that challenge their problem-solving skills, such as puzzle toys or interactive feeders, will help satisfy their need for accomplishment. Teaching them new tricks or introducing them to new challenges can also help keep them mentally stimulated and motivated. They enjoy tasks that allow them to demonstrate their abilities and achieve their goals.
- **A Calm and Organized Environment**: Capricorn cats prefer a calm, organized environment where everything is in its place. They are likely to become stressed or anxious in chaotic or cluttered spaces, so it's important to keep their living area clean and well-organized. Providing them with a quiet, comfortable space where they can retreat when they need to relax or recharge is essential for their well-being.
- **Patience and Respect for Their Process**: Capricorn cats are patient and deliberate in their actions, so it's important to respect their process. They may take their time when making decisions or assessing a situation, and it's important to give them the space they need to do so. Rushing them or trying to force a decision can cause stress and frustration. Allowing them to approach things at their own pace will help build trust and strengthen your bond.
- **Opportunities for Independence and Autonomy**: While Capricorn cats are loyal and committed, they also value their independence. Providing them with opportunities to exercise their autonomy, such as allowing them to explore on their own or giving them the freedom to choose their own activities, will help keep them happy and fulfilled. They appreciate

having the freedom to make their own decisions and are likely to thrive in an environment that supports their independence.

- **Affection on Their Terms**: Capricorn cats may be more reserved in their displays of affection, preferring to show their love in subtle, meaningful ways. It's important to respect their boundaries and allow them to initiate affection on their own terms. They may not seek out attention as frequently as other signs, but when they do, it's a sign of deep trust and commitment. Offering them gentle encouragement and positive reinforcement when they do seek affection will help strengthen your bond.
- **Security and Stability**: Security and stability are crucial for a Capricorn cat's well-being. They need to feel safe and protected in their environment, and they may become anxious if they sense instability or unpredictability. Providing them with a stable, secure home where they can feel in control of their surroundings will help them feel confident and at ease. They also appreciate having a designated space that is exclusively theirs, where they can retreat when they need to relax or recharge.

Conclusion

Capricorn cats are disciplined, ambitious, and practical, bringing a sense of order, determination, and stability to any household. They are goal-oriented, reliable, and deeply committed to their human companions, making them loyal and dependable friends. By understanding their unique traits, behavior, and needs, you can create an environment that supports their desire for structure, achievement, and stability, allowing them to thrive.

Whether it's providing them with a structured and predictable environment, offering opportunities for achievement and success, or respecting their need for independence and security, catering to the needs of a Capricorn cat will help ensure that they remain happy, healthy, and fulfilled. As you continue to explore the astrological influences on your cat, remember that each Capricorn cat is unique, and their individual personality may vary depending on other factors in their astrological chart. However, the disciplined, ambitious, and practical spirit of Capricorn will always be a defining characteristic, making your Capricorn cat a steadfast and cherished member of your family.

Chapter 21: Aquarius Cat: The Quirky, Independent, and Humanitarian Aquarius Cats

Aquarius, the eleventh sign of the zodiac, is ruled by Uranus, the planet of innovation, eccentricity, and change, and traditionally by Saturn, the planet of structure and responsibility. Aquarius cats, born between January 20 and February 18, embody the quirky, independent, and humanitarian qualities of this fixed air sign. These cats are known for their unique personalities, love of freedom, and strong sense of individuality. Understanding the unique traits, behavior, and needs of an Aquarius cat can help you create an environment that fosters their creativity, respects their independence, and supports their desire to make a positive impact on their world.

Aquarius Cat Traits

Aquarius cats are characterized by their quirky, independent, and forward-thinking nature. They are often seen as the free spirits of the feline world, displaying a level of uniqueness and unpredictability that sets them apart from other signs.

- **Quirky and Unconventional**: Aquarius cats are known for their quirky and unconventional personalities. They are likely to have unique behaviors, preferences, and habits that make them stand out from other cats. Whether it's a peculiar way of playing, an unusual favorite toy, or a distinctive way of communicating, Aquarius cats are anything but ordinary. Their eccentricity often makes them endearing and fascinating companions, as they are always full of surprises.

- **Independent and Freedom-Loving**: Ruled by Uranus, the planet of independence and innovation, Aquarius cats value their freedom above all else. They dislike feeling confined or restricted and prefer to have the freedom to explore, play, and think on their own terms. This independent nature means they may resist being overly coddled or controlled, and they thrive in environments that allow them to express their individuality and autonomy.

- **Humanitarian and Altruistic**: Aquarius is often associated with humanitarianism and a desire to improve the world. While this might seem like an abstract concept for a cat, Aquarius cats often display behaviors that suggest a concern for others. They may be particularly sensitive to the needs of their human companions or other animals in the household, showing empathy and a desire to help or comfort those in distress. This altruistic nature makes them compassionate and caring companions.

- **Innovative and Forward-Thinking**: Aquarius cats are highly innovative and enjoy exploring new ideas, toys, and experiences. They are quick to adapt to new situations and are often the first to figure out how to use a new toy or navigate a new environment. Their forward-thinking nature means they are always looking for ways to improve their surroundings or discover something new. This makes them excellent problem-solvers and creative thinkers.
- **Social but Selective**: While Aquarius cats are social and enjoy the company of others, they are also selective about their interactions. They value quality over quantity when it comes to relationships and may form deep bonds with a few chosen individuals rather than seeking out constant attention from everyone. Their social nature is often expressed in unconventional ways, such as choosing to spend time with a particular person or animal who shares their unique interests or energy.
- **Detached and Objective**: Aquarius cats can sometimes appear detached or aloof, as they tend to approach life with an objective, analytical mindset. They are not overly emotional and may prefer to observe from a distance rather than getting caught up in the drama or emotions of those around them. This detached nature allows them to remain calm and level-headed in stressful situations, but it can also make them seem distant or uninterested at times.

Aquarius Cat Behavior

The behavior of an Aquarius cat reflects their quirky, independent, and humanitarian nature. Understanding these behaviors can help you better interact with your Aquarius feline and create an environment that supports their need for freedom, creativity, and social connection.

- **Explorative and Curious**: Aquarius cats are natural explorers. They are always on the lookout for new experiences and enjoy discovering new places, toys, and activities. Their curiosity drives them to investigate every corner of their environment, often leading them to unexpected or unusual places. This explorative behavior is a reflection of their innovative nature, as they are always seeking to expand their knowledge and experience.
- **Playful and Inventive**: Play is an important part of an Aquarius cat's life, but they approach it in their own unique way. They may invent new games, use toys in unconventional ways, or find entertainment in objects that other cats might ignore. Aquarius cats enjoy activities that

challenge their minds and allow them to express their creativity. They are likely to enjoy puzzle toys, interactive games, and anything that encourages them to think outside the box.

- **Independent and Self-Sufficient**: Aquarius cats value their independence and prefer to do things on their own terms. They are self-sufficient and capable of entertaining themselves without relying on constant attention from their human companions. This independence means they may be less likely to seek out affection or companionship compared to other signs, but it also makes them confident and secure in their own company.
- **Socially Selective and Unique**: While Aquarius cats are social, they are selective about their interactions. They may choose to spend time with specific individuals or animals who share their energy or interests, rather than seeking out attention from everyone. This selectiveness means they may form deep, meaningful connections with a few chosen companions rather than spreading their affection widely. Their social interactions are often unique and may involve unconventional ways of showing affection or bonding.
- **Detached and Observant**: Aquarius cats can sometimes appear detached or aloof, as they prefer to observe rather than engage emotionally. They approach life with an analytical mindset, often stepping back to assess a situation before getting involved. This detached nature allows them to remain calm and objective, but it can also make them seem distant or uninterested at times. However, this detachment is not a sign of indifference; it's simply their way of processing and understanding the world around them.
- **Empathetic and Compassionate**: Despite their detached nature, Aquarius cats are often highly empathetic and attuned to the needs of others. They may show concern for their human companions or other animals in the household, offering comfort or support when needed. This humanitarian instinct makes them compassionate and caring, and they are likely to go out of their way to help those in distress.

Needs of an Aquarius Cat

To keep an Aquarius cat happy, healthy, and fulfilled, it's essential to cater to their specific needs. These needs are primarily driven by their love of freedom, creativity, and social connection.

- **Opportunities for Exploration and Discovery**: Aquarius cats need plenty of opportunities to explore and satisfy their curiosity. Providing them with access to new environments, such as a secure outdoor space or a variety of indoor play areas, will allow them to indulge their love of discovery. They enjoy exploring new toys, objects, and spaces, so regularly introducing new items or rearranging their environment can help keep them engaged and prevent boredom.

- **Freedom and Independence**: Independence is crucial for an Aquarius cat's well-being. They need the freedom to make their own choices and explore their environment on their own terms. It's important to respect their need for autonomy and avoid confining them or restricting their movements. Providing them with opportunities to exercise their independence, such as allowing them to explore freely or choose their own activities, will help keep them happy and fulfilled.

- **Mental Stimulation and Creativity**: Aquarius cats are highly intelligent and enjoy activities that challenge their minds. Providing them with puzzle toys, interactive feeders, and games that encourage problem-solving and creativity will help satisfy their need for mental stimulation. They also appreciate activities that allow them to express their unique personality, so offering them a variety of toys and experiences that cater to their creative side is essential.

- **Social Interaction and Connection**: While Aquarius cats are independent, they still value social interaction and connection with their human companions and other pets. They enjoy spending time with those who share their energy and interests, so it's important to provide them with opportunities for social engagement. Spending time playing with them, talking to them, or simply being in their presence can help meet their need for companionship. They may also enjoy forming bonds with specific individuals or animals who understand and appreciate their unique personality.

- **Respect for Their Individuality**: Aquarius cats are unique and have their own way of doing things. It's important to respect their individuality and allow them the freedom to express themselves in their own way. This may mean accepting their quirky behaviors, supporting their unconventional preferences, and giving them the space they need to be themselves. Recognizing and celebrating their individuality will help them feel valued and understood.

- **A Calm and Supportive Environment**: Aquarius cats thrive in environments that are calm, supportive, and free from unnecessary stress. They appreciate having a stable, peaceful home where they can explore and engage with their surroundings without feeling overwhelmed. Providing them with a safe, comfortable space where they can retreat when they need to relax or recharge is essential for their well-being.
- **Opportunities to Help and Comfort Others**: Aquarius cats often have a humanitarian instinct, and they may show concern for others in their household. Providing them with opportunities to help or comfort their human companions or other pets can help satisfy this need. They may appreciate being given a role in the household, such as watching over a new pet or providing comfort during stressful times. Recognizing and supporting their altruistic nature will help them feel fulfilled and appreciated.

Conclusion

Aquarius cats are quirky, independent, and humanitarian, bringing a sense of uniqueness, freedom, and compassion to any household. They are intelligent, creative, and always full of surprises, making them fascinating and engaging companions. By understanding their unique traits, behavior, and needs, you can create an environment that supports their love of freedom, creativity, and social connection, allowing them to thrive.

Whether it's providing them with opportunities for exploration and mental stimulation, respecting their need for independence and individuality, or supporting their desire to help and comfort others, catering to the needs of an Aquarius cat will help ensure that they remain happy, healthy, and fulfilled. As you continue to explore the astrological influences on your cat, remember that each Aquarius cat is unique, and their individual personality may vary depending on other factors in their astrological chart. However, the quirky, independent, and humanitarian spirit of Aquarius will always be a defining characteristic, making your Aquarius cat a fascinating and cherished member of your family.

Chapter 22: Pisces Cat: The Dreamy, Intuitive, and Compassionate Pisces Cats

Pisces, the twelfth and final sign of the zodiac, is ruled by Neptune, the planet of dreams, intuition, and spirituality, as well as traditionally by Jupiter, the planet of expansion and wisdom. Pisces cats, born between February 19 and March 20, embody the dreamy, intuitive, and compassionate qualities of this mutable water sign. These cats are often seen as the mystical, sensitive souls of the feline world, displaying a deep connection to their inner world and an empathetic understanding of the emotions of those around them. Understanding the unique traits, behavior, and needs of a Pisces cat can help you create an environment that nurtures their sensitivity, supports their emotional well-being, and encourages their innate creativity and intuition.

Pisces Cat Traits

Pisces cats are characterized by their dreamy nature, strong intuition, and deep compassion. They are gentle, sensitive, and often have an otherworldly presence that makes them seem more attuned to the spiritual and emotional realms than to the physical world.

- **Dreamy and Imaginative**: Ruled by Neptune, the planet of dreams and illusions, Pisces cats are known for their dreamy and imaginative nature. They often seem to have one paw in another world, lost in thought or absorbed in their own creative imaginings. This can make them appear a bit aloof or distant at times, but it is simply a reflection of their rich inner world. Pisces cats are often drawn to quiet, peaceful environments where they can daydream and let their imagination run wild.

- **Intuitive and Psychic**: Pisces cats are highly intuitive and often display what can only be described as a "sixth sense." They seem to just "know" things, whether it's sensing when someone is upset, predicting changes in the weather, or anticipating events before they happen. This psychic-like ability makes them incredibly in tune with their surroundings and the emotions of those around them. They are often quick to respond to subtle cues and can sense when something is off, even if it's not immediately apparent.

- **Compassionate and Empathetic**: Compassion is a defining trait of Pisces cats. They are deeply empathetic and sensitive to the emotions of others, often acting as a comforting presence in times of need. Pisces cats are known to seek out those who are feeling sad or stressed, offering gentle affection and companionship to help soothe and heal. Their empathetic nature makes them wonderful therapy animals, as they seem to understand and respond to human emotions on a profound level.

- **Gentle and Non-Confrontational**: Pisces cats are gentle and peaceful by nature. They dislike conflict and will go out of their way to avoid confrontational situations. When faced with tension or aggression, they are more likely to retreat to a safe space than to engage in a fight. This non-confrontational attitude makes them easy-going companions who thrive in harmonious environments.

- **Spiritual and Mystical**: Pisces cats have a spiritual and mystical quality about them. They are often drawn to activities and spaces that have a calming, meditative energy, such as lounging in a sunbeam, watching fish swim in a tank, or curling up in a quiet corner of the house. Their connection to the spiritual realm is reflected in their behaviors and preferences, making them seem wise beyond their years and deeply connected to something greater than themselves.

- **Artistic and Creative**: Pisces cats are naturally artistic and creative. They enjoy engaging in activities that allow them to express their creativity, whether it's through play, exploration, or simply the way they interact with their environment. They may have a particular fondness for music, art, or other forms of creative expression, and they often bring a sense of beauty and inspiration to everything they do.

Pisces Cat Behavior

The behavior of a Pisces cat reflects their dreamy, intuitive, and compassionate nature. Understanding these behaviors can help you better interact with your Pisces feline and create an environment that supports their emotional and spiritual needs.

- **Dreamy and Absorbed**: Pisces cats often appear lost in thought, as if they are drifting between the physical and spiritual worlds. They may spend long periods simply gazing out the window, watching the world go by, or lounging in a favorite spot, seemingly deep in contemplation. This dreamy behavior is a reflection of their rich inner life and their need for time to daydream and reflect. They may also display a fascination with water, whether it's playing with a dripping faucet, watching fish in an aquarium, or even splashing in a shallow bowl.

- **Intuitive and Responsive**: Pisces cats are highly intuitive and often respond to subtle cues in their environment. They seem to sense when someone needs comfort or when something is about to happen, and they are quick to offer their support or prepare for change. This intuition makes them incredibly in tune with their human companions, and they often anticipate your needs before you even realize them yourself. They may also show an interest in spiritual activities, such as meditating alongside you or curling up near objects with calming energy, like crystals or candles.

- **Compassionate and Caring**: Pisces cats are deeply compassionate and empathetic, often acting as emotional healers in their households. They are likely to seek out those who are feeling down or stressed, offering gentle purrs, cuddles, or simply their calming presence to help alleviate distress. Their compassion extends to other animals as well, and they may form close bonds with other pets in the household, acting as a comforting companion to those in need.

- **Gentle and Avoidant of Conflict**: Pisces cats are gentle souls who prefer peace and harmony over conflict. When faced with tension or aggression, they are more likely to retreat to a safe, quiet space than to engage in a confrontation. This gentle nature makes them well-suited to calm, stable environments where they can feel secure and at ease. They may also be sensitive to loud noises or chaotic surroundings, so providing them with a peaceful, quiet space to retreat to is essential.

- **Creative and Artistic**: Pisces cats have a natural affinity for creativity and may engage in playful activities that allow them to express their artistic side. They may enjoy exploring their environment in imaginative ways, such as turning everyday objects into toys or creating their own games. They are also likely to be drawn to music, art, or other forms of creative expression, and they may show a preference for activities that involve beauty and aesthetics. This creative streak can make them particularly fun and engaging companions.

- **Spiritual and Connected**: Pisces cats often display behaviors that suggest a deep connection to the spiritual realm. They may be drawn to calming, meditative spaces or show an interest in activities that have a spiritual or mystical quality. This could include sitting quietly near a candle, watching the movement of water, or simply spending time in peaceful, natural surroundings. Their connection to the spiritual world can also be seen in their intuitive behaviors and their ability to sense and respond to the energy of those around them.

Needs of a Pisces Cat

To keep a Pisces cat happy, healthy, and fulfilled, it's essential to cater to their specific needs. These needs are primarily driven by their sensitivity, creativity, and deep connection to the emotional and spiritual realms.

- **A Calm and Peaceful Environment**: Pisces cats thrive in calm, peaceful environments where they can feel secure and at ease. Providing them with a quiet, stable home is essential for their well-being. They may become stressed or anxious in chaotic or noisy surroundings, so it's important to create a space that allows them to relax and unwind. This could include a cozy bed in a quiet corner, a window perch where they can watch the world go by, or a designated area where they can retreat when they need some alone time.
- **Opportunities for Creativity and Play**: Pisces cats are naturally creative and enjoy activities that allow them to express their imagination. Providing them with a variety of toys, including those that encourage creative play, such as interactive toys, puzzle feeders, or even simple objects like cardboard boxes, will help keep them engaged and entertained. They may also enjoy exploring new spaces or engaging in activities that stimulate their artistic side, such as listening to music or watching moving objects like fish or shadows.
- **Emotional Support and Compassion**: Pisces cats are deeply empathetic and sensitive to the emotions of those around them. They need to feel loved and supported by their human companions and may seek out affection and reassurance when they are feeling vulnerable. Spending time with them, offering gentle affection, and providing a comforting presence will help them feel secure and appreciated. They may also appreciate being included in activities that involve emotional bonding, such as cuddling on the couch or sharing a quiet moment together.
- **Spiritual and Meditative Spaces**: Pisces cats have a strong connection to the spiritual realm and may appreciate spaces that have a calming, meditative energy. Providing them with areas where they can relax and connect with their inner world, such as a sunny spot by the window,

a cozy bed near a candle or crystal, or a quiet corner with soft lighting, will help them feel at peace. They may also enjoy spending time in nature, so providing them with access to outdoor spaces, such as a garden or balcony, can be beneficial.

- **Gentle Handling and Patience**: Given their sensitive and gentle nature, Pisces cats need to be handled with care and patience. They may be more easily startled or upset than other signs, so it's important to approach them gently and avoid sudden movements or loud noises. Offering them a calm, reassuring presence and allowing them to come to you on their own terms will help build trust and strengthen your bond.

- **Opportunities for Emotional Expression**: Pisces cats are deeply emotional and may need outlets for expressing their feelings. Providing them with opportunities to bond with you, whether it's through cuddling, playing, or simply spending time together, will help them feel connected and loved. They may also appreciate activities that allow them to express their emotions creatively, such as playing with toys that involve movement or sound, or engaging in activities that stimulate their senses.

- **Protection from Stress and Overstimulation**: Pisces cats are highly sensitive and can be easily overwhelmed by stress or overstimulation. It's important to protect them from chaotic or noisy environments and provide them with a safe, quiet space where they can retreat when needed. This could include a designated room, a cozy bed in a secluded corner, or a covered cat bed that offers privacy and security. Ensuring they have a peaceful place to escape to will help them maintain their emotional and mental well-being.

Conclusion

Pisces cats are dreamy, intuitive, and compassionate, bringing a sense of serenity, empathy, and creativity to any household. They are gentle, sensitive souls who thrive in peaceful, supportive environments where they can connect with their inner world and the emotions of those around them. By understanding their unique traits, behavior, and needs, you can create an environment that nurtures their sensitivity, supports their emotional well-being, and encourages their innate creativity and intuition.

Whether it's providing them with a calm and peaceful environment, offering opportunities for creativity and play, or supporting their need for emotional expression and spiritual connection, catering to the needs of a Pisces cat will help ensure that they remain happy, healthy, and fulfilled. As you continue to explore the astrological influences on your cat, remember that each Pisces cat is unique, and their individual personality may vary depending on other factors in their astrological chart. However, the dreamy, intuitive, and compassionate spirit of Pisces will always be a defining characteristic, making your Pisces cat a mystical and cherished member of your family.

Part III: Celestial Bodies and Their Influence on Cats

Chapter 23: The North Node and South Node: Karmic Lessons and Life Paths for Cats

In astrology, the North Node and South Node, also known as the lunar nodes, represent the points where the moon's orbit intersects the ecliptic, the path of the sun across the sky. These points are not physical bodies like planets but are significant in astrological charts as they indicate karmic lessons, life paths, and the spiritual journey of an individual. When applied to cats, understanding the influence of the North Node and South Node can provide insights into their inherent tendencies, life challenges, and the spiritual growth they are meant to experience during their lifetime.

The North Node: The Future Path and Growth

The North Node is often associated with the future and the path of growth and evolution. It represents qualities and experiences that are new, challenging, and unfamiliar, but necessary for the soul's development. For cats, the North Node can indicate the behaviors, lessons, and experiences that they are meant to explore and embrace in this lifetime. It shows where a cat can grow, develop new skills, and expand their comfort zone.

- **Embracing New Experiences**: The North Node encourages a cat to step outside their comfort zone and explore new experiences that will help them grow. This could involve learning to trust others, adapting to new environments, or developing new social skills. For example, a cat with a North Node in a social sign like Gemini might be encouraged to become more interactive and communicative, while a cat with a North Node in an independent sign like Aquarius might be pushed to embrace their uniqueness and individuality.
- **Overcoming Fears and Insecurities**: The path of the North Node often involves facing fears and insecurities that may have held the cat back in the past. These challenges are essential for growth, as they help the cat build confidence and resilience. For instance, a cat with a North Node in a fire sign like Aries might need to overcome timidity and embrace their inner courage, while a cat with a North Node in an earth sign like Capricorn might need to develop a sense of responsibility and discipline.
- **Developing New Skills and Traits**: The North Node indicates areas where a cat can develop new skills and traits that are important for their evolution. This could involve learning to be more patient, becoming more self-reliant, or developing a stronger sense of empathy.

These traits may not come naturally to the cat, but they are crucial for their spiritual growth and overall well-being.

- **Seeking Balance and Harmony**: The journey of the North Node is also about finding balance and harmony between the new lessons to be learned and the familiar traits represented by the South Node. For example, a cat with a North Node in Libra might need to learn the importance of cooperation and harmony, balancing their natural tendency toward independence or self-focus. The goal is to integrate the lessons of the North Node into the cat's life, creating a more balanced and fulfilled existence.

The South Node: The Past and Comfort Zone

The South Node represents the past, the comfort zone, and the qualities and behaviors that come naturally to the cat. It is associated with karmic patterns and traits that have been carried over from previous lifetimes or early experiences. While the South Node indicates areas of strength and familiarity, it can also signify tendencies that need to be transcended or balanced with the lessons of the North Node.

- **Natural Talents and Strengths**: The South Node represents the cat's natural talents and strengths, the qualities that come easily and without much effort. For example, a cat with a South Node in Taurus might naturally be grounded, patient, and connected to their physical environment, while a cat with a South Node in Sagittarius might have an inherent love for adventure and exploration.
- **Comfort Zone and Familiar Patterns**: The South Node indicates the cat's comfort zone, the behaviors and patterns they naturally fall back on when faced with challenges or stress. While these patterns may provide comfort and security, they can also limit the cat's growth if relied upon too heavily. For instance, a cat with a South Node in Cancer might prefer to stay close to home and be cautious, avoiding new experiences that could lead to growth.
- **Karmic Patterns and Lessons**: The South Node is often associated with karmic patterns that the cat has carried over from previous lifetimes or early experiences. These patterns may need to be recognized and released for the cat to grow and evolve. For example, a cat with a South Node in Leo might have a tendency toward seeking attention or being overly dramatic,

which may need to be balanced with the humility and cooperation of the North Node in Aquarius.

- **Balancing the Past and Future**: The journey of the South Node is about finding a balance between the comfort of the past and the growth required by the future. While the traits of the South Node are valuable and should not be discarded, they must be balanced with the lessons of the North Node to create a harmonious and fulfilling life. For instance, a cat with a South Node in Virgo might need to balance their natural attention to detail and perfectionism with the broader perspective and compassion of a North Node in Pisces.

Interpreting the North Node and South Node for Cats

When interpreting the North Node and South Node for cats, it's important to consider how these points influence the cat's personality, behavior, and life path. While the concepts of karma and spiritual growth are often associated with humans, they can also be applied to animals in a way that acknowledges their unique journeys and contributions to the world.

- **Understanding the Cat's Life Path**: The North Node and South Node can provide insights into the overarching themes and lessons of a cat's life. For example, a cat with a North Node in Scorpio might be on a path of transformation and emotional depth, learning to navigate intense experiences and develop resilience. Conversely, a cat with a South Node in Scorpio might already possess these traits and be encouraged to balance them with the stability and grounding of a North Node in Taurus.
- **Supporting the Cat's Growth**: Understanding the influence of the North Node can help you support your cat's growth and development. If your cat's North Node encourages social interaction, you might introduce them to new pets or people in a gentle and supportive way. If their North Node focuses on independence, you might provide them with opportunities to explore and make decisions on their own.
- **Recognizing and Honoring the Cat's Strengths**: The South Node highlights the cat's natural strengths and talents, which should be recognized and honored. These traits provide a foundation of comfort and security, helping the cat navigate life with confidence. By ac-

knowledging these strengths, you can create an environment that supports both the cat's natural abilities and their journey toward growth.

- **Balancing the Nodes**: The ultimate goal of the North Node and South Node is to achieve balance, integrating the lessons of the future with the strengths of the past. For your cat, this might mean encouraging them to step outside their comfort zone while also providing them with the security and familiarity they need to feel safe. This balance allows for a harmonious life path that honors both the cat's inherent traits and their potential for growth.

Examples of North Node and South Node Influence

Here are some examples of how the North Node and South Node might manifest in a cat's life, providing specific insights into their behavior and development:

- **North Node in Aries, South Node in Libra**: A cat with this placement might naturally be sociable and cooperative (Libra South Node) but may need to develop more independence and assertiveness (Aries North Node). Encouraging this cat to take the lead in play or explore on their own can help them grow.
- **North Node in Taurus, South Node in Scorpio**: This cat may have a deep emotional intensity and a tendency to be secretive or possessive (Scorpio South Node). Their growth path involves finding peace and stability in the material world, embracing a more grounded and contented approach to life (Taurus North Node). Providing them with a calm, stable environment and consistent routines will help them feel secure.
- **North Node in Gemini, South Node in Sagittarius**: Naturally adventurous and independent (Sagittarius South Node), this cat may need to learn to communicate more effectively and engage with others in a social, curious manner (Gemini North Node). Encouraging interaction with different people and pets, and providing mentally stimulating activities, can support their growth.
- **North Node in Cancer, South Node in Capricorn**: A cat with this placement might be naturally disciplined, independent, and focused on their responsibilities (Capricorn South Node). However, they may need to learn to connect emotionally and seek comfort in nurtur-

ing relationships (Cancer North Node). Providing them with a loving, secure environment and opportunities for emotional bonding will help them thrive.

Conclusion

The North Node and South Node provide a unique and profound way to understand the karmic lessons and life paths of cats. These points in the astrological chart highlight the areas where a cat can grow, develop new skills, and overcome challenges, as well as the strengths and tendencies they bring from the past. By understanding and honoring the influence of the North Node and South Node, you can create an environment that supports your cat's spiritual journey, helping them achieve balance, fulfillment, and growth.

Whether it's encouraging them to step outside their comfort zone, recognizing their natural talents, or supporting their emotional and spiritual needs, catering to the lessons of the North Node and South Node will help ensure that your cat remains happy, healthy, and fulfilled. As you continue to explore the astrological influences on your cat, remember that each cat's journey is unique, and their individual experiences may vary depending on other factors in their astrological chart. However, the karmic lessons and life paths represented by the North Node and South Node will always be a defining aspect of their spiritual journey, making your cat's life path a meaningful and cherished part of your shared experience.

Chapter 24: Chiron: The Wounded Healer – Healing and Vulnerability in Your Cat's Life

Chiron, often referred to as the "Wounded Healer," is an asteroid in astrology that represents deep wounds, vulnerabilities, and the potential for healing and wisdom that arises from these experiences. Named after the wise centaur from Greek mythology who was known for his healing abilities but also suffered from a wound that could never heal, Chiron in a natal chart highlights areas where an individual may experience deep pain but also where they can find their greatest strength and capacity for healing others. In the context of your cat's life, understanding the influence of Chiron can provide insights into their vulnerabilities, the challenges they face, and how they can achieve healing and growth through these experiences.

Chiron in Your Cat's Life: Understanding Vulnerability and Healing

Chiron's placement in a cat's astrological chart can reveal areas of vulnerability or pain that they carry with them, whether it's physical, emotional, or even spiritual. However, these wounds also offer the opportunity for profound healing, not only for the cat itself but also for those around them. Cats, like humans, can experience trauma or challenges that shape their behavior and emotional responses. By recognizing these aspects of your cat's life, you can better support their healing process and help them live a more balanced, contented life.

- **Identifying the Wound**: Chiron represents a wound that may never fully heal but offers the potential for deep growth and wisdom. For cats, this wound could manifest as a physical injury, an emotional trauma, or a behavioral challenge. Understanding the nature of this wound can help you provide the care and support your cat needs to navigate their vulnerabilities. For example, a cat that was rescued from a difficult situation might carry emotional scars that influence their trust in humans or other animals. Recognizing this wound allows you to approach them with the patience and compassion needed to help them feel safe and secure.

- **The Potential for Healing**: Despite the pain associated with Chiron, there is also a profound opportunity for healing and transformation. Cats are resilient creatures, and with the right support, they can overcome significant challenges. Healing may involve creating a safe and nurturing environment, providing consistent care and attention, or seeking veterinary or behavioral interventions when necessary. Healing is not always about erasing the wound but rather about helping the cat find peace and comfort despite it.

- **Vulnerability and Trust**: Chiron's influence often highlights areas where a cat may feel vulnerable, whether it's due to past experiences, physical limitations, or emotional sensitivities. These vulnerabilities can lead to behaviors that indicate a need for protection or reassurance. For example, a cat with a deep fear of abandonment might become clingy or anxious when left alone. Understanding these vulnerabilities allows you to create a sense of trust and security for your cat, ensuring that they feel safe in their environment.
- **Compassion and Empathy**: Cats influenced by Chiron often develop a deep sense of empathy, not only for themselves but also for others. They may be particularly sensitive to the emotions of their human companions or other animals in the household. This sensitivity can be a source of strength, as it allows them to offer comfort and companionship to those in need. By fostering this empathetic nature, you can help your cat channel their own experiences of vulnerability into a compassionate and healing presence within your home.
- **The Role of the Caregiver**: As a caregiver, your role in your cat's healing journey is crucial. Understanding Chiron's influence in your cat's chart can guide you in providing the necessary care and support to help them navigate their wounds. This might involve creating a calm and stable environment, offering gentle and consistent affection, or working with a veterinarian or behaviorist to address specific challenges. Your empathy, patience, and love are essential in helping your cat feel secure and supported as they heal.

Interpreting Chiron in Your Cat's Chart

Chiron's placement in your cat's astrological chart can provide specific insights into the nature of their wounds and the areas of life where healing is most needed. Each sign and house placement of Chiron reveals different aspects of this journey, helping you understand how to best support your cat.

- **Chiron in Aries**: A cat with Chiron in Aries may have wounds related to self-confidence or assertiveness. They might struggle with feeling secure in their environment or asserting themselves among other pets. Healing involves helping them build confidence and encouraging them to explore their surroundings in a safe and supportive way.

- **Chiron in Taurus**: Chiron in Taurus may indicate wounds related to physical security or material comfort. A cat with this placement might have experienced neglect or a lack of stability in the past. Healing focuses on providing a consistent, nurturing environment with plenty of physical comfort, such as a cozy bed, regular meals, and a stable routine.

- **Chiron in Gemini**: A cat with Chiron in Gemini may have wounds related to communication or social interaction. They might struggle with expressing their needs or connecting with others, possibly due to early trauma or isolation. Healing involves encouraging gentle socialization, offering clear and consistent communication, and creating a safe space for interaction.

- **Chiron in Cancer**: Chiron in Cancer suggests wounds related to emotional security and nurturing. A cat with this placement might be particularly sensitive to changes in their environment or may have experienced a lack of maternal care. Healing focuses on providing emotional support, a stable home environment, and plenty of affection to help them feel secure and loved.

- **Chiron in Leo**: Chiron in Leo may indicate wounds related to self-expression or recognition. A cat with this placement might struggle with feelings of inadequacy or a fear of not being noticed or appreciated. Healing involves encouraging their natural talents, providing opportunities for play and expression, and offering plenty of positive reinforcement.

- **Chiron in Virgo**: A cat with Chiron in Virgo may have wounds related to health, routine, or a sense of duty. They might have experienced illness or neglect in the past, leading to anxiety or compulsive behaviors. Healing focuses on creating a consistent routine, addressing any health concerns with care, and providing a calm and orderly environment.

- **Chiron in Libra**: Chiron in Libra suggests wounds related to relationships and social harmony. A cat with this placement might have difficulty forming bonds or may be sensitive to conflict in the household. Healing involves fostering positive social interactions, maintaining a peaceful environment, and ensuring that they feel included and valued within the family.

- **Chiron in Scorpio**: Chiron in Scorpio may indicate deep, transformative wounds related to trust, power, or loss. A cat with this placement might have experienced trauma or betrayal, leading to issues with trust or control. Healing focuses on rebuilding trust through consistent care, creating a safe and private space, and allowing them to heal at their own pace.

- **Chiron in Sagittarius**: A cat with Chiron in Sagittarius may have wounds related to freedom, exploration, or a sense of purpose. They might feel confined or restless, particularly if they have experienced restrictions in the past. Healing involves providing opportunities for exploration, ensuring they have plenty of mental and physical stimulation, and fostering a sense of adventure in their life.
- **Chiron in Capricorn**: Chiron in Capricorn suggests wounds related to authority, responsibility, or structure. A cat with this placement might have experienced harsh discipline or a lack of freedom. Healing involves creating a balanced environment with clear boundaries, offering consistent care, and ensuring that they feel secure and respected.
- **Chiron in Aquarius**: A cat with Chiron in Aquarius may have wounds related to individuality, belonging, or innovation. They might struggle with feeling different or misunderstood, particularly if they have unique needs or behaviors. Healing involves embracing their individuality, providing a supportive environment for their quirks, and ensuring that they feel accepted and valued.
- **Chiron in Pisces**: Chiron in Pisces may indicate wounds related to spirituality, empathy, or boundaries. A cat with this placement might be highly sensitive and prone to absorbing the emotions of others, leading to stress or overwhelm. Healing focuses on creating a calm and peaceful environment, offering emotional support, and helping them establish healthy boundaries.

Supporting Healing and Growth in Your Cat

As a caregiver, understanding the influence of Chiron in your cat's life allows you to provide the necessary support and care to help them heal and grow. Here are some ways you can support your cat's healing journey:

- **Create a Safe and Nurturing Environment**: Ensure that your cat has a safe, stable environment where they can feel secure and at ease. This might involve creating quiet spaces where they can retreat, maintaining a consistent routine, and providing plenty of physical and emotional comfort.

- **Be Patient and Understanding**: Healing takes time, and it's important to be patient with your cat as they navigate their wounds. Offer consistent care and affection, and allow them to progress at their own pace. Avoid forcing them into situations that may trigger their vulnerabilities, and instead, provide gentle encouragement and support.
- **Address Physical and Emotional Needs**: Pay attention to both the physical and emotional needs of your cat. Ensure they receive proper veterinary care, a healthy diet, and plenty of opportunities for play and exercise. Emotionally, provide reassurance, affection, and a calm, supportive presence.
- **Encourage Positive Social Interactions**: If your cat struggles with social interactions, encourage gentle and positive experiences with other pets or people. This can help them build trust and confidence, allowing them to form healthy relationships and feel more secure in their environment.
- **Respect Their Individuality**: Every cat is unique, and it's important to respect their individual needs and preferences. Whether they are more introverted, independent, or sensitive, embrace their personality and provide an environment that supports their unique traits and behaviors.
- **Use Healing Modalities**: Consider using additional healing modalities, such as aromatherapy, gentle massage, or calming music, to support your cat's well-being. These tools can help create a peaceful environment and promote relaxation, aiding in their healing process.

Conclusion

Chiron, the "Wounded Healer," plays a significant role in understanding the deeper vulnerabilities and healing journeys of your cat. By recognizing the areas where your cat may carry wounds, whether physical, emotional, or spiritual, you can provide the care and support they need to navigate these challenges and find healing and growth. Chiron's influence highlights the potential for transformation through compassion, empathy, and resilience, making it an essential aspect of your cat's astrological chart.

Whether it's creating a safe and nurturing environment, addressing their physical and emotional needs, or supporting their individuality and unique journey, understanding Chiron's influence will help ensure that your cat remains happy, healthy, and fulfilled. As you continue to explore the astrological influences on your cat, remember that each cat's healing journey is unique, and their experiences may vary depending on other factors in their astrological chart. However, the wisdom and strength that come from navigating the wounds of Chiron will always be a defining aspect of their path, making your cat's journey of healing a meaningful and cherished part of your shared experience.

Chapter 25: The Asteroids (Ceres, Pallas, Juno, Vesta): Specific Influences of These Minor Celestial Bodies on Your Cat's Daily Life

In astrology, the four major asteroids—Ceres, Pallas, Juno, and Vesta—play significant roles in shaping specific aspects of personality, behavior, and life experiences. While often considered "minor" celestial bodies compared to the planets, these asteroids have profound influences that can be reflected in your cat's daily life, affecting their nurturing instincts, creativity, relationships, and devotion to certain routines or behaviors. By understanding the roles of Ceres, Pallas, Juno, and Vesta in your cat's astrological chart, you can gain deeper insights into their behavior and preferences, allowing you to better cater to their needs and enhance their well-being.

Ceres: Nurturing and Care

Ceres, named after the Roman goddess of agriculture and grain, represents nurturing, caregiving, and the sustenance we provide and receive. In your cat's chart, Ceres can reveal how they experience and express nurturing, their relationship with food, and their need for comfort and security.

- **Nurturing Instincts**: Ceres influences how your cat gives and receives care. Cats with a strong Ceres influence may be particularly nurturing, often grooming other animals in the household or seeking to comfort their human companions. They may also have a strong desire to be nurtured themselves, often seeking out affection and closeness.

- **Relationship with Food**: Ceres governs all matters related to nourishment, including your cat's relationship with food. Cats with a prominent Ceres may have particular preferences or sensitivities regarding their diet. They might be more inclined toward specific foods or feeding routines that provide them with comfort and a sense of security. If Ceres is challenged in the chart, your cat might experience issues related to food, such as being picky eaters or showing signs of food-related anxiety.

- **Need for Comfort and Security**: Ceres also represents the need for comfort and security in daily life. Your cat may seek out cozy, nurturing environments where they feel safe and cared for. Providing them with a comfortable bed, regular feeding times, and plenty of affectionate interaction will help satisfy their Ceres-driven needs.

Pallas: Wisdom and Strategy

Pallas (or Pallas Athena), named after the goddess of wisdom, represents intelligence, strategy, and creative problem-solving. In your cat's chart, Pallas reveals how they approach challenges, their ability to strategize, and their intellectual capacities.

- **Strategic Thinking**: Pallas influences your cat's ability to think strategically and solve problems. Cats with a strong Pallas influence are likely to be clever and resourceful, often figuring out how to open doors, access hidden toys, or find creative solutions to obstacles. They may display a high level of mental agility and enjoy activities that challenge their intellect.
- **Creative Play**: Pallas also governs creativity, particularly in how your cat engages in play. A Pallas-influenced cat might invent new games, use toys in unconventional ways, or show a preference for puzzle toys that require strategic thinking. They are likely to enjoy activities that stimulate their mind and allow them to exercise their problem-solving skills.
- **Conflict Resolution**: Pallas is associated with wisdom and the ability to navigate conflicts. Cats with a strong Pallas influence may be adept at mediating disputes between other pets or finding ways to avoid confrontations. They might use their intelligence and strategy to maintain peace in the household, whether by avoiding aggressive situations or subtly asserting their dominance.

Juno: Relationships and Partnerships

Juno, named after the Roman goddess of marriage and partnership, represents relationships, commitment, and the dynamics of partnerships. In your cat's chart, Juno can reveal how they form bonds, their loyalty to others, and their approach to social interactions.

- **Forming Bonds**: Juno influences how your cat forms relationships and bonds with others, whether with their human companions or other animals. Cats with a strong Juno influence may form deep, lasting connections and show a strong sense of loyalty to those they care about. They are likely to be affectionate and committed to their relationships, often seeking out close, regular contact with their bonded companions.

- **Social Harmony**: Juno also governs the dynamics of partnerships and social harmony. A Juno-influenced cat may be particularly sensitive to the social structure of the household and work to maintain balance and harmony in their relationships. They may be more attuned to the needs of others and willing to compromise or adjust their behavior to keep the peace.
- **Commitment and Loyalty**: Cats with a strong Juno influence are often deeply loyal and committed to their human companions or fellow pets. They may display behaviors that reinforce their bond, such as following you around the house, seeking out your company, or showing protectiveness. This loyalty extends to their expectations in relationships; they may expect the same level of commitment in return and can become distressed if they feel neglected or ignored.

Vesta: Devotion and Focus

Vesta, named after the Roman goddess of the hearth and home, represents devotion, focus, and the sacred aspect of daily routines. In your cat's chart, Vesta reveals where they display dedication, their approach to routines, and their connection to their home environment.

- **Devotion and Focus**: Vesta influences your cat's sense of devotion and focus, particularly in areas where they show intense dedication. Cats with a strong Vesta influence may be highly focused on specific tasks or routines, such as grooming, hunting, or even their interactions with you. They may show a level of concentration and commitment that sets them apart from other cats, often becoming deeply absorbed in their chosen activities.
- **Connection to Home**: Vesta is associated with the hearth and home, making it significant in understanding your cat's relationship with their environment. A Vesta-influenced cat is likely to have a strong attachment to their home and may be particularly sensitive to changes in their environment. They might display behaviors that reinforce their connection to their space, such as returning to specific spots or engaging in rituals that give them a sense of security and comfort.

- **Sacred Routines**: Vesta also governs the sacredness of daily routines. Cats with a strong Vesta influence may thrive on routine and find comfort in the predictability of their daily life. They might show a strong preference for regular feeding times, consistent play schedules, or specific grooming habits. Disruptions to these routines can cause stress, so it's important to maintain consistency in their daily activities.

Interpreting the Asteroids in Your Cat's Chart

Each of the four major asteroids—Ceres, Pallas, Juno, and Vesta—offers unique insights into different aspects of your cat's life. Understanding their placement in your cat's chart can help you cater to their specific needs, enhancing their well-being and happiness.

- **Ceres Placement**: Look to Ceres to understand your cat's needs for nurturing, comfort, and food. A cat with Ceres in a nurturing sign like Cancer might require extra affection and a stable home environment, while a cat with Ceres in a more independent sign like Aquarius might seek nurturing in unconventional ways, such as through exploration or mental stimulation.
- **Pallas Placement**: Pallas's placement reveals your cat's approach to problem-solving, creativity, and strategic thinking. A cat with Pallas in an intellectual sign like Gemini might excel in activities that challenge their mind, enjoying puzzle toys and interactive games. On the other hand, a cat with Pallas in a practical sign like Virgo might show a preference for routines and tasks that require attention to detail.
- **Juno Placement**: Juno's placement provides insights into your cat's relationships and social interactions. A cat with Juno in a social sign like Libra might be particularly attuned to the dynamics of the household and work to maintain harmony among pets and people. Conversely, a cat with Juno in a more intense sign like Scorpio might form deep, powerful bonds with a select few individuals, displaying fierce loyalty and protectiveness.
- **Vesta Placement**: Vesta's placement highlights your cat's sense of devotion and their connection to home and routine. A cat with Vesta in a home-oriented sign like Taurus might be deeply attached to their home environment, finding comfort in familiar surroundings and

routines. Meanwhile, a cat with Vesta in a more active sign like Sagittarius might find devotion in exploration, seeking out new experiences and adventures within the safety of their home.

Supporting Your Cat's Needs Based on Asteroid Influences

Understanding the influences of Ceres, Pallas, Juno, and Vesta in your cat's chart allows you to tailor your care to their specific needs and preferences. Here's how you can support your cat based on the insights provided by these asteroids:

- **Nurturing and Care (Ceres)**: Cater to your cat's need for nurturing by providing consistent affection, comfort, and nourishment. Pay attention to their dietary preferences and create a cozy, secure environment where they feel loved and cared for.
- **Mental Stimulation and Creativity (Pallas)**: Encourage your cat's creativity and problem-solving abilities by providing a variety of toys and activities that challenge their intellect. Introduce new games and puzzles that stimulate their mind and allow them to express their natural intelligence.
- **Relationships and Social Harmony (Juno)**: Foster positive social interactions and relationships by ensuring that your cat feels included and valued within the household. Provide opportunities for bonding, whether through play, grooming, or simply spending time together, and be mindful of their need for harmony in their social environment.
- **Devotion and Routine (Vesta)**: Support your cat's devotion to routine by maintaining a consistent daily schedule. Ensure that their environment is stable and that they have access to the spaces and rituals that bring them comfort and security. Respect their need for focus and allow them to engage deeply in their chosen activities.

Conclusion

The asteroids Ceres, Pallas, Juno, and Vesta offer valuable insights into your cat's daily life, revealing their needs for nurturing, creativity, relationships, and routine. By understanding the influence of these minor celestial bodies, you can better cater to your cat's unique personality and preferences, enhancing their overall well-being and happiness.

Whether it's providing the right kind of nourishment and comfort (Ceres), stimulating their mind through creative play (Pallas), fostering deep and meaningful relationships (Juno), or maintaining a consistent and sacred routine (Vesta), understanding these influences allows you to create a more harmonious and fulfilling life for your feline companion. As you continue to explore the astrological influences on your cat, remember that each asteroid adds depth and nuance to their personality, making your cat's life path a rich and cherished experience shared with you.

Chapter 26: Lilith: The Dark Moon – Hidden Desires and the Untamed Aspects of Your Cat's Nature

Lilith, often referred to as the Dark Moon or Black Moon, is a point in astrology that represents the wild, untamed, and primal aspects of nature. In mythological terms, Lilith is associated with the archetype of the independent, rebellious, and sometimes vengeful feminine force, embodying a refusal to be subjugated or controlled. In the context of your cat's astrological chart, Lilith reveals the hidden desires, instincts, and aspects of their nature that are powerful, raw, and sometimes suppressed or misunderstood. Understanding Lilith's influence can provide insights into the more enigmatic and instinctual behaviors of your cat, helping you better appreciate and nurture their wild spirit.

Lilith in Your Cat's Life: Embracing the Untamed Spirit

Lilith in your cat's chart symbolizes the parts of their personality that are wild, instinctual, and sometimes difficult to control or understand. This placement can indicate areas where your cat exhibits fierce independence, deep-rooted instincts, or hidden desires that may not always align with their more domesticated behaviors. Embracing and understanding Lilith's influence allows you to honor your cat's true nature and provide an environment that respects their need for autonomy and self-expression.

- **The Wild and Untamed Nature**: Lilith represents the wild side of your cat's personality—the part that refuses to be tamed or controlled. This might manifest in behaviors that seem rebellious or unpredictable, such as sudden bursts of energy, intense hunting instincts, or a strong desire to escape confinement. These behaviors are not about disobedience but rather a reflection of your cat's deep connection to their primal instincts and natural urges.

- **Hidden Desires and Instincts**: Lilith governs the hidden desires and instincts that drive your cat's behavior. These could be deeply ingrained hunting instincts, a need for territorial dominance, or a desire for freedom and exploration. Cats with a strong Lilith influence may exhibit behaviors that seem intense or unexpected, such as sudden aggression, a fascination with certain objects or activities, or a strong need for independence. Understanding these desires allows you to provide appropriate outlets for your cat's instincts, helping them feel fulfilled and balanced.

- **Independence and Autonomy**: Lilith is often associated with independence and a refusal to be controlled. In your cat, this might manifest as a strong need for autonomy and the ability to make their own choices. They may resist being confined, prefer to explore on their own terms, or show a preference for activities that allow them to assert their independence. Respecting this need for autonomy is crucial in maintaining a healthy relationship with your cat, as it allows them to express their true nature without feeling stifled or restricted.

- **The Shadow Side**: Lilith also represents the shadow side of personality—the aspects that are often hidden or suppressed. In your cat, this could involve behaviors that are not typically seen in their everyday life, such as sudden aggression, territorial disputes, or an intense focus on certain activities or objects. These shadow behaviors can be a response to unmet needs or a reflection of deeper instincts that are not being fully expressed. By acknowledging and understanding these behaviors, you can help your cat find healthier ways to express their Lilith-driven impulses.

- **Sexuality and Sensuality**: Lilith is closely connected to the themes of sexuality and sensuality, even in animals. While this may not be as overt in domesticated cats as in humans, it can still manifest in behaviors related to attraction, mating instincts, and territoriality. For example, a cat with a strong Lilith influence may display more pronounced behaviors during mating seasons, such as vocalizations, territorial marking, or an increased desire for physical contact. Understanding these natural behaviors helps you manage them appropriately, especially in multi-pet households or during breeding seasons.

Interpreting Lilith in Your Cat's Chart

The placement of Lilith in your cat's astrological chart provides specific insights into the areas where their wild instincts, hidden desires, and untamed nature are most likely to manifest. Each sign and house placement of Lilith reveals different aspects of these primal influences.

- **Lilith in Aries**: A cat with Lilith in Aries may exhibit fierce independence and a strong drive for dominance. They are likely to be bold, assertive, and sometimes aggressive, especially when their territory or autonomy is challenged. This placement may also indicate a cat with a powerful hunting instinct, often displaying a relentless pursuit of prey or toys. Providing outlets for their energy and need for dominance, such as interactive play and opportunities for exploration, will help satisfy their Lilith-driven desires.

- **Lilith in Taurus**: Lilith in Taurus suggests a deep connection to physical pleasures and the material world. A cat with this placement might have intense cravings for comfort, food, or sensory experiences. They may display behaviors that reflect a strong attachment to their favorite spots, toys, or food, and could become possessive or territorial over these items. Ensuring they have access to their favorite comforts and respecting their need for space and ownership will help balance their desires.

- **Lilith in Gemini**: A cat with Lilith in Gemini may have a restless, curious nature, always seeking new experiences and stimuli. They are likely to be highly communicative, using a wide range of vocalizations to express their desires. This placement may also indicate a cat with a penchant for mischief or trickery, often finding creative ways to get what they want. Providing mental stimulation, such as puzzle toys and interactive play, will help satisfy their need for novelty and excitement.

- **Lilith in Cancer**: Lilith in Cancer suggests a deep-seated need for emotional security and comfort, but also a strong protective instinct. A cat with this placement may be fiercely protective of their home and family, displaying territorial behaviors or intense loyalty to their human companions. They may also have a strong attachment to their favorite spaces and routines, often seeking comfort in familiar surroundings. Providing a stable, nurturing environment where they feel safe and secure will help soothe their Lilith-driven instincts.

- **Lilith in Leo**: A cat with Lilith in Leo may have a strong need for attention, recognition, and dominance. They are likely to display bold, dramatic behaviors, often seeking to be the center of attention in the household. This placement may also indicate a cat with a strong territorial instinct, often asserting their dominance over other pets or even humans. Ensuring they have opportunities to express their leadership and receive the attention they crave will help balance their desires.

- **Lilith in Virgo**: Lilith in Virgo suggests a focus on precision, routine, and control. A cat with this placement may have specific rituals or behaviors that they follow meticulously, and they may become anxious or upset if these routines are disrupted. They may also have a heightened awareness of their surroundings, often reacting strongly to changes or disruptions. Providing a stable, orderly environment with consistent routines will help satisfy their need for control and precision.

- **Lilith in Libra**: A cat with Lilith in Libra may have a strong desire for balance, harmony, and social interaction, but also a hidden side that seeks independence and autonomy. They are likely to be charming and sociable, often forming close bonds with their human companions or other pets. However, they may also have a rebellious streak, sometimes seeking to disrupt the harmony they usually crave. Providing opportunities for social interaction, while also respecting their need for space and independence, will help balance their Lilith-driven desires.
- **Lilith in Scorpio**: Lilith in Scorpio suggests intense, passionate behaviors and a strong connection to the darker, more mysterious aspects of life. A cat with this placement may exhibit powerful territorial instincts, often displaying aggressive or possessive behaviors when their space is threatened. They may also have a deep, intuitive connection to their surroundings, often sensing things that others cannot. Providing a secure, private space where they can retreat and feel in control will help satisfy their Lilith-driven instincts.
- **Lilith in Sagittarius**: A cat with Lilith in Sagittarius may have a strong desire for freedom, exploration, and adventure. They are likely to be independent, restless, and always seeking new experiences. This placement may also indicate a cat with a strong hunting instinct, often displaying a relentless pursuit of prey or toys. Providing opportunities for exploration, whether through outdoor access or a stimulating indoor environment, will help satisfy their need for freedom and adventure.
- **Lilith in Capricorn**: Lilith in Capricorn suggests a strong focus on control, authority, and structure. A cat with this placement may exhibit behaviors that reflect a need for dominance and order, often asserting their control over their environment and those within it. They may also have a strong attachment to routines and traditions, often displaying behaviors that reflect a need for consistency and stability. Providing a structured, orderly environment where they feel in control will help satisfy their Lilith-driven instincts.
- **Lilith in Aquarius**: A cat with Lilith in Aquarius may have a strong need for individuality, independence, and unconventional behaviors. They are likely to be unique and unpredictable, often displaying behaviors that defy expectations or norms. This placement may also indicate a cat with a strong connection to technology or innovation, often showing interest

in unusual or high-tech toys. Providing opportunities for self-expression and respecting their need for independence will help balance their Lilith-driven desires.

- **Lilith in Pisces**: Lilith in Pisces suggests a deep connection to the spiritual, mystical aspects of life, but also a tendency toward escapism and withdrawal. A cat with this placement may exhibit behaviors that reflect a strong sensitivity to their environment, often retreating to quiet, peaceful spaces when they feel overwhelmed. They may also have a strong attachment to water, often displaying behaviors that involve water or other fluid, flowing elements. Providing a calm, serene environment where they can retreat and recharge will help satisfy their Lilith-driven instincts.

Supporting Your Cat's Lilith Influences

Understanding the influence of Lilith in your cat's life allows you to cater to their hidden desires, untamed instincts, and need for autonomy. Here are some ways you can support your cat based on the insights provided by Lilith:

- **Respect Their Wild Side**: Acknowledge and respect the wild, untamed aspects of your cat's nature. Provide them with opportunities to express their instincts, whether through hunting games, exploration, or simply allowing them the freedom to make their own choices. Understanding that these behaviors are natural and not necessarily a sign of disobedience will help you create a more harmonious relationship with your cat.
- **Create a Secure Environment**: Ensure that your cat has a secure, private space where they can retreat when they need to feel safe and in control. This could be a quiet room, a cozy bed in a secluded corner, or a high perch where they can observe their surroundings. Providing a sense of security will help them feel more balanced and less likely to act out their Lilith-driven instincts in disruptive ways.
- **Provide Mental and Physical Stimulation**: Cats with a strong Lilith influence often need plenty of mental and physical stimulation to satisfy their intense desires and instincts. Provide them with toys, puzzles, and activities that challenge their mind and body, helping them burn off excess energy and focus their instincts in positive ways.

- **Maintain a Balanced Routine**: While Lilith represents the wild, untamed aspects of nature, cats still benefit from a balanced routine that provides consistency and stability. Ensure that their daily needs are met, including regular feeding times, play sessions, and opportunities for rest and relaxation. A balanced routine will help them feel more secure and less likely to act out in unpredictable ways.
- **Support Their Independence**: Respect your cat's need for independence and autonomy, allowing them the freedom to explore and make their own choices. Avoid confining them unnecessarily or forcing them into situations that make them feel trapped or controlled. Supporting their independence will help them feel more secure and less likely to rebel against perceived restrictions.
- **Embrace Their Uniqueness**: Every cat is unique, and Lilith's influence highlights the aspects of their personality that are most individual and unconventional. Embrace and celebrate these traits, whether it's their quirky behaviors, intense instincts, or strong desire for freedom. Recognizing and honoring their individuality will help you create a stronger bond with your cat, based on mutual respect and understanding.

Conclusion

Lilith, the Dark Moon, reveals the hidden desires, untamed instincts, and primal aspects of your cat's nature. By understanding and respecting the influence of Lilith in your cat's life, you can create an environment that honors their wild spirit, supports their need for autonomy, and provides appropriate outlets for their intense desires.

Whether it's respecting their need for independence, providing opportunities for mental and physical stimulation, or creating a secure space where they can retreat and recharge, catering to Lilith's influence will help ensure that your cat remains happy, healthy, and fulfilled. As you continue to explore the astrological influences on your cat, remember that Lilith adds depth and complexity to their personality, making your cat's life path a rich and fascinating experience shared with you.

Part IV: Moon Phases and Feline Behavior

Chapter 27: New Moon: Initiation and New Beginnings in Your Cat's Life

The New Moon in astrology represents a time of initiation, new beginnings, and setting intentions. It marks the start of a new lunar cycle, a time when the moon is positioned between the Earth and the Sun, leaving the night sky dark and seemingly void of the moon's light. This phase is symbolic of a fresh start, an opportunity to plant seeds for the future, and to embark on new journeys. In the context of your cat's life, the New Moon can signify times when your cat is particularly receptive to changes, new experiences, and the beginning of new cycles of growth and development. Understanding the influence of the New Moon can help you align with your cat's natural rhythms and support them during periods of transition and renewal.

The Significance of the New Moon in Your Cat's Life

The New Moon is a powerful time for setting intentions and embracing new beginnings. Just as this phase encourages growth and change in the natural world, it also influences your cat's behavior, energy levels, and receptiveness to new experiences. This is a time when your cat may be more open to exploring new environments, learning new behaviors, or starting new routines. It's also a period where changes you introduce may take root more effectively, as the New Moon's energy supports fresh starts and the establishment of new habits.

- **Initiation and New Beginnings**: The New Moon symbolizes the start of a new cycle, making it an ideal time for initiating new experiences or changes in your cat's life. This could include introducing a new diet, starting a new routine, or even welcoming a new pet into the household. During this phase, your cat may be more open to exploring and adapting to these changes, as the energy of the New Moon supports the process of beginning anew.

- **Setting Intentions**: The New Moon is traditionally a time for setting intentions and making plans for the future. For your cat, this could mean setting goals related to their health, behavior, or overall well-being. Whether it's improving their diet, encouraging more play and exercise, or working on a specific behavioral issue, the New Moon is an auspicious time to set these intentions and begin working toward them.

- **Increased Sensitivity and Intuition**: During the New Moon, your cat may experience heightened sensitivity and intuition. This phase is often associated with introspection and a deeper connection to inner feelings and instincts. Your cat may be more attuned to subtle changes in their environment or more responsive to your emotions and energy. This increased sensitivity can make them more receptive to training, bonding activities, or any efforts to strengthen your relationship.

- **Rejuvenation and Renewal**: The New Moon also symbolizes renewal and rejuvenation. This is a time when your cat may naturally seek out rest and relaxation, preparing themselves for the new cycle ahead. Providing a calm, nurturing environment during this phase can help them recharge and prepare for the growth and changes that the new lunar cycle will bring. Activities that promote relaxation, such as gentle grooming, quiet time in a cozy space, or low-energy play, can be particularly beneficial during this time.

- **Adaptation to Change**: The energy of the New Moon supports adaptation to change. If you've been considering introducing something new into your cat's life—whether it's a new routine, a change in diet, or the introduction of another pet—this is an ideal time to do so. The New Moon's influence helps your cat adapt more smoothly to these changes, making transitions easier and less stressful.

Interpreting the New Moon in Your Cat's Chart

The placement of the New Moon in your cat's astrological chart can provide specific insights into how this phase influences their behavior and life experiences. Each sign and house placement of the New Moon offers different aspects of its energy, helping you understand how to best support your cat during this phase.

- **New Moon in Aries**: A New Moon in Aries signifies a time of bold action and new beginnings related to independence and leadership. Your cat may feel more energetic and assertive during this phase, eager to explore new territories or assert their dominance. This is a good time to introduce new activities that challenge their physical abilities or encourage them to take the lead in play.

- **New Moon in Taurus**: The New Moon in Taurus emphasizes new beginnings related to comfort, security, and material well-being. Your cat may focus on finding new favorite spots to relax or showing increased interest in food and treats. This is an ideal time to introduce new bedding, toys, or treats that cater to their sense of comfort and pleasure.

- **New Moon in Gemini**: A New Moon in Gemini brings new opportunities for communication, curiosity, and mental stimulation. Your cat may be more inquisitive and eager to explore their environment, interact with others, or engage in new forms of play. Introducing puzzle toys, new interactive games, or socializing with other pets can be particularly stimulating during this time.
- **New Moon in Cancer**: The New Moon in Cancer highlights new beginnings related to home, family, and emotional security. Your cat may seek out more nurturing and affectionate interactions or become more attached to their home environment. This is a good time to strengthen your bond through cuddling, grooming, or simply spending quality time together in a comforting space.
- **New Moon in Leo**: A New Moon in Leo emphasizes creativity, playfulness, and self-expression. Your cat may be more playful and outgoing during this phase, eager to engage in activities that allow them to show off or express themselves. Introducing new toys that encourage active play or engaging in interactive games can help them channel this energy positively.
- **New Moon in Virgo**: The New Moon in Virgo brings new opportunities for health, routine, and organization. Your cat may be more focused on their daily routines, showing an interest in maintaining order and cleanliness. This is an ideal time to establish or reinforce healthy habits, such as regular grooming, feeding schedules, or litter box maintenance.
- **New Moon in Libra**: A New Moon in Libra highlights new beginnings related to relationships, balance, and harmony. Your cat may be more social and cooperative during this phase, seeking out interactions with you or other pets. This is a good time to introduce new social experiences, such as playdates with other pets or spending time with different family members.
- **New Moon in Scorpio**: The New Moon in Scorpio emphasizes transformation, intensity, and deep emotional connections. Your cat may show a stronger focus on their surroundings, exhibiting more intense or focused behaviors. This is an ideal time to introduce new experiences that allow for deep exploration, such as new hiding spots, sensory toys, or engaging in activities that tap into their instincts.

- **New Moon in Sagittarius**: A New Moon in Sagittarius brings opportunities for adventure, exploration, and learning. Your cat may be more eager to explore new environments or engage in activities that stimulate their mind. This is a good time to introduce new toys, outdoor experiences, or activities that encourage exploration and discovery.
- **New Moon in Capricorn**: The New Moon in Capricorn emphasizes new beginnings related to discipline, structure, and responsibility. Your cat may be more focused on routines and may benefit from the introduction of new habits that promote discipline and order. This is an ideal time to establish or reinforce training, introduce new feeding routines, or create a more structured daily schedule.
- **New Moon in Aquarius**: A New Moon in Aquarius brings new opportunities for innovation, independence, and unconventional behaviors. Your cat may be more interested in exploring new ways of doing things or engaging in activities that challenge the status quo. Introducing new, innovative toys or creating opportunities for independent exploration can help satisfy their curiosity during this time.
- **New Moon in Pisces**: The New Moon in Pisces highlights new beginnings related to spirituality, creativity, and emotional sensitivity. Your cat may be more introspective and attuned to the emotional energies around them. This is a good time to create a calming, serene environment where they can relax and recharge. Activities that promote relaxation, such as gentle grooming or listening to calming music, can be particularly beneficial during this phase.

Supporting Your Cat During the New Moon

Understanding the influence of the New Moon in your cat's life allows you to provide the necessary support and care to help them navigate new beginnings and transitions. Here are some ways you can support your cat during this phase:

- **Introduce New Routines or Habits**: The New Moon is an ideal time to introduce new routines or habits that you want your cat to adopt. Whether it's a new feeding schedule, a regular playtime routine, or a new grooming ritual, the energy of the New Moon supports the establishment of these new practices.

- **Encourage Exploration and Curiosity**: During the New Moon, your cat may be more open to exploring new environments or trying new activities. Encourage this curiosity by providing opportunities for exploration, such as introducing new toys, setting up a new play area, or allowing them to explore different parts of the house or garden.
- **Focus on Bonding and Connection**: The New Moon is a powerful time for strengthening bonds and deepening connections. Spend quality time with your cat, engaging in activities that promote bonding, such as gentle grooming, cuddling, or simply being present with them. This is also a good time to introduce new pets or family members, as the energy supports the development of new relationships.
- **Create a Calm and Nurturing Environment**: As the New Moon is also a time for introspection and renewal, it's important to create a calm and nurturing environment where your cat can relax and recharge. Ensure that they have access to a quiet, comfortable space where they can retreat when they need to rest. Consider using calming elements such as soft lighting, soothing music, or aromatherapy to enhance their sense of well-being.
- **Set Intentions for Growth and Development**: Use the energy of the New Moon to set intentions for your cat's growth and development. Whether it's improving their diet, encouraging more physical activity, or working on a specific behavioral issue, the New Moon is an ideal time to focus on these goals and start working toward them.
- **Monitor and Support Emotional Sensitivity**: The New Moon can heighten your cat's emotional sensitivity, making them more attuned to the energies around them. Be mindful of their emotional state during this phase, offering extra comfort and reassurance if they seem more sensitive or withdrawn. Creating a peaceful environment and maintaining a consistent routine can help them feel secure and supported.

Conclusion

The New Moon represents a powerful time of initiation, new beginnings, and setting intentions, both in the natural world and in your cat's life. By understanding and aligning with the energy of the New Moon, you can support your cat during times of transition and renewal, helping them embrace new experiences and grow in positive ways.

Whether it's introducing new routines, encouraging exploration, or focusing on bonding and connection, the New Moon offers an opportunity to enhance your cat's well-being and support their development. As you continue to explore the astrological influences on your cat, remember that the New Moon's energy is a dynamic and ever-present force, guiding your cat through cycles of growth, renewal, and transformation, making their life journey a rich and fulfilling experience shared with you.

Chapter 28: Waxing Crescent Moon: Growth and Development Phases for Your Cat

The Waxing Crescent Moon is the phase that follows the New Moon and precedes the First Quarter Moon. This phase represents the period of growth and expansion, where the intentions set during the New Moon begin to take form. It is a time of gradual increase in light and energy, symbolizing the development of new ideas, habits, and experiences. For your cat, the Waxing Crescent Moon is a time when their natural instincts for growth and exploration are heightened. Understanding the influence of this lunar phase can help you support your cat's growth and development, ensuring they thrive during this period of expansion.

The Significance of the Waxing Crescent Moon in Your Cat's Life

The Waxing Crescent Moon marks a period of increasing energy and momentum. It's a time when the seeds planted during the New Moon start to sprout, and your cat's desire for exploration, learning, and growth is at its peak. During this phase, your cat may show increased curiosity, energy, and a willingness to engage in new activities. It's an ideal time to introduce new experiences, reinforce positive behaviors, and support your cat's ongoing development.

- **Growth and Expansion**: The Waxing Crescent Moon is a time of growth and expansion. Just as the moon's light begins to increase, your cat's energy and desire for growth also rise. This is an excellent time to focus on activities that promote physical, mental, and emotional development. Your cat may be more active, playful, and eager to explore their environment, making it an ideal time to introduce new toys, games, or experiences that challenge them in positive ways.

- **Building on New Beginnings**: Following the New Moon, where new intentions and goals are set, the Waxing Crescent Moon is the time to build on those foundations. For your cat, this might involve reinforcing new routines, habits, or behaviors introduced during the New Moon. This phase is all about nurturing these beginnings, ensuring they take root and grow strong. Whether it's encouraging a new diet, a play routine, or a training regimen, the Waxing Crescent Moon supports the continuation and strengthening of these efforts.

- **Increased Curiosity and Exploration**: Cats are naturally curious creatures, and during the Waxing Crescent Moon, this curiosity is often heightened. Your cat may be more interested in exploring new areas, investigating unfamiliar objects, or engaging in more interactive play. This phase is an ideal time to stimulate their curiosity by introducing them to new environments, toys, or activities that engage their senses and intellect.

- **Encouraging Positive Behaviors**: The Waxing Crescent Moon is also a time to encourage and reinforce positive behaviors in your cat. Whether you're working on training, socialization, or simply encouraging good habits, this phase offers an excellent opportunity to build on these behaviors. Positive reinforcement, consistency, and patience are key during this time, as your cat is more receptive to learning and adapting to new expectations.
- **Physical and Emotional Development**: As the moon waxes, your cat's physical and emotional development is also supported. This is a time when your cat may exhibit increased energy levels, making it important to provide outlets for physical activity and play. Additionally, their emotional development is also in focus, so activities that strengthen your bond, such as grooming, cuddling, or interactive play, are particularly beneficial.
- **Gradual Progress and Patience**: The Waxing Crescent Moon is a time of gradual progress. While growth is occurring, it's important to remember that this phase is about steady development rather than immediate results. Patience is key as your cat navigates this period of expansion. Allow them to explore at their own pace, offering guidance and support as they grow and develop.

Interpreting the Waxing Crescent Moon in Your Cat's Chart

The placement of the Waxing Crescent Moon in your cat's astrological chart can provide specific insights into how this phase influences their growth and development. Each sign and house placement of the Waxing Crescent Moon offers different aspects of its energy, helping you understand how to best support your cat during this phase.

- **Waxing Crescent Moon in Aries**: A Waxing Crescent Moon in Aries emphasizes growth related to independence, courage, and action. Your cat may exhibit increased energy and assertiveness, eager to explore and take on new challenges. This is a good time to introduce activities that require physical exertion, such as active play, climbing, or hunting games, allowing them to channel their energy in positive ways.

- **Waxing Crescent Moon in Taurus**: The Waxing Crescent Moon in Taurus highlights growth related to comfort, security, and material well-being. Your cat may focus on finding new favorite spots to relax or show increased interest in food and treats. This is an ideal time to introduce new comforts, such as a cozy bed, high-quality treats, or a favorite toy that provides sensory pleasure.
- **Waxing Crescent Moon in Gemini**: A Waxing Crescent Moon in Gemini brings growth opportunities related to communication, curiosity, and mental stimulation. Your cat may be more inquisitive and eager to explore their environment, interact with others, or engage in new forms of play. Introducing puzzle toys, new interactive games, or socializing with other pets can be particularly stimulating during this time.
- **Waxing Crescent Moon in Cancer**: The Waxing Crescent Moon in Cancer emphasizes growth related to home, family, and emotional security. Your cat may seek out more nurturing and affectionate interactions or become more attached to their home environment. This is a good time to strengthen your bond through cuddling, grooming, or simply spending quality time together in a comforting space.
- **Waxing Crescent Moon in Leo**: A Waxing Crescent Moon in Leo emphasizes creativity, playfulness, and self-expression. Your cat may be more playful and outgoing during this phase, eager to engage in activities that allow them to show off or express themselves. Introducing new toys that encourage active play or engaging in interactive games can help them channel this energy positively.
- **Waxing Crescent Moon in Virgo**: The Waxing Crescent Moon in Virgo brings growth opportunities related to health, routine, and organization. Your cat may be more focused on their daily routines, showing an interest in maintaining order and cleanliness. This is an ideal time to establish or reinforce healthy habits, such as regular grooming, feeding schedules, or litter box maintenance.
- **Waxing Crescent Moon in Libra**: A Waxing Crescent Moon in Libra highlights growth related to relationships, balance, and harmony. Your cat may be more social and cooperative during this phase, seeking out interactions with you or other pets. This is a good time to introduce new social experiences, such as playdates with other pets or spending time with different family members.

- **Waxing Crescent Moon in Scorpio**: The Waxing Crescent Moon in Scorpio emphasizes transformation, intensity, and deep emotional connections. Your cat may show a stronger focus on their surroundings, exhibiting more intense or focused behaviors. This is an ideal time to introduce new experiences that allow for deep exploration, such as new hiding spots, sensory toys, or engaging in activities that tap into their instincts.
- **Waxing Crescent Moon in Sagittarius**: A Waxing Crescent Moon in Sagittarius brings opportunities for adventure, exploration, and learning. Your cat may be more eager to explore new environments or engage in activities that stimulate their mind. This is a good time to introduce new toys, outdoor experiences, or activities that encourage exploration and discovery.
- **Waxing Crescent Moon in Capricorn**: The Waxing Crescent Moon in Capricorn emphasizes growth related to discipline, structure, and responsibility. Your cat may be more focused on routines and may benefit from the introduction of new habits that promote discipline and order. This is an ideal time to establish or reinforce training, introduce new feeding routines, or create a more structured daily schedule.
- **Waxing Crescent Moon in Aquarius**: A Waxing Crescent Moon in Aquarius brings new opportunities for innovation, independence, and unconventional behaviors. Your cat may be more interested in exploring new ways of doing things or engaging in activities that challenge the status quo. Introducing new, innovative toys or creating opportunities for independent exploration can help satisfy their curiosity during this time.
- **Waxing Crescent Moon in Pisces**: The Waxing Crescent Moon in Pisces highlights growth related to spirituality, creativity, and emotional sensitivity. Your cat may be more introspective and attuned to the emotional energies around them. This is a good time to create a calming, serene environment where they can relax and recharge. Activities that promote relaxation, such as gentle grooming or listening to calming music, can be particularly beneficial during this phase.

Supporting Your Cat During the Waxing Crescent Moon

Understanding the influence of the Waxing Crescent Moon in your cat's life allows you to provide the necessary support and care to help them navigate their growth and development during this phase. Here are some ways you can support your cat during the Waxing Crescent Moon:

- **Encourage Exploration and Learning**: The Waxing Crescent Moon is a time of curiosity and exploration. Encourage your cat to explore their environment by introducing new toys, allowing access to different areas of the house, or taking them on supervised outdoor adventures. Providing new experiences that engage their senses and intellect will help them grow and develop.

- **Reinforce Positive Behaviors and Routines**: As your cat's energy and curiosity increase, this is an ideal time to reinforce positive behaviors and routines. Whether you're working on training, establishing feeding schedules, or encouraging healthy habits, consistency and positive reinforcement are key during this phase. Celebrate small successes and provide rewards that motivate your cat to continue their progress.

- **Provide Physical and Mental Stimulation**: During the Waxing Crescent Moon, your cat's energy levels are likely to be higher, making it important to provide outlets for physical and mental stimulation. Engage them in interactive play sessions, offer puzzle toys that challenge their mind, and ensure they have plenty of opportunities for physical exercise. This will help them channel their energy in positive ways and prevent boredom.

- **Foster Emotional Bonding**: This lunar phase is also a time to strengthen the emotional bond between you and your cat. Spend quality time together, engaging in activities that promote trust and connection. Whether it's grooming, cuddling, or simply being present, your cat will benefit from the emotional support and reassurance you provide during this time of growth.

- **Monitor and Support Development**: Pay attention to your cat's development during the Waxing Crescent Moon, observing any changes in behavior, energy levels, or interests. Use this time to address any challenges that arise, providing guidance and support as needed. If your cat is showing signs of stress or frustration, consider adjusting their environment or routine to better suit their needs.

- **Embrace Gradual Progress**: Remember that the Waxing Crescent Moon is a time of gradual growth and development. Be patient with your cat as they navigate this phase, allowing them to progress at their own pace. Celebrate small milestones and continue to provide a supportive environment that encourages their natural curiosity and desire to grow.

Conclusion

The Waxing Crescent Moon represents a powerful time of growth, expansion, and development in your cat's life. By understanding and aligning with the energy of this lunar phase, you can support your cat's natural instincts for exploration, learning, and positive behavior reinforcement.

Whether it's encouraging them to explore new environments, reinforcing healthy habits, or providing physical and mental stimulation, the Waxing Crescent Moon offers an opportunity to enhance your cat's well-being and support their ongoing development. As you continue to explore the astrological influences on your cat, remember that the Waxing Crescent Moon's energy is a dynamic and nurturing force, guiding your cat through cycles of growth and helping them thrive in their journey of life.

Chapter 29: First Quarter Moon: Challenges and Action in Your Cat's Activities

The First Quarter Moon is the halfway point between the New Moon and the Full Moon, marking a significant phase of action, decision-making, and overcoming challenges. During this phase, the moon is half-illuminated, symbolizing the duality of growth and resistance, where the initial seeds planted during the New Moon face their first real tests. For your cat, the First Quarter Moon represents a time when they may encounter challenges in their activities or behavior, requiring them to take action, assert their will, and navigate obstacles. Understanding the influence of the First Quarter Moon can help you support your cat through these challenges, encouraging their growth and resilience.

The Significance of the First Quarter Moon in Your Cat's Life

The First Quarter Moon is a time of friction and momentum, where the energy that has been building since the New Moon now encounters resistance. This resistance is not necessarily negative; it's a natural part of the growth process that forces your cat to take action, make decisions, and confront challenges. This phase is characterized by increased energy, determination, and a focus on overcoming obstacles. Your cat may be more assertive, active, and driven to achieve their goals, making it an ideal time to support them in their activities and help them navigate any difficulties they encounter.

- **Action and Decision-Making**: The First Quarter Moon is a time for taking action and making decisions. For your cat, this might involve asserting their dominance, exploring new territories, or resolving conflicts with other pets. During this phase, your cat may display more decisive behavior, showing a strong sense of purpose and determination in their activities. This is an ideal time to encourage proactive behaviors, such as engaging in physical play, exploring new environments, or tackling new challenges.

- **Overcoming Challenges**: As the first major phase of resistance in the lunar cycle, the First Quarter Moon often brings challenges that need to be overcome. Your cat may encounter obstacles in their daily routine, such as difficulty adapting to new environments, conflicts with other pets, or frustration with certain activities. These challenges are opportunities for growth, as they push your cat to develop resilience and problem-solving skills. Supporting your cat through these challenges by providing guidance, encouragement, and appropriate outlets for their energy will help them navigate this phase successfully.

- **Increased Energy and Assertiveness**: The First Quarter Moon is associated with heightened energy levels and assertiveness. Your cat may be more active, playful, and eager to engage in physical activities during this time. They may also be more assertive in their interactions with others, whether it's claiming their favorite spot, seeking out attention, or asserting their dominance over other pets. This is a good time to channel their energy into constructive activities, such as interactive play, training, or exploration.

- **Testing Boundaries and Limits**: During the First Quarter Moon, your cat may be more inclined to test boundaries and limits. This could involve challenging the established order in the household, pushing back against rules, or exploring areas they previously avoided. While this behavior can sometimes be frustrating, it's a natural part of their development and an opportunity to reinforce boundaries and expectations. Consistency and positive reinforcement are key during this phase, helping your cat understand the limits while also encouraging their growth and independence.

- **Building Confidence and Resilience**: The challenges and obstacles encountered during the First Quarter Moon are essential for building confidence and resilience in your cat. By facing and overcoming these challenges, your cat develops a stronger sense of self-assurance and the ability to handle future difficulties. Encourage your cat to take on new challenges, whether it's learning a new trick, navigating a new environment, or resolving a conflict with another pet. Your support and encouragement will help them build the confidence they need to thrive.

- **Taking Initiative**: The First Quarter Moon is a time for taking initiative and moving forward with plans and intentions. Your cat may be more driven to take the lead in their activities, whether it's initiating play, exploring new territories, or asserting their presence in the household. Encourage this initiative by providing opportunities for leadership and independence, allowing your cat to make decisions and take charge of their environment.

Interpreting the First Quarter Moon in Your Cat's Chart

The placement of the First Quarter Moon in your cat's astrological chart can provide specific insights into how this phase influences their behavior and life experiences. Each sign and house placement of the First Quarter Moon offers different aspects of its energy, helping you understand how to best support your cat during this phase.

- **First Quarter Moon in Aries**: A First Quarter Moon in Aries emphasizes action, assertiveness, and the need to overcome challenges related to independence and leadership. Your cat may be more energetic, bold, and eager to assert their dominance during this phase. This is an ideal time to encourage physical activities that allow them to channel their energy and assert their independence, such as active play, climbing, or exploring new territories.
- **First Quarter Moon in Taurus**: The First Quarter Moon in Taurus highlights challenges related to comfort, security, and material well-being. Your cat may focus on asserting their ownership of certain spaces, toys, or food, and may resist changes to their routine or environment. This is a good time to reinforce boundaries and expectations while also providing comfort and security to help them feel safe and supported.
- **First Quarter Moon in Gemini**: A First Quarter Moon in Gemini brings challenges related to communication, curiosity, and mental stimulation. Your cat may be more vocal, inquisitive, and eager to explore their environment during this phase. Encourage their curiosity by providing new toys, interactive games, or opportunities for social interaction, while also addressing any challenges related to communication or socialization.
- **First Quarter Moon in Cancer**: The First Quarter Moon in Cancer emphasizes challenges related to home, family, and emotional security. Your cat may seek to assert their position in the household or become more protective of their territory during this phase. This is a good time to reinforce their sense of belonging and security, providing them with consistent care, affection, and a stable environment.
- **First Quarter Moon in Leo**: A First Quarter Moon in Leo emphasizes challenges related to self-expression, creativity, and leadership. Your cat may be more playful, outgoing, and eager to take the lead in their activities during this phase. Encourage their self-expression by providing opportunities for creative play, interactive games, or activities that allow them to show off and take charge.
- **First Quarter Moon in Virgo**: The First Quarter Moon in Virgo brings challenges related to health, routine, and organization. Your cat may be more focused on maintaining order in

their environment or may resist changes to their routine during this phase. This is an ideal time to reinforce healthy habits, such as regular grooming, feeding schedules, or litter box maintenance, while also addressing any challenges related to routine or cleanliness.

- **First Quarter Moon in Libra**: A First Quarter Moon in Libra highlights challenges related to relationships, balance, and harmony. Your cat may be more social and cooperative during this phase, but may also face challenges related to maintaining balance in their interactions with others. This is a good time to reinforce positive social behaviors, provide opportunities for bonding, and address any conflicts or imbalances in their relationships.
- **First Quarter Moon in Scorpio**: The First Quarter Moon in Scorpio emphasizes challenges related to transformation, intensity, and deep emotional connections. Your cat may show more intense or focused behaviors during this phase, particularly related to their surroundings or relationships. This is an ideal time to support their emotional growth by providing opportunities for deep exploration, such as new hiding spots, sensory toys, or engaging in activities that tap into their instincts.
- **First Quarter Moon in Sagittarius**: A First Quarter Moon in Sagittarius brings challenges related to adventure, exploration, and learning. Your cat may be more eager to explore new environments or engage in activities that stimulate their mind during this phase. Encourage their sense of adventure by introducing new toys, outdoor experiences, or activities that encourage exploration and discovery.
- **First Quarter Moon in Capricorn**: The First Quarter Moon in Capricorn emphasizes challenges related to discipline, structure, and responsibility. Your cat may be more focused on routines and may face challenges related to maintaining order in their environment during this phase. This is an ideal time to reinforce training, establish new habits, or create a more structured daily schedule that promotes discipline and responsibility.
- **First Quarter Moon in Aquarius**: A First Quarter Moon in Aquarius brings challenges related to innovation, independence, and unconventional behaviors. Your cat may be more interested in exploring new ways of doing things or engaging in activities that challenge the status quo during this phase. Encourage their individuality by providing opportunities for independent exploration, introducing innovative toys, or creating activities that challenge their intellect.

- **First Quarter Moon in Pisces**: The First Quarter Moon in Pisces highlights challenges related to spirituality, creativity, and emotional sensitivity. Your cat may be more introspective and attuned to the emotional energies around them during this phase. This is a good time to create a calming, serene environment where they can relax and recharge, while also addressing any challenges related to their emotional well-being.

Supporting Your Cat During the First Quarter Moon

Understanding the influence of the First Quarter Moon in your cat's life allows you to provide the necessary support and care to help them navigate challenges and take action during this phase. Here are some ways you can support your cat during the First Quarter Moon:

- **Encourage Action and Initiative**: The First Quarter Moon is a time for taking action and making decisions. Encourage your cat to take the lead in their activities, whether it's initiating play, exploring new environments, or asserting their presence in the household. Provide opportunities for leadership and independence, allowing your cat to make decisions and take charge of their environment.
- **Reinforce Positive Behaviors**: As your cat faces challenges during this phase, it's important to reinforce positive behaviors and provide guidance. Use positive reinforcement to encourage good habits, such as rewarding them for using the litter box, playing nicely with others, or following routines. Consistency and patience are key to helping your cat navigate this phase successfully.
- **Provide Physical and Mental Stimulation**: During the First Quarter Moon, your cat's energy levels are likely to be higher, making it important to provide outlets for physical and mental stimulation. Engage them in interactive play sessions, offer puzzle toys that challenge their mind, and ensure they have plenty of opportunities for physical exercise. This will help them channel their energy in positive ways and prevent boredom.
- **Support Emotional Well-Being**: As your cat faces challenges, it's important to provide emotional support and reassurance. Spend quality time together, engaging in activities that promote bonding and trust. If your cat seems stressed or anxious, create a calm, comforting environment where they can feel secure and relaxed.

- **Address Conflicts and Challenges**: The First Quarter Moon may bring conflicts or challenges in your cat's relationships or environment. Be proactive in addressing these issues, whether it's resolving conflicts with other pets, reinforcing boundaries, or providing additional support in areas where your cat is struggling. Your guidance and intervention can help them navigate these challenges with confidence.
- **Monitor and Support Growth**: Pay attention to your cat's behavior during the First Quarter Moon, observing how they respond to challenges and take action. Use this time to support their growth and development, offering encouragement and guidance as needed. Celebrate their successes and provide comfort and reassurance when they encounter difficulties.

Conclusion

The First Quarter Moon represents a powerful time of action, decision-making, and overcoming challenges in your cat's life. By understanding and aligning with the energy of this lunar phase, you can support your cat as they navigate obstacles, take initiative, and assert their will.

Whether it's encouraging them to take action, reinforcing positive behaviors, or providing physical and mental stimulation, the First Quarter Moon offers an opportunity to enhance your cat's well-being and support their ongoing development. As you continue to explore the astrological influences on your cat, remember that the First Quarter Moon's energy is a dynamic and motivating force, guiding your cat through cycles of growth and helping them build the confidence and resilience they need to thrive.

Chapter 30: Waxing Gibbous Moon: Refinement and Adjustment Periods for Your Cat

The Waxing Gibbous Moon is the phase that occurs between the First Quarter Moon and the Full Moon. During this period, the moon is almost fully illuminated, symbolizing a time of refinement, adjustment, and preparation. The seeds planted during the New Moon have grown and developed, and now it's time to refine and perfect these efforts before reaching full fruition at the Full Moon. For your cat, the Waxing Gibbous Moon represents a period of fine-tuning behaviors, making adjustments, and preparing for the culmination of their efforts. Understanding the influence of the Waxing Gibbous Moon can help you support your cat during this critical phase of growth, ensuring they continue to thrive and develop in a balanced way.

The Significance of the Waxing Gibbous Moon in Your Cat's Life

The Waxing Gibbous Moon is a time of refinement, when the initial growth and development from earlier phases are fine-tuned and perfected. This phase is characterized by a focus on details, adjustments, and making the necessary changes to ensure that efforts come to fruition successfully. For your cat, this might involve refining certain behaviors, adjusting to new routines or environments, and preparing for the culmination of their actions and growth. It's a period of increased focus, attention to detail, and a readiness to make the final push toward achieving goals.

- **Refinement of Behaviors**: The Waxing Gibbous Moon is an ideal time for refining and perfecting behaviors that have been developing during the previous lunar phases. This might involve fine-tuning training efforts, reinforcing positive habits, or addressing minor behavioral issues. Your cat may show a greater ability to focus and adapt during this phase, making it an excellent time to work on specific behaviors or routines that need adjustment or improvement.

- **Adjustment and Adaptation**: As your cat progresses toward the Full Moon, they may encounter areas where adjustments are necessary. This could involve adapting to new environments, adjusting to changes in routine, or making small tweaks to their behavior. The Waxing Gibbous Moon supports these adjustments, helping your cat find balance and harmony in their daily life. During this phase, your cat may be more open to making changes and refining their approach to various activities.

- **Increased Focus and Attention to Detail**: The energy of the Waxing Gibbous Moon encourages a heightened focus on details and precision. Your cat may display more careful and deliberate behavior, paying closer attention to their surroundings and the tasks at hand. This is a good time to introduce activities that require concentration, such as puzzle toys, interactive games, or training exercises that challenge their mind and body.
- **Preparation for Culmination**: As the Full Moon approaches, the Waxing Gibbous Moon is a time of preparation and final adjustments. Your cat may be more focused on completing tasks, reaching goals, or solidifying their position in the household. This phase is about getting everything in order before the Full Moon, ensuring that your cat is ready to fully embrace the culmination of their efforts. Providing support and guidance during this period will help them feel prepared and confident.
- **Balancing Energy and Rest**: The Waxing Gibbous Moon represents a time of increased energy, but also the need for balance and rest. While your cat may be more active and focused during this phase, it's important to ensure they have opportunities for relaxation and recovery. Providing a balanced routine that includes both physical activity and rest will help your cat maintain their energy and well-being as they approach the Full Moon.
- **Attention to Health and Well-Being**: During the Waxing Gibbous Moon, your cat's health and well-being may also come into focus. This is an ideal time to address any minor health concerns, adjust their diet, or reinforce grooming habits. Ensuring that your cat's physical and emotional needs are met during this phase will help them feel balanced and supported as they continue to grow and develop.

Interpreting the Waxing Gibbous Moon in Your Cat's Chart

The placement of the Waxing Gibbous Moon in your cat's astrological chart can provide specific insights into how this phase influences their behavior and life experiences. Each sign and house placement of the Waxing Gibbous Moon offers different aspects of its energy, helping you understand how to best support your cat during this phase.

- **Waxing Gibbous Moon in Aries**: A Waxing Gibbous Moon in Aries emphasizes refinement and adjustment related to independence, action, and leadership. Your cat may be focused on fine-tuning their assertive behaviors or making adjustments to their approach in interactions with others. Encourage them to channel their energy into activities that promote confidence and independence, while also reinforcing positive social behaviors.
- **Waxing Gibbous Moon in Taurus**: The Waxing Gibbous Moon in Taurus highlights refinement related to comfort, security, and material well-being. Your cat may be focused on perfecting their routines related to food, sleep, or relaxation. This is an ideal time to make adjustments to their environment or routine that enhance their comfort and sense of security, such as introducing a new bed or refining their diet.
- **Waxing Gibbous Moon in Gemini**: A Waxing Gibbous Moon in Gemini brings refinement opportunities related to communication, curiosity, and mental stimulation. Your cat may be more focused on fine-tuning their social interactions or adjusting to new forms of play. Encourage their curiosity by providing new toys, interactive games, or opportunities for socialization, while also reinforcing positive communication behaviors.
- **Waxing Gibbous Moon in Cancer**: The Waxing Gibbous Moon in Cancer emphasizes refinement related to home, family, and emotional security. Your cat may be focused on making adjustments to their routines or behaviors related to their home environment and relationships. This is a good time to strengthen your bond through consistent care, affection, and creating a stable, nurturing environment.
- **Waxing Gibbous Moon in Leo**: A Waxing Gibbous Moon in Leo emphasizes refinement related to self-expression, creativity, and leadership. Your cat may be focused on perfecting their play behaviors or adjusting their approach to interactions with others. Encourage their self-expression by providing opportunities for creative play and leadership, while also reinforcing positive social behaviors.
- **Waxing Gibbous Moon in Virgo**: The Waxing Gibbous Moon in Virgo brings refinement opportunities related to health, routine, and organization. Your cat may be more focused on fine-tuning their daily routines or making adjustments to their habits. This is an ideal time to reinforce healthy behaviors, such as regular grooming, feeding schedules, or litter box maintenance, while also addressing any minor health concerns.

- **Waxing Gibbous Moon in Libra**: A Waxing Gibbous Moon in Libra highlights refinement related to relationships, balance, and harmony. Your cat may be focused on making adjustments to their social interactions or refining their approach to maintaining balance in their relationships. Encourage positive social behaviors by providing opportunities for bonding and addressing any conflicts or imbalances in their relationships.

- **Waxing Gibbous Moon in Scorpio**: The Waxing Gibbous Moon in Scorpio emphasizes refinement related to transformation, intensity, and deep emotional connections. Your cat may be focused on fine-tuning their behaviors related to their surroundings or relationships. This is an ideal time to support their emotional growth by providing opportunities for deep exploration and addressing any challenges related to their emotional well-being.

- **Waxing Gibbous Moon in Sagittarius**: A Waxing Gibbous Moon in Sagittarius brings refinement opportunities related to adventure, exploration, and learning. Your cat may be focused on making adjustments to their activities related to exploration or learning. Encourage their sense of adventure by introducing new toys, outdoor experiences, or activities that stimulate their mind and body, while also reinforcing positive behaviors.

- **Waxing Gibbous Moon in Capricorn**: The Waxing Gibbous Moon in Capricorn emphasizes refinement related to discipline, structure, and responsibility. Your cat may be focused on perfecting their routines related to discipline and order. This is an ideal time to reinforce training, establish new habits, or create a more structured daily schedule that promotes discipline and responsibility.

- **Waxing Gibbous Moon in Aquarius**: A Waxing Gibbous Moon in Aquarius brings refinement opportunities related to innovation, independence, and unconventional behaviors. Your cat may be focused on fine-tuning their approach to independence or making adjustments to their unique behaviors. Encourage their individuality by providing opportunities for independent exploration and introducing innovative toys or activities that challenge their intellect.

- **Waxing Gibbous Moon in Pisces**: The Waxing Gibbous Moon in Pisces highlights refinement related to spirituality, creativity, and emotional sensitivity. Your cat may be more introspective and focused on making adjustments to their behaviors related to emotional well-being. This is a good time to create a calming, serene environment where they can relax and recharge, while also reinforcing positive emotional behaviors.

Supporting Your Cat During the Waxing Gibbous Moon

Understanding the influence of the Waxing Gibbous Moon in your cat's life allows you to provide the necessary support and care to help them navigate this period of refinement and adjustment. Here are some ways you can support your cat during the Waxing Gibbous Moon:

- **Encourage Refinement and Precision**: The Waxing Gibbous Moon is a time for fine-tuning and perfecting behaviors. Encourage your cat to focus on details and refine their approach to various activities, whether it's through training, play, or social interactions. Use positive reinforcement to guide them toward more precise and deliberate behaviors, helping them build confidence and skill.

- **Facilitate Adjustments and Adaptations**: As your cat navigates this phase, they may need to make adjustments to their routines or behaviors. Be patient and supportive as they adapt, offering guidance and encouragement as needed. Whether it's adjusting to a new environment, refining their diet, or tweaking their daily routine, your support will help them find balance and harmony.

- **Provide Physical and Mental Stimulation**: During the Waxing Gibbous Moon, your cat's focus and attention to detail may be heightened, making it important to provide activities that challenge their mind and body. Engage them in interactive play sessions, offer puzzle toys that require concentration, and ensure they have plenty of opportunities for physical exercise. This will help them channel their energy in positive ways and prevent boredom.

- **Support Emotional Well-Being**: As your cat focuses on refinement and adjustment, it's important to provide emotional support and reassurance. Spend quality time together, engaging in activities that promote bonding and trust. If your cat seems stressed or anxious, create a calm, comforting environment where they can feel secure and relaxed.

- **Monitor and Support Health and Well-Being**: The Waxing Gibbous Moon is an ideal time to address any minor health concerns and reinforce healthy habits. Pay attention to your cat's physical and emotional well-being, making adjustments to their diet, grooming routine, or daily activities as needed. Ensuring that their health and well-being are prioritized during this phase will help them feel balanced and supported.

- **Celebrate Progress and Success**: As your cat makes adjustments and refinements during the Waxing Gibbous Moon, take the time to celebrate their progress and successes. Acknowledge their efforts and provide positive reinforcement for their achievements. This will help build their confidence and motivation as they continue to grow and develop.

Conclusion

The Waxing Gibbous Moon represents a powerful time of refinement, adjustment, and preparation in your cat's life. By understanding and aligning with the energy of this lunar phase, you can support your cat as they fine-tune their behaviors, adapt to new routines, and prepare for the culmination of their efforts at the Full Moon.

Whether it's encouraging them to refine their approach to various activities, facilitating adjustments to their environment or routine, or providing physical and mental stimulation, the Waxing Gibbous Moon offers an opportunity to enhance your cat's well-being and support their ongoing development. As you continue to explore the astrological influences on your cat, remember that the Waxing Gibbous Moon's energy is a dynamic and nurturing force, guiding your cat through cycles of growth and helping them achieve balance and harmony in their journey of life.

Chapter 31: Full Moon: Heightened Emotions and Behaviors in Your Cat

The Full Moon is a powerful and intense phase in the lunar cycle, representing the culmination of the intentions and efforts set during the New Moon. During this phase, the moon is fully illuminated, symbolizing a time of clarity, heightened emotions, and peak energy. For your cat, the Full Moon can bring about significant changes in behavior, emotions, and energy levels. Understanding the influence of the Full Moon can help you navigate these heightened states in your cat, ensuring that you provide the necessary support and care during this intense period.

The Significance of the Full Moon in Your Cat's Life

The Full Moon is a time of fruition, where the efforts and intentions set earlier in the lunar cycle come to a peak. This phase is often associated with heightened emotions, increased activity, and a sense of completion or resolution. For your cat, the Full Moon can amplify their natural behaviors and instincts, leading to increased activity, emotional sensitivity, and sometimes unpredictable behavior. It's a time when your cat may be more expressive, assertive, and in tune with their environment, making it important to understand and support them through this phase.

- **Heightened Emotions**: The Full Moon is known for its ability to amplify emotions, and this effect is often seen in cats as well. Your cat may become more sensitive, reactive, or expressive during this phase. They may display stronger emotional responses to their surroundings, whether it's seeking more affection, displaying signs of agitation, or reacting more intensely to stimuli. It's important to be mindful of their emotional state during the Full Moon, providing extra comfort and reassurance as needed.

- **Increased Activity and Energy**: The Full Moon is also associated with increased energy and activity levels. Your cat may be more playful, restless, or eager to engage in physical activities during this phase. They may display a stronger desire to explore, hunt, or assert their presence in the household. Providing outlets for this increased energy, such as interactive play, climbing activities, or opportunities for exploration, will help them channel their energy in positive ways.

- **Intensified Instincts**: During the Full Moon, your cat's natural instincts may be heightened. This could include a stronger drive to hunt, mark territory, or engage in territorial behaviors. They may also be more attuned to changes in their environment, reacting more strongly to new scents, sounds, or movements. Understanding these intensified instincts allows you to provide appropriate outlets, such as toys that simulate hunting or secure spaces where they can retreat if they feel overwhelmed.

- **Increased Social Interaction**: Some cats may seek out more social interaction during the Full Moon, displaying a stronger need for companionship and attention. They may follow you around the house, seek out physical contact, or vocalize more frequently. This increased need for social interaction can be a way for your cat to seek comfort and reassurance during this emotionally charged phase. Spending quality time with your cat, engaging in bonding activities, or simply being present with them can help fulfill their social needs.
- **Heightened Sensitivity to Environment**: The Full Moon often brings a heightened sensitivity to the environment, and your cat may be more aware of changes in their surroundings. They may react more strongly to unfamiliar objects, new people, or changes in routine. This sensitivity can sometimes lead to stress or anxiety, so it's important to maintain a stable and consistent environment during this phase. Providing a safe, familiar space where your cat can retreat and feel secure will help them manage their heightened sensitivity.
- **Behavioral Changes and Unpredictability**: The Full Moon can sometimes lead to unpredictable behavior in cats. They may display behaviors that are out of character, such as sudden bursts of energy, increased aggression, or a change in their usual routines. These behavioral changes are often temporary and related to the heightened energy and emotions of the Full Moon. Being patient and understanding during this phase, and providing appropriate outlets for their energy, will help your cat navigate this period of intensity.

Interpreting the Full Moon in Your Cat's Chart

The placement of the Full Moon in your cat's astrological chart can provide specific insights into how this phase influences their behavior and life experiences. Each sign and house placement of the Full Moon offers different aspects of its energy, helping you understand how to best support your cat during this phase.

- **Full Moon in Aries**: A Full Moon in Aries emphasizes heightened emotions and behaviors related to independence, assertiveness, and action. Your cat may display increased energy, confidence, and a stronger desire to assert their dominance during this phase. This is an ideal time to engage in activities that allow them to channel their energy and assertiveness, such as interactive play, climbing, or hunting games.

- **Full Moon in Taurus**: The Full Moon in Taurus highlights heightened emotions and behaviors related to comfort, security, and material well-being. Your cat may seek out more comfort and stability during this phase, displaying a stronger attachment to their favorite spots, toys, or food. Providing a stable and comforting environment, along with their favorite treats or activities, will help them feel secure and content.
- **Full Moon in Gemini**: A Full Moon in Gemini brings heightened emotions and behaviors related to communication, curiosity, and social interaction. Your cat may be more vocal, inquisitive, and eager to engage with their surroundings during this phase. Encourage their curiosity by providing new toys, interactive games, or opportunities for socialization, while also being mindful of their need for mental stimulation.
- **Full Moon in Cancer**: The Full Moon in Cancer emphasizes heightened emotions and behaviors related to home, family, and emotional security. Your cat may become more attached to their home environment and may seek out more affectionate interactions during this phase. This is a good time to strengthen your bond through cuddling, grooming, or simply spending quality time together in a comforting space.
- **Full Moon in Leo**: A Full Moon in Leo emphasizes heightened emotions and behaviors related to self-expression, creativity, and leadership. Your cat may be more playful, outgoing, and eager to show off during this phase. Encourage their self-expression by providing opportunities for creative play, interactive games, or activities that allow them to take the lead and assert their presence.
- **Full Moon in Virgo**: The Full Moon in Virgo brings heightened emotions and behaviors related to health, routine, and organization. Your cat may become more focused on their daily routines and may display heightened sensitivity to changes in their environment. This is an ideal time to reinforce healthy habits, such as regular grooming, feeding schedules, or litter box maintenance, while also providing a stable and organized environment.
- **Full Moon in Libra**: A Full Moon in Libra highlights heightened emotions and behaviors related to relationships, balance, and harmony. Your cat may be more social and cooperative

during this phase, seeking out interactions with you or other pets. This is a good time to reinforce positive social behaviors, provide opportunities for bonding, and maintain balance in their relationships.

- **Full Moon in Scorpio**: The Full Moon in Scorpio emphasizes heightened emotions and behaviors related to transformation, intensity, and deep emotional connections. Your cat may display more intense or focused behaviors during this phase, particularly related to their surroundings or relationships. This is an ideal time to support their emotional growth by providing opportunities for deep exploration, such as new hiding spots, sensory toys, or engaging in activities that tap into their instincts.

- **Full Moon in Sagittarius**: A Full Moon in Sagittarius brings heightened emotions and behaviors related to adventure, exploration, and learning. Your cat may be more eager to explore new environments or engage in activities that stimulate their mind during this phase. Encourage their sense of adventure by introducing new toys, outdoor experiences, or activities that promote exploration and discovery.

- **Full Moon in Capricorn**: The Full Moon in Capricorn emphasizes heightened emotions and behaviors related to discipline, structure, and responsibility. Your cat may become more focused on maintaining order in their environment and may display a stronger attachment to their routines. This is an ideal time to reinforce training, establish new habits, or create a more structured daily schedule that promotes discipline and responsibility.

- **Full Moon in Aquarius**: A Full Moon in Aquarius brings heightened emotions and behaviors related to innovation, independence, and unconventional actions. Your cat may be more interested in exploring new ways of doing things or engaging in activities that challenge the status quo during this phase. Encourage their individuality by providing opportunities for independent exploration, introducing innovative toys, or creating activities that challenge their intellect.

- **Full Moon in Pisces**: The Full Moon in Pisces highlights heightened emotions and behaviors related to spirituality, creativity, and emotional sensitivity. Your cat may be more introspective and attuned to the emotional energies around them during this phase. This is a good time to create a calming, serene environment where they can relax and recharge, while also supporting their creative and emotional needs.

Supporting Your Cat During the Full Moon

Understanding the influence of the Full Moon in your cat's life allows you to provide the necessary support and care to help them navigate heightened emotions and behaviors during this intense phase. Here are some ways you can support your cat during the Full Moon:

- **Provide Emotional Support and Reassurance**: The Full Moon can bring heightened emotions, making it important to provide extra comfort and reassurance to your cat. Spend quality time together, engaging in activities that promote bonding and trust. If your cat seems more sensitive or reactive, create a calm and comforting environment where they can feel safe and secure.
- **Channel Energy Through Physical Activity**: The Full Moon often increases energy levels, so it's important to provide outlets for physical activity. Engage your cat in interactive play sessions, offer toys that simulate hunting or climbing, and ensure they have plenty of opportunities for exercise. This will help them channel their energy in positive ways and prevent restlessness or frustration.
- **Support Instinctual Behaviors**: During the Full Moon, your cat's instincts may be heightened, leading to stronger territorial behaviors, hunting drives, or other natural instincts. Provide appropriate outlets for these behaviors, such as toys that satisfy their hunting instincts, secure spaces where they can retreat, or activities that allow them to mark their territory in a positive way.
- **Maintain a Stable Environment**: The heightened sensitivity of the Full Moon can make your cat more reactive to changes in their environment. Maintain a stable and consistent environment during this phase, avoiding major changes or disruptions. Ensure that your cat has access to familiar spaces, routines, and comforts that help them feel secure.
- **Monitor Behavioral Changes**: The Full Moon can sometimes lead to unpredictable behavior, so it's important to monitor your cat closely during this phase. If you notice significant changes in their behavior, such as increased aggression, restlessness, or anxiety, provide additional support and consider adjusting their routine or environment to help them manage these changes.

- **Promote Relaxation and Rest**: While the Full Moon is a time of heightened energy, it's also important to promote relaxation and rest. Ensure that your cat has access to quiet, comfortable spaces where they can retreat and recharge. Consider using calming aids, such as soothing music, aromatherapy, or gentle grooming, to help them relax during this intense phase.
- **Celebrate Achievements and Milestones**: The Full Moon is a time of culmination and completion, making it an ideal time to celebrate your cat's achievements and milestones. Whether it's mastering a new trick, overcoming a behavioral challenge, or simply maintaining their well-being, take the time to acknowledge and reward their efforts. Positive reinforcement during this phase can help build their confidence and motivation.

Conclusion

The Full Moon represents a powerful time of heightened emotions, increased activity, and intensified behaviors in your cat's life. By understanding and aligning with the energy of this lunar phase, you can support your cat as they navigate the challenges and opportunities that come with the Full Moon.

Whether it's providing emotional support, channeling their energy through physical activity, or maintaining a stable environment, the Full Moon offers an opportunity to enhance your cat's well-being and support their ongoing development. As you continue to explore the astrological influences on your cat, remember that the Full Moon's energy is a dynamic and transformative force, guiding your cat through cycles of growth and helping them reach their fullest potential in their journey of life.

Chapter 32: Waning Gibbous Moon: Reflection and Gratitude in Your Cat's Life

The Waning Gibbous Moon is the phase that follows the Full Moon and precedes the Last Quarter Moon. This phase represents a time of reflection, release, and gratitude as the moon begins to decrease in light. The energy of the Waning Gibbous Moon is more introspective, encouraging a focus on what has been accomplished, what needs to be released, and how to move forward with a sense of gratitude and understanding. For your cat, the Waning Gibbous Moon is a period where they may naturally slow down, reflect on their experiences, and show signs of contentment or the need for emotional release. Understanding the influence of the Waning Gibbous Moon can help you support your cat during this reflective phase, ensuring they continue to feel balanced, secure, and appreciated.

The Significance of the Waning Gibbous Moon in Your Cat's Life

The Waning Gibbous Moon marks a shift from the active, high-energy phase of the Full Moon to a more reflective and introspective period. It is a time to process the events and experiences that have transpired, to release what is no longer needed, and to cultivate a sense of gratitude for the growth and lessons learned. For your cat, this phase may manifest as a period of reduced activity, increased contentment, and a need for comfort and reassurance. Your cat may show a greater appreciation for the familiar and may seek out more quiet, nurturing environments. It's a time to honor their need for rest, reflection, and emotional connection.

- **Reflection on Accomplishments and Experiences**: The Waning Gibbous Moon is a time to reflect on what has been achieved during the previous lunar phases. Your cat may exhibit a sense of satisfaction or contentment, indicating that they are processing the experiences and challenges they have faced. This reflection may manifest as a quieter, more introspective demeanor, where your cat seems to be more thoughtful or reflective in their actions. It's an ideal time to acknowledge their progress, reinforce positive behaviors, and provide them with a peaceful environment to process their experiences.

- **Emotional Release and Letting Go**: As the moon's light begins to wane, there is an emphasis on release and letting go of what is no longer serving. For your cat, this might involve the release of pent-up energy, stress, or emotions. You may notice behaviors that indicate a need for emotional release, such as increased grooming, resting, or a desire to be close to you. Providing a calm and supportive environment where your cat feels safe to relax and release any tension is essential during this phase.

- **Increased Need for Comfort and Security**: The Waning Gibbous Moon often brings a heightened need for comfort and security. Your cat may seek out familiar spaces, favorite toys, or preferred routines that provide a sense of stability and reassurance. They may also show a greater appreciation for physical affection, such as cuddling, gentle grooming, or simply being close to you. Ensuring that your cat has access to their favorite comfort items and maintaining a consistent routine will help them feel secure and content during this reflective phase.

- **Gratitude and Contentment**: The energy of the Waning Gibbous Moon encourages a focus on gratitude and contentment. Your cat may express a sense of satisfaction with their environment, relationships, and daily routines. This is a time to celebrate the bond you share with your cat, acknowledging the joy and fulfillment they bring to your life. You may notice your cat displaying behaviors that indicate contentment, such as purring, kneading, or resting in their favorite spots. Expressing your own gratitude for your cat's presence and companionship can deepen your connection and enhance their sense of well-being.

- **Rest and Recovery**: After the high-energy phase of the Full Moon, the Waning Gibbous Moon is a time for rest and recovery. Your cat may naturally slow down, seeking more opportunities for sleep and relaxation. This phase is essential for recharging and preparing for the next cycle of growth and activity. Providing a quiet, comfortable space where your cat can rest undisturbed will help them recuperate and maintain their overall health.

- **Maintaining Emotional Balance**: The introspective nature of the Waning Gibbous Moon also emphasizes the importance of maintaining emotional balance. Your cat may be more sensitive to changes in their environment or routine, making it important to provide consistency and emotional support. Being attuned to your cat's needs during this phase, offering extra affection, and ensuring that they feel secure and loved will help them navigate this reflective period with ease.

Interpreting the Waning Gibbous Moon in Your Cat's Chart

The placement of the Waning Gibbous Moon in your cat's astrological chart can provide specific insights into how this phase influences their behavior and life experiences. Each sign and house placement of the Waning Gibbous Moon offers different aspects of its energy, helping you understand how to best support your cat during this phase.

- **Waning Gibbous Moon in Aries**: A Waning Gibbous Moon in Aries emphasizes reflection and release related to independence, assertiveness, and action. Your cat may show a need to process their recent activities and may become more introspective regarding their interactions with others. This is an ideal time to provide a peaceful environment where they can rest and reflect on their actions, reinforcing positive behaviors while encouraging emotional release.
- **Waning Gibbous Moon in Taurus**: The Waning Gibbous Moon in Taurus highlights reflection and gratitude related to comfort, security, and material well-being. Your cat may seek out more comfort and stability during this phase, displaying a greater attachment to their favorite spots, toys, or food. Providing a stable and comforting environment, along with their favorite treats or activities, will help them feel secure and content as they reflect on their experiences.
- **Waning Gibbous Moon in Gemini**: A Waning Gibbous Moon in Gemini brings reflection and adjustment related to communication, curiosity, and social interaction. Your cat may become more introspective about their social interactions or may seek out quieter, more contemplative activities. Encouraging gentle play, quiet exploration, and providing opportunities for mental stimulation will help them process their experiences and maintain balance.
- **Waning Gibbous Moon in Cancer**: The Waning Gibbous Moon in Cancer emphasizes reflection and release related to home, family, and emotional security. Your cat may seek out more nurturing and affectionate interactions during this phase, displaying a stronger attachment to their home environment and loved ones. This is a good time to strengthen your bond through consistent care, affection, and creating a stable, nurturing environment where they can feel secure and loved.
- **Waning Gibbous Moon in Leo**: A Waning Gibbous Moon in Leo emphasizes reflection and gratitude related to self-expression, creativity, and leadership. Your cat may become more introspective about their recent actions and may seek out quieter forms of self-expression. Encouraging creative but low-energy activities, such as gentle play or relaxing in a favorite spot, will help them maintain balance while reflecting on their achievements.

- **Waning Gibbous Moon in Virgo**: The Waning Gibbous Moon in Virgo brings reflection and adjustment related to health, routine, and organization. Your cat may become more focused on maintaining order in their environment and may display heightened sensitivity to changes in their routine. This is an ideal time to reinforce healthy habits, such as regular grooming, feeding schedules, or litter box maintenance, while also providing a stable and organized environment.
- **Waning Gibbous Moon in Libra**: A Waning Gibbous Moon in Libra highlights reflection and gratitude related to relationships, balance, and harmony. Your cat may become more introspective about their social interactions and may seek out more balanced and harmonious relationships during this phase. Encouraging positive social behaviors and providing opportunities for bonding and relaxation will help them maintain emotional balance and contentment.
- **Waning Gibbous Moon in Scorpio**: The Waning Gibbous Moon in Scorpio emphasizes reflection and release related to transformation, intensity, and deep emotional connections. Your cat may display more intense or focused behaviors during this phase, particularly related to their surroundings or relationships. This is an ideal time to support their emotional growth by providing opportunities for deep exploration and addressing any challenges related to their emotional well-being.
- **Waning Gibbous Moon in Sagittarius**: A Waning Gibbous Moon in Sagittarius brings reflection and adjustment related to adventure, exploration, and learning. Your cat may become more introspective about their recent experiences and may seek out quieter forms of exploration or learning during this phase. Encouraging gentle exploration, providing mental stimulation, and creating a serene environment will help them process their experiences and maintain balance.
- **Waning Gibbous Moon in Capricorn**: The Waning Gibbous Moon in Capricorn emphasizes reflection and gratitude related to discipline, structure, and responsibility. Your cat may become more focused on maintaining order and may display a stronger attachment to their routines and responsibilities. This is an ideal time to reinforce training, establish new habits, or create a more structured daily schedule that promotes discipline and responsibility, while also providing opportunities for rest and reflection.

- **Waning Gibbous Moon in Aquarius**: A Waning Gibbous Moon in Aquarius brings reflection and adjustment related to innovation, independence, and unconventional behaviors. Your cat may become more introspective about their unique behaviors and may seek out quieter, more contemplative activities during this phase. Encouraging gentle exploration, providing innovative but low-energy toys, and creating opportunities for independent reflection will help them maintain balance.
- **Waning Gibbous Moon in Pisces**: The Waning Gibbous Moon in Pisces highlights reflection and release related to spirituality, creativity, and emotional sensitivity. Your cat may become more introspective and attuned to the emotional energies around them during this phase. This is a good time to create a calming, serene environment where they can relax and recharge, while also supporting their creative and emotional needs.

Supporting Your Cat During the Waning Gibbous Moon

Understanding the influence of the Waning Gibbous Moon in your cat's life allows you to provide the necessary support and care to help them navigate this reflective and introspective phase. Here are some ways you can support your cat during the Waning Gibbous Moon:

- **Encourage Reflection and Relaxation**: The Waning Gibbous Moon is a time for reflection and relaxation. Encourage your cat to take it easy by providing a calm, quiet environment where they can rest and reflect on their recent experiences. Offer gentle, low-energy activities that promote relaxation, such as grooming, cuddling, or simply being present with them.
- **Facilitate Emotional Release**: As your cat processes their experiences, they may need to release pent-up emotions or tension. Be mindful of their emotional state and provide opportunities for emotional release, whether it's through gentle play, comforting interactions, or creating a safe space where they can retreat and relax. Offering extra affection and reassurance during this phase will help them feel secure and supported.
- **Provide Comfort and Security**: The Waning Gibbous Moon often brings a heightened need for comfort and security. Ensure that your cat has access to their favorite comfort items, such as a cozy bed, familiar toys, or their preferred resting spots. Maintaining a consistent rou-

tine and environment will help them feel secure and content as they reflect on their experiences.

- **Express Gratitude and Appreciation**: This phase is also a time to express gratitude and appreciation for your cat's presence and companionship. Acknowledge the joy and fulfillment they bring to your life, and let them know they are loved and appreciated. Positive reinforcement, gentle praise, and affection will deepen your bond and enhance your cat's sense of well-being.
- **Support Rest and Recovery**: After the active phase of the Full Moon, your cat may need more rest and recovery during the Waning Gibbous Moon. Ensure they have plenty of opportunities for sleep and relaxation, providing a quiet, comfortable space where they can rest undisturbed. This will help them recharge and prepare for the next cycle of growth and activity.
- **Maintain Emotional Balance**: The introspective nature of the Waning Gibbous Moon emphasizes the importance of maintaining emotional balance. Be attuned to your cat's needs during this phase, offering extra affection and ensuring they feel secure and loved. Providing a stable and nurturing environment will help them navigate this reflective period with ease.

Conclusion

The Waning Gibbous Moon represents a powerful time of reflection, release, and gratitude in your cat's life. By understanding and aligning with the energy of this lunar phase, you can support your cat as they process their experiences, release what is no longer needed, and cultivate a sense of contentment and appreciation.

Whether it's encouraging them to relax and reflect, facilitating emotional release, or providing comfort and security, the Waning Gibbous Moon offers an opportunity to enhance your cat's well-being and support their ongoing development. As you continue to explore the astrological influences on your cat, remember that the Waning Gibbous Moon's energy is a gentle and introspective force, guiding your cat through cycles of growth and helping them find peace, balance, and fulfillment in their journey of life.

Chapter 33: Last Quarter Moon: Release and Letting Go Processes for Your Cat

The Last Quarter Moon is a critical phase in the lunar cycle, occurring between the Waning Gibbous Moon and the New Moon. This phase represents a time of release, letting go, and clearing out old energy to make space for new beginnings. The Last Quarter Moon is often associated with reflection on the past cycle, evaluating what has been learned, and consciously releasing what no longer serves a positive purpose. For your cat, this phase can manifest as a period of emotional and physical release, where they may naturally let go of certain behaviors, routines, or stressors. Understanding the influence of the Last Quarter Moon can help you support your cat during this transformative phase, ensuring they continue to feel balanced and ready for the next cycle of growth.

The Significance of the Last Quarter Moon in Your Cat's Life

The Last Quarter Moon is a time of transition, where the focus shifts from the activity and reflection of the previous phases to a process of letting go and preparing for renewal. It's a period where your cat may instinctively release old patterns, behaviors, or energy that is no longer beneficial. This phase is about shedding the old to make room for the new, both physically and emotionally. Your cat may display behaviors that reflect this need to release, such as increased grooming, changes in sleep patterns, or a desire to be alone. It's a time for you to support your cat in this natural process, helping them move through it with ease and comfort.

- **Releasing Old Behaviors and Patterns**: The Last Quarter Moon is an ideal time for your cat to release old behaviors or patterns that may have been holding them back. This could include letting go of certain habits, adjusting routines, or moving away from activities that no longer bring them joy or fulfillment. You may notice your cat naturally moving away from certain behaviors or showing less interest in activities that were once a focus. Supporting them in this process by gently encouraging new behaviors or routines can help them transition smoothly.

- **Emotional Cleansing and Letting Go**: Just as the moon begins to decrease in light, your cat may experience a natural emotional cleansing during the Last Quarter Moon. This phase is often associated with letting go of pent-up emotions, stress, or anxiety. Your cat might display behaviors that indicate they are processing and releasing these emotions, such as increased grooming, sleeping more, or seeking solitude. Providing a calm and supportive environment where they can feel safe to release and process their emotions is essential during this phase.

- **Physical Detox and Renewal**: The Last Quarter Moon also represents a time for physical detox and renewal. Your cat's body may go through a natural process of shedding old energy and toxins, which might be reflected in their behavior or physical state. They may show signs of wanting to cleanse or purify themselves, such as drinking more water, being more selective with their food, or spending more time grooming. Ensuring that your cat has access to fresh water, a healthy diet, and a clean environment will support their physical renewal during this phase.

- **Decreased Activity and Increased Rest**: As the moon's light wanes, your cat may show a natural decrease in activity and an increased need for rest. The Last Quarter Moon is a time for conserving energy and preparing for the new cycle that will begin with the New Moon. Your cat may be less interested in active play and more focused on resting, sleeping, or simply being still. Providing a quiet, comfortable space where your cat can rest undisturbed is important during this phase, as it allows them to recharge and prepare for the upcoming cycle.

- **Evaluating and Letting Go of Attachments**: The Last Quarter Moon encourages evaluation and release of attachments that are no longer beneficial. For your cat, this might mean letting go of certain toys, routines, or even relationships that no longer bring them joy or fulfillment. You may notice your cat losing interest in a favorite toy or changing their behavior toward other pets or people in the household. This is a natural part of the letting go process, and it's important to support your cat by respecting their need to move on from these attachments.

- **Preparing for New Beginnings**: As the Last Quarter Moon phase comes to an end, your cat will be preparing for the new beginnings that come with the New Moon. This phase is about clearing out the old to make space for the new, both emotionally and physically. Supporting your cat in this process by helping them let go of what is no longer serving them, while gently encouraging new experiences and behaviors, will help them transition smoothly into the next cycle.

Interpreting the Last Quarter Moon in Your Cat's Chart

The placement of the Last Quarter Moon in your cat's astrological chart can provide specific insights into how this phase influences their behavior and life experiences. Each sign and house placement of the Last Quarter Moon offers different aspects of its energy, helping you understand how to best support your cat during this phase.

- **Last Quarter Moon in Aries**: A Last Quarter Moon in Aries emphasizes the release of behaviors related to independence, assertiveness, and action. Your cat may be letting go of old ways of asserting dominance or may be reevaluating their need for independence. This is an ideal time to support them in finding a balance between assertiveness and cooperation, helping them release any overly aggressive behaviors.
- **Last Quarter Moon in Taurus**: The Last Quarter Moon in Taurus highlights the release of attachments related to comfort, security, and material well-being. Your cat may be letting go of certain comfort items or routines that no longer serve them, such as a favorite toy or sleeping spot. Supporting them in finding new sources of comfort and security will help them transition smoothly during this phase.
- **Last Quarter Moon in Gemini**: A Last Quarter Moon in Gemini brings the release of behaviors related to communication, curiosity, and social interaction. Your cat may be letting go of certain social behaviors or patterns of curiosity that no longer serve them. Encouraging new forms of communication and social interaction, while allowing them to release old habits, will help them adapt to the changing energy of this phase.
- **Last Quarter Moon in Cancer**: The Last Quarter Moon in Cancer emphasizes the release of attachments related to home, family, and emotional security. Your cat may be letting go of certain attachments to their home environment or relationships within the household. Supporting them in finding new sources of emotional security and nurturing will help them feel safe and supported during this phase of release.
- **Last Quarter Moon in Leo**: A Last Quarter Moon in Leo emphasizes the release of behaviors related to self-expression, creativity, and leadership. Your cat may be letting go of old ways of asserting their presence or expressing themselves. Encouraging new forms of creative ex-

pression, while allowing them to release old habits, will help them adapt to the changing energy of this phase.

- **Last Quarter Moon in Virgo**: The Last Quarter Moon in Virgo brings the release of behaviors related to health, routine, and organization. Your cat may be letting go of old routines or habits that no longer serve their health and well-being. This is an ideal time to introduce new, healthier routines, while supporting them in releasing any patterns that are no longer beneficial.

- **Last Quarter Moon in Libra**: A Last Quarter Moon in Libra highlights the release of behaviors related to relationships, balance, and harmony. Your cat may be letting go of certain social behaviors or attachments that no longer serve their relationships or sense of balance. Encouraging new forms of social interaction and harmony, while allowing them to release old habits, will help them maintain emotional balance during this phase.

- **Last Quarter Moon in Scorpio**: The Last Quarter Moon in Scorpio emphasizes the release of behaviors related to transformation, intensity, and deep emotional connections. Your cat may be letting go of certain intense behaviors or attachments that no longer serve them. Supporting them in finding new ways to explore their emotions and connections, while allowing them to release old patterns, will help them adapt to the changing energy of this phase.

- **Last Quarter Moon in Sagittarius**: A Last Quarter Moon in Sagittarius brings the release of behaviors related to adventure, exploration, and learning. Your cat may be letting go of certain exploratory behaviors or patterns of curiosity that no longer serve them. Encouraging new forms of exploration and learning, while allowing them to release old habits, will help them adapt to the changing energy of this phase.

- **Last Quarter Moon in Capricorn**: The Last Quarter Moon in Capricorn emphasizes the release of behaviors related to discipline, structure, and responsibility. Your cat may be letting go of old routines or habits that no longer serve their sense of discipline and structure. Supporting them in finding new routines or responsibilities, while allowing them to release old patterns, will help them adapt to the changing energy of this phase.

- **Last Quarter Moon in Aquarius**: A Last Quarter Moon in Aquarius brings the release of behaviors related to innovation, independence, and unconventional actions. Your cat may be letting go of certain independent or unconventional behaviors that no longer serve them. Encouraging new forms of independence and innovation, while allowing them to release old habits, will help them adapt to the changing energy of this phase.

- **Last Quarter Moon in Pisces**: The Last Quarter Moon in Pisces highlights the release of behaviors related to spirituality, creativity, and emotional sensitivity. Your cat may be letting go of certain emotional or creative behaviors that no longer serve them. Supporting them in finding new ways to explore their emotions and creativity, while allowing them to release old patterns, will help them adapt to the changing energy of this phase.

Supporting Your Cat During the Last Quarter Moon

Understanding the influence of the Last Quarter Moon in your cat's life allows you to provide the necessary support and care to help them navigate this phase of release and letting go. Here are some ways you can support your cat during the Last Quarter Moon:

- **Encourage Emotional and Physical Release**: The Last Quarter Moon is a time for letting go of old energy, both emotionally and physically. Encourage your cat to release any pent-up emotions or stress by providing a calm and supportive environment. Offer gentle activities that promote relaxation, such as grooming, cuddling, or quiet play, to help them release and process their emotions.

- **Support Changes in Routine**: As your cat lets go of old habits or routines, be supportive of any changes they naturally make. This might involve adjusting their feeding schedule, changing their sleeping arrangements, or introducing new activities that better align with their current needs. Be patient and flexible, allowing your cat to guide the changes they need during this phase.

- **Provide a Safe and Comforting Environment**: During the Last Quarter Moon, your cat may seek out familiar and comforting spaces where they can process their emotions and let go of old energy. Ensure that your cat has access to their favorite spots, toys, and routines that provide a sense of security and comfort. A stable environment will help them feel safe as they navigate this transformative phase.

- **Encourage Rest and Recovery**: The Last Quarter Moon is a time for conserving energy and preparing for the next cycle of growth. Encourage your cat to rest and recover by providing a quiet, comfortable space where they can sleep undisturbed. Reducing stimulation and allowing for plenty of downtime will help them recharge and prepare for the upcoming New Moon.

- **Facilitate New Beginnings**: As your cat releases old behaviors and attachments, they will be preparing for new beginnings that come with the New Moon. Gently introduce new experiences, toys, or routines that align with their current needs and interests. Supporting them in this transition will help them feel confident and ready to embrace the next phase of growth.
- **Be Attuned to Emotional Needs**: The introspective nature of the Last Quarter Moon emphasizes the importance of being attuned to your cat's emotional needs. Offer extra affection, reassurance, and support as they process their experiences and release old energy. Your presence and understanding will help them feel loved and secure during this phase.

Conclusion

The Last Quarter Moon represents a powerful time of release, letting go, and preparation for new beginnings in your cat's life. By understanding and aligning with the energy of this lunar phase, you can support your cat as they navigate the challenges and opportunities of releasing old patterns and preparing for the next cycle of growth.

Whether it's encouraging emotional and physical release, supporting changes in routine, or providing a safe and comforting environment, the Last Quarter Moon offers an opportunity to enhance your cat's well-being and support their ongoing development. As you continue to explore the astrological influences on your cat, remember that the Last Quarter Moon's energy is a transformative and cleansing force, guiding your cat through cycles of growth and helping them shed what no longer serves them in their journey of life.

Chapter 34: Waning Crescent Moon: Rest and Recuperation Phases for Your Cat

The Waning Crescent Moon, also known as the Balsamic Moon, is the final phase in the lunar cycle before the New Moon. This phase is characterized by a sliver of the moon's light, signaling a time of deep rest, introspection, and preparation for renewal. The Waning Crescent Moon is a period of winding down, letting go of the last remnants of the past cycle, and conserving energy for the new beginnings that will come with the New Moon. For your cat, this phase is essential for rest, recuperation, and the final release of any lingering stresses or tensions. Understanding the influence of the Waning Crescent Moon can help you provide the necessary support and care to ensure your cat remains balanced, relaxed, and ready to embrace the next cycle.

The Significance of the Waning Crescent Moon in Your Cat's Life

The Waning Crescent Moon represents a time of deep rest and recuperation, where the focus shifts from action and growth to quiet reflection and conservation of energy. For your cat, this phase is crucial for maintaining physical and emotional well-being, as it allows them to recover from the demands of the previous lunar cycle and prepare for the new cycle ahead. Your cat may naturally seek out more rest, solitude, and quiet during this phase, making it important to create an environment that supports their need for calm and relaxation.

- **Deep Rest and Recovery**: The Waning Crescent Moon is the ideal time for deep rest and recovery. Your cat may spend more time sleeping, napping, or simply resting in their favorite spots. This phase allows your cat to recharge both physically and emotionally, ensuring they are fully rested and ready for the new beginnings that will come with the New Moon. Providing a quiet, comfortable space where your cat can rest undisturbed is essential during this phase, as it helps them recover from the previous cycle and prepare for the next.

- **Introspection and Emotional Processing**: As the final phase of the lunar cycle, the Waning Crescent Moon is also a time for introspection and emotional processing. Your cat may become more introspective during this phase, reflecting on their experiences and emotions from the past cycle. This introspection may manifest as a quieter, more contemplative demeanor, where your cat seems to be more thoughtful or reflective in their actions. Supporting your cat's need for introspection by providing a calm, supportive environment will help them process their emotions and release any lingering stress.

- **Final Release of Tension and Stress**: The Waning Crescent Moon is the last opportunity to release any remaining tension, stress, or emotional baggage before the new cycle begins. Your cat may display behaviors that indicate they are releasing these final remnants, such as increased grooming, seeking solitude, or engaging in gentle play. Encouraging your cat to let go of any remaining stress by offering comfort, reassurance, and quiet activities will help them feel balanced and relaxed as they move into the New Moon phase.

- **Conserving Energy for New Beginnings**: During the Waning Crescent Moon, your cat may instinctively conserve their energy, preparing for the new cycle that will begin with the New Moon. This phase is about winding down, reducing activity, and focusing on rest and recuperation. Your cat may be less interested in active play and more focused on resting, sleeping, or simply being still. Providing opportunities for quiet time and minimizing stimulation will help your cat conserve their energy and prepare for the upcoming cycle.

- **Increased Sensitivity and Need for Solitude**: The introspective nature of the Waning Crescent Moon often brings increased sensitivity and a greater need for solitude. Your cat may seek out quiet, secluded spaces where they can be alone and undisturbed. This is a time when your cat may prefer to be by themselves, processing their thoughts and emotions in their own way. Respecting your cat's need for solitude and providing them with a safe, quiet space where they can retreat will help them feel secure and supported during this phase.

- **Preparation for Renewal and Rebirth**: As the Waning Crescent Moon phase comes to an end, your cat will be preparing for the renewal and rebirth that comes with the New Moon. This phase is about letting go of the old and making space for the new, both emotionally and physically. Supporting your cat in this process by helping them release any remaining tension and encouraging quiet reflection will help them transition smoothly into the new cycle.

Interpreting the Waning Crescent Moon in Your Cat's Chart

The placement of the Waning Crescent Moon in your cat's astrological chart can provide specific insights into how this phase influences their behavior and life experiences. Each sign and house placement of the Waning Crescent Moon offers different aspects of its energy, helping you understand how to best support your cat during this phase.

- **Waning Crescent Moon in Aries**: A Waning Crescent Moon in Aries emphasizes the need for rest and recuperation related to independence, assertiveness, and action. Your cat may be winding down from a period of high energy and assertiveness, seeking out rest and solitude to recover. Providing a quiet space where they can rest and recharge will help them release any remaining tension and prepare for the new cycle.
- **Waning Crescent Moon in Taurus**: The Waning Crescent Moon in Taurus highlights the need for comfort, security, and material well-being during the rest and recuperation phase. Your cat may seek out their favorite comfort items or routines that provide a sense of stability and reassurance. Ensuring that your cat has access to their favorite spots, toys, and treats will help them feel secure and content as they rest and recover.
- **Waning Crescent Moon in Gemini**: A Waning Crescent Moon in Gemini brings the need for rest and recuperation related to communication, curiosity, and social interaction. Your cat may become more introspective and less interested in socializing during this phase, preferring quiet, solitary activities. Encouraging gentle play, quiet exploration, and providing opportunities for mental relaxation will help them process their experiences and maintain balance.
- **Waning Crescent Moon in Cancer**: The Waning Crescent Moon in Cancer emphasizes the need for rest and recuperation related to home, family, and emotional security. Your cat may seek out more nurturing and affectionate interactions during this phase, displaying a stronger attachment to their home environment and loved ones. This is a good time to strengthen your bond through consistent care, affection, and creating a stable, nurturing environment where they can feel secure and loved.
- **Waning Crescent Moon in Leo**: A Waning Crescent Moon in Leo emphasizes the need for rest and recuperation related to self-expression, creativity, and leadership. Your cat may be winding down from a period of active self-expression and may seek out quieter, more reflective activities. Encouraging creative but low-energy activities, such as gentle play or relaxing in a favorite spot, will help them maintain balance while resting and recovering.

- **Waning Crescent Moon in Virgo**: The Waning Crescent Moon in Virgo brings the need for rest and recuperation related to health, routine, and organization. Your cat may become more focused on maintaining order in their environment and may display heightened sensitivity to changes in their routine. This is an ideal time to reinforce healthy habits, such as regular grooming, feeding schedules, or litter box maintenance, while also providing a stable and organized environment.

- **Waning Crescent Moon in Libra**: A Waning Crescent Moon in Libra highlights the need for rest and recuperation related to relationships, balance, and harmony. Your cat may become more introspective about their social interactions and may seek out more balanced and harmonious relationships during this phase. Encouraging positive social behaviors and providing opportunities for bonding and relaxation will help them maintain emotional balance and contentment.

- **Waning Crescent Moon in Scorpio**: The Waning Crescent Moon in Scorpio emphasizes the need for rest and recuperation related to transformation, intensity, and deep emotional connections. Your cat may display more intense or focused behaviors during this phase, particularly related to their surroundings or relationships. This is an ideal time to support their emotional growth by providing opportunities for deep exploration and addressing any challenges related to their emotional well-being.

- **Waning Crescent Moon in Sagittarius**: A Waning Crescent Moon in Sagittarius brings the need for rest and recuperation related to adventure, exploration, and learning. Your cat may become more introspective about their recent experiences and may seek out quieter forms of exploration or learning during this phase. Encouraging gentle exploration, providing mental stimulation, and creating a serene environment will help them process their experiences and maintain balance.

- **Waning Crescent Moon in Capricorn**: The Waning Crescent Moon in Capricorn emphasizes the need for rest and recuperation related to discipline, structure, and responsibility. Your cat may become more focused on maintaining order and may display a stronger attachment to their routines and responsibilities. This is an ideal time to reinforce training, establish new habits, or create a more structured daily schedule that promotes discipline and responsibility, while also providing opportunities for rest and reflection.

- **Waning Crescent Moon in Aquarius**: A Waning Crescent Moon in Aquarius brings the need for rest and recuperation related to innovation, independence, and unconventional behaviors. Your cat may become more introspective about their unique behaviors and may seek out quieter, more contemplative activities during this phase. Encouraging gentle exploration, providing innovative but low-energy toys, and creating opportunities for independent reflection will help them maintain balance.
- **Waning Crescent Moon in Pisces**: The Waning Crescent Moon in Pisces highlights the need for rest and recuperation related to spirituality, creativity, and emotional sensitivity. Your cat may become more introspective and attuned to the emotional energies around them during this phase. This is a good time to create a calming, serene environment where they can relax and recharge, while also supporting their creative and emotional needs.

Supporting Your Cat During the Waning Crescent Moon

Understanding the influence of the Waning Crescent Moon in your cat's life allows you to provide the necessary support and care to help them navigate this phase of rest and recuperation. Here are some ways you can support your cat during the Waning Crescent Moon:

- **Provide Ample Rest and Relaxation**: The Waning Crescent Moon is a time for deep rest and recovery. Ensure that your cat has access to quiet, comfortable spaces where they can rest undisturbed. Reducing stimulation and allowing for plenty of downtime will help them recharge and prepare for the upcoming New Moon.
- **Support Emotional and Physical Release**: As your cat winds down from the previous cycle, they may need to release any remaining tension or stress. Be mindful of their emotional state and provide opportunities for emotional release, whether it's through gentle play, comforting interactions, or creating a safe space where they can retreat and relax. Offering extra affection and reassurance during this phase will help them feel secure and supported.
- **Maintain a Stable and Comforting Environment**: The Waning Crescent Moon often brings a heightened need for comfort and security. Ensure that your cat has access to their favorite comfort items, such as a cozy bed, familiar toys, or their preferred resting spots. Main-

taining a consistent routine and environment will help them feel secure and content as they rest and recuperate.

- **Encourage Solitude and Introspection**: During the Waning Crescent Moon, your cat may seek out quiet, secluded spaces where they can be alone and undisturbed. Respect their need for solitude and provide them with a safe, quiet space where they can retreat and reflect. This will help them process their thoughts and emotions and prepare for the new cycle ahead.
- **Facilitate Quiet Activities**: While the Waning Crescent Moon is a time for rest, your cat may still benefit from gentle, low-energy activities that promote relaxation and mental stimulation. Offer toys that encourage quiet play, such as puzzle toys or soft, interactive toys that don't require much physical exertion. These activities can help your cat maintain mental balance while conserving their energy.
- **Prepare for New Beginnings**: As the Waning Crescent Moon phase comes to an end, your cat will be preparing for the new beginnings that come with the New Moon. Support them in this transition by helping them release any remaining tension and encouraging quiet reflection. This will help them feel ready and rejuvenated as they move into the new cycle.

Conclusion

The Waning Crescent Moon represents a powerful time of rest, recuperation, and preparation for new beginnings in your cat's life. By understanding and aligning with the energy of this lunar phase, you can support your cat as they navigate the challenges and opportunities of resting, reflecting, and recharging for the next cycle of growth.

Whether it's providing ample rest and relaxation, supporting emotional and physical release, or maintaining a stable and comforting environment, the Waning Crescent Moon offers an opportunity to enhance your cat's well-being and support their ongoing development. As you continue to explore the astrological influences on your cat, remember that the Waning Crescent Moon's energy is a soothing and nurturing force, guiding your cat through cycles of rest and helping them find peace, balance, and renewal in their journey of life.

Part V: Celestial Events and Their Impact on Cats

Chapter 35: Solar Eclipses: Major Changes and Revelations in Your Cat's Life

Solar eclipses are powerful celestial events that occur when the Moon passes between the Earth and the Sun, temporarily obscuring the Sun's light. In astrology, solar eclipses are associated with significant changes, breakthroughs, and revelations that can alter the course of life. These events often signal a time of intense energy, where new beginnings are initiated, and old patterns are eclipsed by fresh perspectives. For your cat, solar eclipses can bring about shifts in behavior, energy levels, and even their environment, leading to transformative experiences that may unfold over time. Understanding the influence of solar eclipses on your cat's life can help you navigate these periods of change with awareness and care, ensuring your cat remains balanced and supported during these potent times.

The Significance of Solar Eclipses in Your Cat's Life

Solar eclipses are rare and powerful events that mark the end of one cycle and the beginning of another. In your cat's life, these eclipses can herald significant changes, whether in their daily routine, behavior, or overall environment. The energy of a solar eclipse is often intense and can bring about sudden shifts or new insights that weren't previously visible. These changes may not always be immediately apparent but can unfold over the weeks and months following the eclipse. It's a time of revelation, where hidden aspects of your cat's life may come to the forefront, prompting new behaviors, attitudes, or circumstances.

- **Initiating Major Changes**: Solar eclipses are known for initiating major changes in life, and this can apply to your cat's world as well. These changes might be sudden and unexpected, such as a shift in their behavior, a change in their routine, or even an alteration in their environment. Your cat may react to these changes by exhibiting new behaviors or adapting to their surroundings in different ways. It's important to be observant and supportive during this time, helping your cat navigate these changes with ease and confidence.

- **Revelations and Insights**: Just as solar eclipses can bring hidden truths to light, they can also reveal new insights about your cat's behavior, needs, or preferences. You might notice previously hidden aspects of your cat's personality emerging, or discover new ways to interact with them that deepen your bond. These revelations can lead to a greater understanding of your cat's needs and desires, allowing you to make adjustments that enhance their well-being.

- **Sudden Shifts in Behavior**: The energy of a solar eclipse can sometimes result in sudden shifts in your cat's behavior. They may exhibit new habits, preferences, or reactions that seem out of character. These changes could be temporary, lasting only during the eclipse season, or they might signal the beginning of a longer-term transformation. Being attentive to these shifts and providing a stable, supportive environment will help your cat adjust to these changes more smoothly.

- **Heightened Sensitivity and Energy**: Solar eclipses often bring heightened sensitivity and energy, both in humans and animals. Your cat may become more alert, reactive, or sensitive to changes in their environment during this time. They might display increased energy levels, restlessness, or a desire for more activity. Providing outlets for this heightened energy, such as interactive play or exploration, will help them channel it in positive ways.

- **Clearing Out the Old to Make Way for the New**: Solar eclipses are powerful times for clearing out old patterns, behaviors, or attachments that no longer serve a positive purpose. Your cat may instinctively let go of certain habits or preferences, making way for new experiences or routines. This could involve a change in their sleeping habits, diet, or the way they interact with their environment. Supporting your cat through this clearing process by offering new opportunities for growth and exploration will help them embrace the changes with enthusiasm.

- **Long-Term Impact and Transformation**: The effects of a solar eclipse can unfold over several months, leading to long-term transformations in your cat's life. The changes initiated during the eclipse may develop gradually, leading to significant shifts in their behavior, health, or environment. Being aware of these potential transformations allows you to monitor your cat's progress and provide the necessary support as they adapt to their new circumstances.

Interpreting Solar Eclipses in Your Cat's Chart

The impact of a solar eclipse on your cat's life can be better understood by examining the astrological sign and house in which the eclipse occurs in their chart. Each sign and house placement offers different insights into the areas of life that may be affected, helping you anticipate and support the changes that may arise.

- **Solar Eclipse in Aries**: A solar eclipse in Aries suggests that changes may occur related to independence, assertiveness, and action. Your cat may become more confident, assertive, or eager to explore their surroundings. They might develop new behaviors that reflect their need for autonomy or leadership. Supporting them in expressing their newfound independence while maintaining a balanced routine will help them adapt to these changes.
- **Solar Eclipse in Taurus**: A solar eclipse in Taurus highlights changes related to comfort, security, and material well-being. Your cat may experience shifts in their environment or daily routines that affect their sense of security. They might become more attached to certain comfort items or develop new preferences for food, bedding, or toys. Ensuring that your cat's environment remains stable and comforting during this time will help them adjust to these changes.
- **Solar Eclipse in Gemini**: A solar eclipse in Gemini brings changes related to communication, curiosity, and social interaction. Your cat may become more vocal, inquisitive, or interested in exploring new areas. They might develop new ways of interacting with you or other pets, reflecting a shift in their social behaviors. Encouraging positive communication and providing opportunities for exploration will help them embrace these changes.
- **Solar Eclipse in Cancer**: A solar eclipse in Cancer suggests changes related to home, family, and emotional security. Your cat may experience shifts in their attachment to their home environment or the relationships within the household. They might seek out more affection or become more sensitive to changes in their surroundings. Providing extra emotional support and maintaining a stable home environment will help them feel secure during these changes.
- **Solar Eclipse in Leo**: A solar eclipse in Leo emphasizes changes related to self-expression, creativity, and leadership. Your cat may become more playful, outgoing, or eager to assert their presence. They might develop new ways of expressing themselves, whether through play, vocalizations, or interactions with others. Encouraging their creativity and leadership qualities while maintaining a balanced routine will help them adapt to these changes.

- **Solar Eclipse in Virgo**: A solar eclipse in Virgo brings changes related to health, routine, and organization. Your cat may experience shifts in their daily routines, diet, or grooming habits. They might develop new preferences for certain activities or become more focused on maintaining order in their environment. Supporting them in establishing healthy routines and providing a clean, organized space will help them navigate these changes.
- **Solar Eclipse in Libra**: A solar eclipse in Libra highlights changes related to relationships, balance, and harmony. Your cat may experience shifts in their interactions with others, whether with you, other pets, or even new additions to the household. They might become more social, cooperative, or interested in forming new bonds. Encouraging positive social behaviors and maintaining harmony in their environment will help them adjust to these changes.
- **Solar Eclipse in Scorpio**: A solar eclipse in Scorpio suggests changes related to transformation, intensity, and deep emotional connections. Your cat may undergo a period of intense change, whether in their behavior, health, or environment. They might become more introspective, focused, or attached to certain people or objects. Supporting them through this transformative period by providing stability and reassurance will help them adapt to the changes.
- **Solar Eclipse in Sagittarius**: A solar eclipse in Sagittarius brings changes related to adventure, exploration, and learning. Your cat may become more adventurous, curious, or eager to explore new territories. They might develop new interests or behaviors that reflect a desire for growth and expansion. Encouraging exploration and providing opportunities for mental and physical stimulation will help them embrace these changes.
- **Solar Eclipse in Capricorn**: A solar eclipse in Capricorn emphasizes changes related to discipline, structure, and responsibility. Your cat may experience shifts in their routines, behaviors, or environment that require greater discipline or responsibility. They might become more focused on certain tasks or develop new habits that reflect a need for order. Supporting them in maintaining a structured routine while allowing for flexibility will help them adapt to these changes.
- **Solar Eclipse in Aquarius**: A solar eclipse in Aquarius brings changes related to innovation, independence, and unconventional behaviors. Your cat may develop new, unexpected be-

haviors or show a stronger desire for independence. They might become more interested in exploring new ways of interacting with their environment or expressing their individuality. Encouraging their uniqueness while providing a stable foundation will help them navigate these changes.

- **Solar Eclipse in Pisces**: A solar eclipse in Pisces suggests changes related to spirituality, creativity, and emotional sensitivity. Your cat may become more sensitive to their environment or develop new behaviors that reflect a deeper emotional connection. They might become more introspective, creative, or attuned to the energies around them. Supporting their emotional well-being and providing a calming environment will help them adapt to these changes.

Supporting Your Cat During a Solar Eclipse

Understanding the influence of a solar eclipse on your cat's life allows you to provide the necessary support and care to help them navigate these periods of major change and revelation. Here are some ways you can support your cat during a solar eclipse:

- **Provide Stability During Change**: Solar eclipses can bring sudden and significant changes, so it's important to provide stability and reassurance during this time. Ensure that your cat's environment remains consistent, with familiar routines and comfort items that help them feel secure. Being present and attentive to their needs will help them adjust to any changes more smoothly.
- **Encourage Exploration and New Experiences**: Solar eclipses often signal new beginnings, making it an ideal time to introduce your cat to new experiences or environments. Whether it's a new toy, a different play area, or a new routine, encouraging exploration and curiosity will help your cat embrace the changes initiated by the eclipse.
- **Monitor Behavior and Adjust as Needed**: Pay close attention to any changes in your cat's behavior during and after a solar eclipse. If you notice shifts in their habits, energy levels, or interactions, be prepared to adjust their routine or environment to better support their needs. Flexibility and adaptability are key to helping your cat navigate these periods of transformation.

- **Support Emotional Well-Being**: Solar eclipses can bring heightened sensitivity and emotional intensity, so it's important to provide emotional support and reassurance. Spend quality time with your cat, engaging in activities that promote bonding and trust. If your cat seems anxious or unsettled, offer extra comfort and affection to help them feel secure.
- **Facilitate the Release of Old Patterns**: As solar eclipses often signal the end of old patterns, be supportive of your cat's need to let go of certain behaviors, routines, or attachments. Encourage them to release what no longer serves them by offering new opportunities for growth and exploration. Providing a safe and supportive environment will help them move forward with confidence.
- **Prepare for Long-Term Changes**: The effects of a solar eclipse can unfold over several months, leading to long-term transformations in your cat's life. Be mindful of these potential changes and be prepared to support your cat as they adapt to new circumstances. Consistency, patience, and understanding will help them navigate these transitions with ease.

Conclusion

Solar eclipses represent powerful times of major change, revelation, and new beginnings in your cat's life. By understanding and aligning with the energy of these celestial events, you can support your cat as they navigate the challenges and opportunities of transformation and growth.

Whether it's providing stability during change, encouraging exploration and new experiences, or supporting emotional well-being, solar eclipses offer an opportunity to enhance your cat's well-being and support their ongoing development. As you continue to explore the astrological influences on your cat, remember that solar eclipses are potent catalysts for change, guiding your cat through cycles of transformation and helping them embrace new possibilities in their journey of life.

Chapter 36: Lunar Eclipses: Emotional Highs and Lows for Your Cat

Lunar eclipses are profound celestial events that occur when the Earth passes between the Sun and the Moon, casting a shadow over the Moon. In astrology, lunar eclipses are associated with intense emotional experiences, powerful shifts in perception, and the culmination of cycles. These eclipses can bring about a period of heightened emotional intensity, where unresolved feelings and hidden aspects of the self come to the surface. For your cat, a lunar eclipse can manifest as a time of emotional highs and lows, where they may display more pronounced reactions to their environment and experiences. Understanding the influence of lunar eclipses on your cat's life can help you navigate these periods of emotional fluctuation with compassion and care, ensuring your cat remains balanced and supported during these transformative times.

The Significance of Lunar Eclipses in Your Cat's Life

Lunar eclipses mark the culmination of emotional cycles, bringing hidden feelings and unresolved issues to the forefront. This phase is often characterized by emotional intensity, where deep-seated emotions rise to the surface, leading to significant shifts in behavior and perception. For your cat, a lunar eclipse can be a time of emotional turbulence, where they may experience heightened sensitivity, mood swings, or changes in their usual behavior. These emotional highs and lows can be both challenging and transformative, offering an opportunity for your cat to release pent-up emotions and realign with their true self.

- **Heightened Emotional Sensitivity**: During a lunar eclipse, your cat may become more emotionally sensitive, reacting more strongly to changes in their environment or interactions with others. They may display heightened awareness of your emotions, other pets' behaviors, or subtle changes in their surroundings. This increased sensitivity can lead to more pronounced emotional reactions, such as becoming more affectionate, anxious, or irritable. Being mindful of your cat's emotional state and providing extra comfort and reassurance during this time can help them navigate these intense feelings.

- **Emotional Highs and Lows**: Lunar eclipses often bring emotional highs and lows, where your cat may swing between periods of contentment and restlessness. One moment they might be purring and seeking affection, while the next, they could be more distant or withdrawn. These emotional fluctuations are a natural response to the energy of the eclipse, which stirs up underlying feelings that need to be processed and released. Supporting your cat through these emotional waves by maintaining a calm and stable environment will help them feel more secure.

- **Release of Pent-Up Emotions**: The energy of a lunar eclipse encourages the release of pent-up emotions and unresolved feelings. Your cat may exhibit behaviors that indicate they are processing and releasing these emotions, such as increased grooming, vocalization, or seeking solitude. This release is a necessary part of the emotional healing process, allowing your cat to let go of what no longer serves them. Providing a safe space where your cat can retreat and feel comfortable expressing their emotions is essential during this phase.

- **Increased Need for Comfort and Security**: As emotions run high during a lunar eclipse, your cat may seek out more comfort and security. They might show a greater attachment to familiar objects, routines, or people, seeking reassurance in the face of emotional turbulence. Offering extra affection, maintaining consistent routines, and ensuring that your cat has access to their favorite comfort items will help them feel more grounded and supported during this time.

- **Behavioral Changes and Unpredictability**: The emotional intensity of a lunar eclipse can lead to temporary changes in your cat's behavior, making them more unpredictable. They might display behaviors that are out of character, such as increased aggression, restlessness, or sudden shifts in their usual routines. These behavioral changes are often a reflection of the emotional highs and lows brought on by the eclipse. Being patient and understanding, and providing appropriate outlets for their energy, will help your cat navigate these temporary fluctuations.

- **Culmination and Closure**: Lunar eclipses are often associated with the culmination of emotional cycles, bringing closure to unresolved issues. For your cat, this might involve the resolution of lingering emotional conflicts, changes in their relationships, or the completion of a behavioral pattern. This phase offers an opportunity for emotional healing and realignment, allowing your cat to move forward with a renewed sense of balance and clarity. Supporting your cat through this process by acknowledging and addressing any emotional issues that arise will help them find closure and peace.

Interpreting Lunar Eclipses in Your Cat's Chart

The impact of a lunar eclipse on your cat's life can be better understood by examining the astrological sign and house in which the eclipse occurs in their chart. Each sign and house placement offers different insights into the areas of life that may be affected, helping you anticipate and support the emotional changes that may arise.

- **Lunar Eclipse in Aries**: A lunar eclipse in Aries suggests emotional highs and lows related to independence, assertiveness, and self-expression. Your cat may experience fluctuations in their desire for autonomy or in their assertive behaviors. They might become more protective of their space or more demanding of attention. Supporting them in finding a balance between independence and connection will help them navigate these emotional shifts.
- **Lunar Eclipse in Taurus**: A lunar eclipse in Taurus highlights emotional highs and lows related to comfort, security, and material well-being. Your cat may become more attached to their favorite comfort items or routines, seeking reassurance in the familiar. They might also experience emotional fluctuations related to food, bedding, or their environment. Providing a stable and comforting environment will help them feel secure during these emotional highs and lows.
- **Lunar Eclipse in Gemini**: A lunar eclipse in Gemini brings emotional highs and lows related to communication, curiosity, and social interaction. Your cat may become more vocal, inquisitive, or reactive to social stimuli. They might experience fluctuations in their desire for interaction, swinging between being highly social and more withdrawn. Encouraging positive communication and providing mental stimulation will help them navigate these emotional changes.
- **Lunar Eclipse in Cancer**: A lunar eclipse in Cancer suggests emotional highs and lows related to home, family, and emotional security. Your cat may become more sensitive to changes in their home environment or more attached to their loved ones. They might experience emotional fluctuations related to their relationships or their sense of security. Providing extra emotional support and maintaining a stable home environment will help them feel secure during these emotional highs and lows.

- **Lunar Eclipse in Leo**: A lunar eclipse in Leo emphasizes emotional highs and lows related to self-expression, creativity, and leadership. Your cat may experience fluctuations in their desire to assert themselves or in their playful behaviors. They might swing between being highly expressive and more reserved. Encouraging creative expression while providing opportunities for rest and reflection will help them navigate these emotional shifts.
- **Lunar Eclipse in Virgo**: A lunar eclipse in Virgo brings emotional highs and lows related to health, routine, and organization. Your cat may become more sensitive to changes in their routines or more focused on maintaining order in their environment. They might experience emotional fluctuations related to their daily habits or grooming behaviors. Supporting them in maintaining healthy routines while being flexible with their needs will help them feel balanced during these emotional highs and lows.
- **Lunar Eclipse in Libra**: A lunar eclipse in Libra highlights emotional highs and lows related to relationships, balance, and harmony. Your cat may experience fluctuations in their social interactions or their desire for connection. They might swing between seeking out companionship and preferring solitude. Encouraging positive social behaviors and providing a harmonious environment will help them navigate these emotional changes.
- **Lunar Eclipse in Scorpio**: A lunar eclipse in Scorpio suggests emotional highs and lows related to transformation, intensity, and deep emotional connections. Your cat may experience intense emotional fluctuations, particularly related to their surroundings or relationships. They might become more introspective, focused, or attached to certain people or objects. Supporting them through this transformative period by providing stability and reassurance will help them navigate these emotional highs and lows.
- **Lunar Eclipse in Sagittarius**: A lunar eclipse in Sagittarius brings emotional highs and lows related to adventure, exploration, and learning. Your cat may experience fluctuations in their desire for exploration or in their curiosity about their environment. They might swing between being highly adventurous and more cautious. Encouraging exploration while providing a safe and familiar environment will help them navigate these emotional shifts.
- **Lunar Eclipse in Capricorn**: A lunar eclipse in Capricorn emphasizes emotional highs and lows related to discipline, structure, and responsibility. Your cat may experience fluctuations in their routines or in their desire for structure and order. They might swing between being

highly focused on their tasks and more relaxed or detached. Supporting them in maintaining a balanced routine while allowing for flexibility will help them feel secure during these emotional highs and lows.

- **Lunar Eclipse in Aquarius**: A lunar eclipse in Aquarius brings emotional highs and lows related to innovation, independence, and unconventional behaviors. Your cat may experience fluctuations in their desire for independence or in their interest in exploring new behaviors. They might swing between being highly independent and more dependent on you for comfort. Encouraging their unique behaviors while providing a stable foundation will help them navigate these emotional shifts.

- **Lunar Eclipse in Pisces**: A lunar eclipse in Pisces suggests emotional highs and lows related to spirituality, creativity, and emotional sensitivity. Your cat may experience heightened sensitivity to their environment or to the emotions of others. They might swing between being highly introspective and more outwardly expressive. Supporting their emotional well-being by providing a calming and supportive environment will help them navigate these emotional highs and lows.

Supporting Your Cat During a Lunar Eclipse

Understanding the influence of a lunar eclipse on your cat's life allows you to provide the necessary support and care to help them navigate these periods of emotional highs and lows. Here are some ways you can support your cat during a lunar eclipse:

- **Provide Emotional Reassurance and Comfort**: Lunar eclipses can bring heightened emotions, making it important to provide extra comfort and reassurance to your cat. Spend quality time together, engaging in activities that promote bonding and trust. If your cat seems more sensitive or reactive, offer extra affection and create a calm, soothing environment where they can feel safe and secure.

- **Monitor Behavior and Adapt as Needed**: Pay close attention to any changes in your cat's behavior during and after a lunar eclipse. If you notice fluctuations in their mood, energy levels, or interactions, be prepared to adapt their routine or environment to better support their emotional needs. Flexibility and understanding are key to helping your cat navigate these emotional highs and lows.

- **Support Emotional Release**: The energy of a lunar eclipse encourages the release of pent-up emotions. Be mindful of your cat's emotional state and provide opportunities for emotional release, whether through gentle play, comforting interactions, or creating a safe space where they can retreat and express their emotions. Offering extra affection and reassurance during this phase will help them feel secure and supported.
- **Maintain a Stable Environment**: The emotional intensity of a lunar eclipse can make your cat more sensitive to changes in their environment. Maintaining a stable and consistent environment during this time is important for helping your cat feel grounded and secure. Ensure that your cat has access to familiar spaces, routines, and comforts that help them feel more at ease during this emotional phase.
- **Facilitate Quiet Time and Solitude**: During a lunar eclipse, your cat may seek out quiet, secluded spaces where they can process their emotions undisturbed. Respect their need for solitude and provide them with a safe, quiet space where they can retreat and reflect. This will help them process their thoughts and emotions and maintain emotional balance.
- **Encourage Emotional Healing**: Lunar eclipses are a time for emotional healing and realignment. Support your cat in this process by acknowledging and addressing any emotional issues that arise. Providing a nurturing and supportive environment, along with positive reinforcement for healthy emotional expression, will help your cat heal and find closure during this phase.

Conclusion

Lunar eclipses represent powerful times of emotional intensity, bringing both highs and lows in your cat's life. By understanding and aligning with the energy of these celestial events, you can support your cat as they navigate the challenges and opportunities of emotional release and healing.

Whether it's providing emotional reassurance and comfort, supporting emotional release, or maintaining a stable environment, lunar eclipses offer an opportunity to enhance your cat's well-being and support their ongoing development. As you continue to explore the astrological influences on your cat, remember that lunar eclipses are potent catalysts for emotional transformation, guiding your cat through cycles of healing and helping them realign with their true emotional self in their journey of life.

Chapter 37: Retrogrades: How Planetary Retrogrades Influence Your Cat's Behavior and Health

Planetary retrogrades occur when a planet appears to move backward in its orbit from our perspective on Earth. While this is an optical illusion, astrologically, retrogrades are significant events that influence introspection, reflection, and revisiting past issues. Each planet's retrograde can have distinct effects, influencing various aspects of life, including behavior, health, and relationships. For your cat, planetary retrogrades can manifest as shifts in behavior, changes in routine, or even temporary health issues. Understanding the influence of retrogrades on your cat's life can help you navigate these periods with awareness and care, ensuring your cat remains balanced and healthy during these reflective times.

The Significance of Planetary Retrogrades in Your Cat's Life

During a retrograde period, the energy of the retrograding planet is turned inward, leading to a time of reflection, reassessment, and possible delays or disruptions. For your cat, this can translate into noticeable changes in their behavior, health, or daily routine. Retrogrades often bring up unresolved issues, whether they are behavioral patterns, health concerns, or changes in the home environment. These periods are an opportunity to address and resolve these issues, allowing for growth and healing once the retrograde ends.

- **General Effects of Retrogrades on Behavior and Health**: Retrogrades can cause your cat to behave differently than usual, sometimes becoming more introspective, lethargic, or reactive. Health issues that may have been dormant can resurface, or your cat might exhibit signs of stress or discomfort. Understanding the general effects of retrogrades can help you anticipate these changes and provide the necessary support.
  - **Behavioral Shifts**: Your cat may exhibit changes in their usual behavior, such as becoming more withdrawn, restless, or clingy. They might revisit old habits or display behaviors that seem out of character. These shifts are often temporary and reflect the introspective nature of the retrograde period.
  - **Health Concerns**: Retrogrades can sometimes bring up health issues, either by exacerbating existing conditions or revealing underlying problems. Your cat might seem more fatigued, experience digestive issues, or show signs of discomfort. Being attentive to

these potential health concerns and consulting with a veterinarian if necessary will help you manage your cat's well-being during this time.

- **Mercury Retrograde**: Mercury retrograde is one of the most well-known retrogrades, associated with communication breakdowns, misunderstandings, and disruptions in routine. For your cat, this can manifest as increased sensitivity to changes in their environment, communication challenges (such as not responding to cues as usual), and disruptions in their daily routine.

  - **Communication and Interaction**: Your cat may become more confused or less responsive during Mercury retrograde, leading to misunderstandings between you and your pet. They might ignore commands, seem more aloof, or react unexpectedly to stimuli. Maintaining clear and consistent communication, using positive reinforcement, and being patient with your cat during this time will help reduce confusion.

  - **Routine Disruptions**: Mercury retrograde can also disrupt your cat's daily routine, leading to changes in their sleep patterns, feeding times, or play behavior. Your cat may seem more restless or anxious, particularly if their routine is altered. Keeping their environment as consistent as possible and minimizing changes during this time can help mitigate these effects.

- **Venus Retrograde**: Venus retrograde affects relationships, affection, and comfort, which can influence your cat's interactions with you and other pets. During this period, your cat may become more distant or, conversely, more needy for attention and affection. Issues related to comfort, such as their sleeping environment or favorite resting spots, may also come to the forefront.

  - **Changes in Affection**: Your cat may exhibit fluctuating levels of affection during Venus retrograde, ranging from being overly clingy to suddenly seeking more independence. They might show less interest in cuddling or become more sensitive to touch. Respecting their space while offering comfort when needed will help them feel secure during this time.

  - **Comfort and Environment**: Your cat may also be more particular about their comfort during Venus retrograde, possibly rejecting their usual bedding or becoming more fussy about their food. Ensuring that your cat's environment is comfortable and addressing any changes they might be responding to will help them feel more at ease.

- **Mars Retrograde**: Mars retrograde is associated with energy, aggression, and action, which can lead to fluctuations in your cat's activity levels and assertiveness. Your cat may experience bursts of energy followed by periods of lethargy, or they may become more territorial and assertive than usual.
  - **Fluctuating Energy Levels**: During Mars retrograde, your cat's energy levels may become unpredictable. They might have sudden bursts of activity, followed by longer periods of rest or inactivity. Providing outlets for their energy, such as interactive toys or play sessions, while allowing for plenty of rest will help them balance these fluctuations.
  - **Increased Aggression or Assertiveness**: Mars retrograde can also amplify your cat's territorial instincts, leading to increased aggression toward other pets or even you. They may become more protective of their space or belongings. Ensuring that your cat feels secure and avoiding situations that might trigger aggression will help manage these behaviors during the retrograde.
- **Jupiter Retrograde**: Jupiter retrograde influences growth, expansion, and optimism. During this period, your cat may exhibit changes in their appetite, mood, or overall enthusiasm. They might be less interested in exploring new areas or trying new things, and could show signs of lethargy or reduced curiosity.
  - **Changes in Appetite**: Your cat's appetite may fluctuate during Jupiter retrograde, with periods of overeating or reduced interest in food. Monitoring their diet and ensuring they have access to nutritious food that meets their needs will help maintain their health during this time.
  - **Mood and Curiosity**: Jupiter retrograde may also cause your cat to become less curious or adventurous, preferring to stick to familiar routines and spaces. Encouraging gentle exploration and providing stimulating environments will help keep their spirits up while respecting their need for comfort.
- **Saturn Retrograde**: Saturn retrograde is linked to discipline, structure, and boundaries. Your cat may show changes in their response to training, routine, and boundaries during this

period. They might become more stubborn, resistant to commands, or show a preference for solitude.

- ◦ **Resistance to Routine**: During Saturn retrograde, your cat may resist their usual routines or show disinterest in training exercises. They might ignore commands or become more independent in their behaviors. Being patient and consistent with training, while allowing some flexibility, will help them navigate this period of resistance.
- ◦ **Increased Need for Solitude**: Saturn retrograde can also lead to a greater need for solitude and reflection. Your cat might seek out quiet, isolated spaces where they can be alone. Respecting their need for solitude and ensuring they have access to a safe, comfortable space will help them feel secure during this time.

- **Uranus Retrograde**: Uranus retrograde is associated with change, innovation, and unpredictability. Your cat may exhibit sudden, unexpected behaviors or react differently to their environment during this period. They might become more independent, explore new areas, or exhibit unusual behaviors.
- ◦ **Unpredictable Behavior**: Your cat's behavior may become more unpredictable during Uranus retrograde. They might suddenly become more adventurous, exploring areas they usually avoid, or they could display new behaviors that seem out of character. Providing a safe environment where they can explore and express themselves will help them feel secure while navigating these changes.
- ◦ **Increased Independence**: Uranus retrograde may also lead to increased independence in your cat. They might prefer to spend more time alone or become less interested in social interaction. Encouraging their independence while being available for support when needed will help them balance these tendencies.

- **Neptune Retrograde**: Neptune retrograde influences dreams, intuition, and sensitivity. During this period, your cat may become more sensitive to their environment and may display changes in their sleep patterns or emotional state. They might have vivid dreams, become more introspective, or react more strongly to changes in their surroundings.
- ◦ **Changes in Sleep Patterns**: Neptune retrograde can affect your cat's sleep patterns, leading to more restless nights or unusual napping behaviors. They might have vivid

dreams or seem more unsettled during sleep. Providing a calm, peaceful environment for rest will help them feel more secure and improve their sleep quality.

- **Heightened Sensitivity**: Your cat may also become more sensitive to their environment during Neptune retrograde, reacting strongly to sounds, smells, or changes in routine. Being mindful of their sensitivities and providing a stable, comforting environment will help them feel more at ease during this introspective period.

- **Pluto Retrograde**: Pluto retrograde is associated with transformation, power, and deep emotional processes. Your cat may undergo profound changes during this period, whether in behavior, health, or emotional state. They might become more introspective, exhibit signs of stress or anxiety, or display behaviors related to past experiences.

  - **Profound Behavioral Changes**: Pluto retrograde can bring deep, transformative changes in your cat's behavior. They might revisit old habits, become more introspective, or display new behaviors that reflect underlying emotional processes. Supporting your cat through these changes by providing stability and reassurance will help them navigate this transformative period.

  - **Emotional Release and Healing**: Pluto retrograde is also a time for emotional release and healing. Your cat may display signs of stress, anxiety, or emotional turmoil as they process past experiences. Offering extra comfort, affection, and a safe environment for emotional release will help them heal and emerge stronger from this period of transformation.

Supporting Your Cat During Planetary Retrogrades

Understanding the influence of planetary retrogrades on your cat's life allows you to provide the necessary support and care to help them navigate these periods of introspection and change. Here are some ways you can support your cat during planetary retrogrades:

- **Provide Stability and Consistency**: Retrogrades can bring uncertainty and disruption, making it important to provide stability and consistency in your cat's environment. Maintaining familiar routines, offering comfort items, and minimizing changes will help your cat feel secure during these reflective times.

- **Monitor Health and Behavior**: Pay close attention to any changes in your cat's health and behavior during retrogrades. If you notice fluctuations in appetite, energy levels, or emotional state, be prepared to adjust their routine or seek veterinary advice if necessary. Being proactive in monitoring your cat's well-being will help you address any issues before they become more significant.

- **Encourage Rest and Reflection**: Retrogrades are a time for introspection and healing, so it's important to encourage rest and reflection for your cat. Providing quiet, comfortable spaces where your cat can retreat and relax will help them process the energy of the retrograde and emerge feeling more balanced.

- **Support Emotional Well-Being**: Retrogrades can bring up unresolved emotions or trigger stress in your cat. Being attuned to your cat's emotional needs and offering extra comfort, affection, and reassurance will help them feel supported during these times. Creating a calm and nurturing environment will promote emotional healing and well-being.

- **Be Patient and Flexible**: Retrogrades often require a more patient and flexible approach to your cat's care. Your cat's behavior and needs may change during these periods, and being adaptable will help you support them more effectively. Whether it's adjusting routines, providing extra rest, or offering new forms of stimulation, being responsive to your cat's needs will help them navigate retrogrades with greater ease.

- **Facilitate Healing and Transformation**: Retrogrades are powerful times for healing and transformation. Supporting your cat through these processes by providing opportunities for emotional release, addressing any unresolved issues, and offering a safe space for growth will help them emerge from the retrograde period feeling more balanced and renewed.

Conclusion

Planetary retrogrades represent significant times of introspection, reflection, and change in your cat's life. By understanding and aligning with the energy of these celestial events, you can support your cat as they navigate the challenges and opportunities of retrogrades, helping them to grow, heal, and transform.

Whether it's providing stability during periods of uncertainty, monitoring health and behavior, or supporting emotional well-being, planetary retrogrades offer an opportunity to enhance your cat's well-being and support their ongoing development. As you continue to explore the astrological influences on your cat, remember that retrogrades are powerful catalysts for introspection and healing, guiding your cat through cycles of reflection and helping them realign with their true self in their journey of life.

Chapter 38: Meteor Showers: Energetic Bursts and Playful Behavior in Your Cat

Meteor showers are spectacular celestial events where numerous meteors streak across the sky as Earth passes through the debris trail left by a comet. These showers are associated with bursts of energy, excitement, and heightened activity. Astrologically, meteor showers are believed to influence sudden changes, unexpected developments, and a surge in energy and enthusiasm. For your cat, meteor showers can manifest as periods of heightened energy, increased playfulness, and spontaneous behavior. Understanding the influence of meteor showers on your cat's behavior can help you make the most of these vibrant times, ensuring your cat stays engaged, stimulated, and healthy.

The Significance of Meteor Showers in Your Cat's Life

Meteor showers are times of dynamic energy and excitement, often bringing a sense of renewal, inspiration, and spontaneity. For your cat, these periods can be marked by bursts of energy, increased curiosity, and a desire to explore and engage in playful activities. These showers offer an opportunity for your cat to express their natural instincts, such as hunting, chasing, and pouncing, in a more intense and focused way. Understanding and supporting your cat's needs during a meteor shower can help channel this energy positively, leading to a more enriched and fulfilling experience for your feline companion.

- **Increased Energy Levels**: During a meteor shower, your cat may exhibit heightened energy levels, characterized by more frequent and intense bursts of activity. This can include running around the house, chasing toys, or engaging in play behavior that is more vigorous than usual. These periods of increased energy are a natural response to the dynamic and stimulating energy of the meteor shower, and providing appropriate outlets for this energy will help your cat stay healthy and happy.

- **Playful and Spontaneous Behavior**: Meteor showers are often associated with a surge in playful behavior. Your cat may become more interested in interactive play, showing a greater enthusiasm for games that involve chasing, pouncing, or hunting. This spontaneous behavior can be an expression of your cat's instinctual drive to explore and engage with their environment. Encouraging and participating in these playful activities will help strengthen your bond and keep your cat mentally and physically stimulated.

- **Heightened Curiosity and Exploration**: The energy of a meteor shower can also ignite your cat's curiosity, leading to increased exploration of their surroundings. They may show more interest in investigating new areas of the house, playing with unfamiliar objects, or engaging in activities that they usually overlook. This heightened curiosity is a sign that your cat is responding to the stimulating energy of the meteor shower, and providing safe opportunities for exploration will help satisfy their inquisitive nature.

- **Short Bursts of Intensity**: Meteor showers are characterized by short, intense bursts of activity, and this can be mirrored in your cat's behavior. They may experience sudden surges of energy where they engage in rapid, intense play sessions, followed by periods of rest or calm. These bursts of intensity are a way for your cat to release pent-up energy and express their natural hunting instincts. Ensuring that your cat has access to toys and activities that allow for these bursts of play will help them channel their energy in positive ways.

- **Increased Social Interaction**: During a meteor shower, your cat may seek out more social interaction, either with you or other pets in the household. They might initiate play sessions, follow you around more closely, or engage in behaviors that invite interaction, such as bringing toys to you. This increased desire for social engagement is a reflection of the heightened energy and excitement associated with the meteor shower, and participating in these interactions will help strengthen your bond with your cat.

- **Enhanced Sensory Awareness**: The energetic influence of a meteor shower can also heighten your cat's sensory awareness. They may become more attuned to sounds, movements, and changes in their environment, reacting more quickly or intensely to stimuli. This enhanced sensory awareness is part of your cat's natural response to the dynamic energy of the meteor shower, and providing a stimulating environment with new toys, scents, or textures will help them fully engage with their surroundings.

Interpreting the Influence of Meteor Showers on Your Cat

The impact of a meteor shower on your cat's behavior can vary depending on the astrological context and the specific characteristics of the meteor shower. Here's how different factors might influence your cat's response to these celestial events:

- **Meteor Showers in Aries**: A meteor shower occurring in Aries is likely to amplify your cat's natural assertiveness and drive. They may become more energetic, displaying a strong desire to chase, pounce, and engage in physical play. Providing toys that encourage active play, such as balls or interactive wands, will help them channel this energy constructively.

- **Meteor Showers in Taurus**: A meteor shower in Taurus may influence your cat to seek comfort and pleasure through sensory experiences. They might be more interested in activities that involve tactile stimulation, such as playing with soft or textured toys. Offering opportunities for sensory exploration, such as new bedding or toys with different textures, will help satisfy their heightened sensory awareness.

- **Meteor Showers in Gemini**: A meteor shower in Gemini can enhance your cat's curiosity and social engagement. They may become more vocal, interactive, and eager to explore new areas of the house. Providing interactive toys, puzzle feeders, or new areas to explore will help keep their mind engaged and satisfy their need for mental stimulation.

- **Meteor Showers in Cancer**: A meteor shower in Cancer may lead to increased affection and a desire for closeness with you or other pets. Your cat may seek more cuddles, engage in kneading behavior, or follow you around the house. Providing comfort and engaging in gentle, nurturing play will help them feel secure and loved during this time.

- **Meteor Showers in Leo**: A meteor shower in Leo can amplify your cat's desire for attention and self-expression. They may become more playful, seeking out interactive games that allow them to show off their skills. Providing toys that encourage active play and offering plenty of praise and attention will help them feel appreciated and engaged.

- **Meteor Showers in Virgo**: A meteor shower in Virgo might influence your cat to engage in more methodical and precise play. They may focus on tasks that require concentration, such as solving puzzle toys or engaging in activities that involve hunting or foraging. Offering toys that challenge their problem-solving skills will help keep them mentally stimulated and satisfied.

- **Meteor Showers in Libra**: A meteor shower in Libra may enhance your cat's social interactions and desire for balance. They may seek out play with other pets or engage in activities that involve cooperation and sharing. Encouraging play that involves interaction with other pets or family members will help them feel connected and balanced during this time.

- **Meteor Showers in Scorpio**: A meteor shower in Scorpio can intensify your cat's focus and determination during play. They may become more interested in games that involve hunting or stalking, displaying a more intense and focused demeanor. Providing toys that mimic prey or encourage stealthy play will help them channel this energy effectively.

- **Meteor Showers in Sagittarius**: A meteor shower in Sagittarius is likely to amplify your cat's adventurous spirit. They may become more eager to explore new territories, engage in high-energy play, or try new activities. Providing opportunities for exploration, such as introducing new toys or rearranging their play space, will help satisfy their need for adventure.

- **Meteor Showers in Capricorn**: A meteor shower in Capricorn may lead your cat to engage in more structured and goal-oriented play. They may focus on tasks that involve achieving specific outcomes, such as retrieving toys or completing a puzzle. Offering toys that involve challenges or rewards will help them stay motivated and engaged.

- **Meteor Showers in Aquarius**: A meteor shower in Aquarius can inspire your cat to engage in more unconventional or creative play. They may explore new ways of interacting with their environment, showing a preference for novel toys or activities. Providing a variety of toys and allowing them to explore different play styles will help them express their creativity.

- **Meteor Showers in Pisces**: A meteor shower in Pisces may enhance your cat's sensitivity and intuition during play. They may become more attuned to the emotions of those around them, engaging in play that reflects a more gentle and nurturing nature. Offering toys that promote calm, soothing play, such as soft or slow-moving toys, will help them feel relaxed and content.

Supporting Your Cat During Meteor Showers

Understanding the influence of meteor showers on your cat's behavior allows you to provide the necessary support and care to help them navigate these periods of heightened energy and playfulness. Here are some ways you can support your cat during a meteor shower:

- **Provide Interactive and Stimulating Toys**: Meteor showers are a time of increased energy and playfulness, making it important to provide toys that encourage active engagement. Interactive toys, such as laser pointers, feather wands, or puzzle feeders, will help channel your cat's energy in positive ways and keep them mentally stimulated.
- **Encourage Exploration and New Experiences**: The dynamic energy of a meteor shower can ignite your cat's curiosity and desire to explore. Encourage exploration by introducing new toys, rearranging their play area, or allowing them to explore new parts of the house. Providing opportunities for safe exploration will satisfy their curiosity and keep them engaged.
- **Engage in Playtime Together**: During a meteor shower, your cat may seek out more social interaction and playtime with you. Take advantage of this time by engaging in interactive play sessions that allow your cat to express their natural instincts, such as chasing, pouncing, or stalking. This will strengthen your bond and provide your cat with the mental and physical stimulation they crave.
- **Monitor Energy Levels and Provide Rest**: While meteor showers can lead to bursts of energy, it's also important to monitor your cat's activity levels and ensure they get enough rest. After intense play sessions, provide a quiet, comfortable space where your cat can rest and recharge. Balancing play with rest will help them maintain their energy and well-being.
- **Create a Safe and Stimulating Environment**: Meteor showers can heighten your cat's sensory awareness, making it important to create an environment that is both safe and stimulating. Ensure that your cat's play area is free of hazards, and provide toys or activities that engage their senses, such as toys with different textures, scents, or sounds.
- **Be Responsive to Your Cat's Needs**: Each cat may respond differently to the energy of a meteor shower, so it's important to be attuned to your cat's individual needs and preferences.

Whether they seek out more social interaction, prefer solitary play, or need extra comfort, being responsive to their needs will help them feel supported and secure during this time.

Conclusion

Meteor showers represent powerful times of energetic bursts and playful behavior in your cat's life. By understanding and aligning with the energy of these celestial events, you can support your cat as they navigate the challenges and opportunities of increased energy, curiosity, and playfulness.

Whether it's providing interactive and stimulating toys, encouraging exploration and new experiences, or engaging in playtime together, meteor showers offer an opportunity to enhance your cat's well-being and support their ongoing development. As you continue to explore the astrological influences on your cat, remember that meteor showers are moments of dynamic energy and excitement, guiding your cat through cycles of play and discovery, and helping them express their true nature in their journey of life.

Chapter 39: Comets: Rare and Extraordinary Influences on Your Cat's Life

Comets are celestial wanderers that travel through space, often visible from Earth as bright objects with long, glowing tails. Unlike planets or regular meteor showers, comets are rare occurrences, each one unique in its path and visibility. Astrologically, comets are associated with significant, rare, and often unexpected influences that can bring about profound changes, insights, and transformations. For your cat, the influence of a comet can be seen as a time of rare and extraordinary experiences that may lead to notable shifts in behavior, health, or overall energy. Understanding the influence of comets on your cat's life can help you navigate these unique moments with awareness and care, ensuring your cat remains balanced and well-supported during these transformative times.

The Significance of Comets in Your Cat's Life

Comets, with their rare appearances, symbolize extraordinary events or influences that can disrupt the ordinary flow of life. These celestial visitors often herald moments of intense energy, transformation, and revelation, which can manifest in your cat's life in unexpected ways. A comet's influence may lead to profound changes in your cat's behavior, health, or environment, marking a time of significant growth or transition. While these influences may be fleeting, they often leave a lasting impact, guiding your cat through a period of change that can shape their future behavior and well-being.

- **Sudden and Unexpected Changes**: The arrival of a comet can symbolize sudden and unexpected changes in your cat's life. These changes might manifest as shifts in behavior, new habits, or even alterations in your cat's health or routine. Your cat may suddenly develop a new interest, behavior, or preference that seems to come out of nowhere. These changes can be both exciting and challenging, as they often require quick adaptation and flexibility. Being aware of these potential shifts and providing the necessary support can help your cat navigate these changes with confidence.

- **Profound Emotional Shifts**: Comets are often associated with deep, transformative energy that can trigger profound emotional shifts. Your cat may experience heightened emotions during this time, displaying behaviors that reflect a deeper level of introspection or sensitivity. They may become more affectionate, more withdrawn, or exhibit signs of stress or anxiety.

Understanding these emotional shifts and providing a stable, comforting environment will help your cat feel secure as they process these powerful energies.

- **Rare Health Fluctuations**: Just as comets are rare, your cat may experience unusual health fluctuations during the influence of a comet. These health changes might be subtle, such as shifts in appetite or energy levels, or they could be more pronounced, such as a sudden illness or recovery. It's important to monitor your cat's health closely during this time and consult with a veterinarian if you notice any significant changes. These rare health fluctuations often reflect the deeper transformative processes that a comet's energy can bring.

- **Increased Curiosity and Exploration**: The extraordinary energy of a comet can ignite your cat's curiosity and desire to explore. They may become more adventurous, seeking out new experiences or exploring parts of the house they usually avoid. This heightened curiosity is a natural response to the comet's influence, as your cat taps into the rare and extraordinary energy that the comet brings. Encouraging safe exploration and providing new stimuli will help satisfy your cat's inquisitive nature during this time.

- **Enhanced Intuition and Sensitivity**: Comets are also linked to heightened intuition and sensitivity. Your cat may become more attuned to the emotions and energies around them, displaying a greater awareness of subtle changes in their environment or in your behavior. They might respond more intensely to your mood, react to changes in the household, or even anticipate events before they happen. Supporting your cat's heightened intuition by maintaining a calm, stable environment will help them feel more at ease during this time.

- **Catalyst for Long-Term Change**: While a comet's influence is temporary, it often serves as a catalyst for long-term change. The shifts and transformations that occur during this time can have lasting effects on your cat's behavior, health, or overall well-being. Whether it's the development of a new habit, a change in their relationship with you, or a shift in their routine, these changes are often profound and can shape your cat's future in meaningful ways. Being mindful of these long-term effects and supporting your cat through the transition will help them adapt and thrive.

Interpreting the Influence of Comets on Your Cat

The impact of a comet on your cat's life can vary depending on the astrological context and the specific characteristics of the comet. Here's how different factors might influence your cat's response to these rare celestial events:

- **Comet in Aries**: A comet in Aries may influence your cat to become more assertive, energetic, and bold. They might exhibit sudden bursts of activity, a desire to assert their independence, or a newfound confidence in their interactions. Providing opportunities for active play and exploration will help channel this intense energy constructively.
- **Comet in Taurus**: A comet in Taurus may bring changes related to comfort, security, and material well-being. Your cat might suddenly show a preference for different bedding, toys, or food, or they may become more possessive of their favorite items. Ensuring that your cat's environment remains comfortable and addressing any changes in their preferences will help them feel secure.
- **Comet in Gemini**: A comet in Gemini can amplify your cat's curiosity and social interaction. They may become more communicative, exploring new ways to interact with you or other pets. This influence might also spark a desire for mental stimulation, leading them to engage more with puzzle toys or other mentally challenging activities.
- **Comet in Cancer**: A comet in Cancer may heighten your cat's emotional sensitivity and attachment to their home environment. They might seek out more comfort, become more affectionate, or display a stronger attachment to their favorite resting spots. Providing extra emotional support and maintaining a stable home environment will help them feel secure during this time.
- **Comet in Leo**: A comet in Leo can enhance your cat's desire for attention and self-expression. They may become more playful, demanding more interaction and praise from you. This influence might also bring out their creative side, encouraging them to engage in activities that allow them to show off their skills. Providing plenty of attention and opportunities for creative play will help them thrive.
- **Comet in Virgo**: A comet in Virgo may bring changes related to routine, health, and organization. Your cat might suddenly develop new habits, become more focused on grooming,

or show a preference for a more structured routine. Supporting these changes by maintaining a clean, organized environment and encouraging healthy habits will help them adapt to the comet's influence.

- **Comet in Libra**: A comet in Libra may influence your cat's social interactions and desire for balance. They may become more cooperative, seeking out interaction with other pets or family members. This influence might also prompt a need for harmony in their environment, leading them to avoid conflict or seek out peaceful resting spots.
- **Comet in Scorpio**: A comet in Scorpio can bring intense emotional experiences and deep transformation. Your cat may become more introspective, displaying behaviors that reflect a deeper emotional process. They might also exhibit signs of stress or anxiety as they process these intense energies. Providing a calm, secure environment and offering extra comfort will help them navigate this transformative time.
- **Comet in Sagittarius**: A comet in Sagittarius may amplify your cat's sense of adventure and curiosity. They might become more eager to explore new areas, try new toys, or engage in high-energy play. Encouraging exploration and providing a variety of stimulating activities will help satisfy their adventurous spirit during this time.
- **Comet in Capricorn**: A comet in Capricorn may influence your cat to become more disciplined, focused, and determined. They might show a stronger attachment to their routines or become more goal-oriented in their play. Supporting their need for structure and providing opportunities for achievement, such as puzzle toys or training exercises, will help them feel accomplished and balanced.
- **Comet in Aquarius**: A comet in Aquarius can inspire your cat to explore new, unconventional behaviors or preferences. They may show an interest in new types of toys, engage in unusual play behaviors, or develop a preference for different types of interactions. Providing a variety of toys and allowing them to explore their unique preferences will help them express their individuality.
- **Comet in Pisces**: A comet in Pisces may heighten your cat's sensitivity, intuition, and emotional depth. They might become more attuned to the emotions of those around them, showing empathy or reacting more strongly to changes in their environment. Providing a calm,

nurturing environment and supporting their emotional needs will help them feel secure and connected during this time.

Supporting Your Cat During a Comet's Influence

Understanding the influence of a comet on your cat's life allows you to provide the necessary support and care to help them navigate these rare and extraordinary experiences. Here are some ways you can support your cat during a comet's influence:

- **Provide Stability During Change**: Comets can bring sudden and unexpected changes, making it important to provide stability and reassurance. Ensure that your cat's environment remains consistent, with familiar routines and comfort items that help them feel secure. Being present and attentive to their needs will help them adapt to any changes more smoothly.
- **Encourage Exploration and New Experiences**: The dynamic energy of a comet can ignite your cat's curiosity and desire to explore. Encourage exploration by introducing new toys, rearranging their play area, or allowing them to explore new parts of the house. Providing opportunities for safe exploration will satisfy their curiosity and keep them engaged.
- **Support Emotional and Physical Well-Being**: Comets can trigger profound emotional and physical shifts, so it's important to support your cat's well-being during this time. Be attuned to any changes in their behavior or health, and provide extra comfort, affection, and reassurance. Creating a calm and nurturing environment will promote emotional healing and physical health.
- **Monitor Health and Behavior**: Pay close attention to any unusual changes in your cat's health and behavior during a comet's influence. If you notice significant fluctuations in appetite, energy levels, or emotional state, be prepared to adjust their routine or consult with a veterinarian if necessary. Being proactive in monitoring your cat's well-being will help you address any issues before they become more significant.
- **Facilitate Long-Term Growth and Transformation**: While a comet's influence may be temporary, it often serves as a catalyst for long-term growth and transformation. Support your cat through these changes by helping them release any old patterns, encouraging new experiences, and offering a safe space for emotional and physical growth.

• **Be Patient and Adaptable**: Comets are rare events that can bring unexpected changes, so it's important to be patient and adaptable. Your cat's behavior and needs may change during this time, and being responsive to their needs will help them navigate these extraordinary experiences with greater ease.

Conclusion

Comets represent rare and extraordinary influences in your cat's life, bringing moments of profound change, growth, and transformation. By understanding and aligning with the energy of these celestial events, you can support your cat as they navigate the challenges and opportunities of these unique experiences.

Whether it's providing stability during periods of change, encouraging exploration and new experiences, or supporting emotional and physical well-being, comets offer an opportunity to enhance your cat's development and well-being. As you continue to explore the astrological influences on your cat, remember that comets are powerful catalysts for growth and transformation, guiding your cat through rare and extraordinary moments that shape their journey of life in meaningful ways.

Part VI: Integration and Practical Applications

Chapter 40: Creating a Cat Horoscope: Step-by-Step Guide to Casting and Interpreting Your Cat's Horoscope

Astrology offers a fascinating lens through which we can explore the personalities, behaviors, and destinies of not only humans but also our beloved pets. Creating a horoscope for your cat involves the same principles as creating one for a human, with a focus on understanding your cat's unique personality, behavior, and life experiences. A cat horoscope can provide insights into your cat's natural instincts, preferences, and potential challenges, helping you better support and care for them. This chapter provides a step-by-step guide to casting and interpreting your cat's horoscope, offering you a deeper connection with your feline companion.

Step 1: Gather Essential Information

Before you can cast your cat's horoscope, you'll need to gather some essential information. The accuracy and depth of the horoscope depend on how much of this information you can obtain.

- **Birth Date**: The most important piece of information is your cat's birth date. If you know the exact date, you can create a more precise horoscope. If you don't know the exact date, you can approximate based on your cat's adoption date or when they were found.
- **Birth Time**: If you know the time of your cat's birth, this will allow you to determine their exact Ascendant (Rising Sign) and the house placements of the planets. This can provide more detailed insights. If you don't know the exact time, you can use a solar chart, which places the Sun on the Ascendant and provides a general overview.
- **Birthplace**: The location where your cat was born helps in determining the precise positions of the planets at the time of their birth. This is particularly important if you're using an astrology software or an ephemeris to cast the chart.

Step 2: Cast Your Cat's Natal Chart

With the essential information in hand, the next step is to cast your cat's natal chart. The natal chart, or birth chart, is a snapshot of the sky at the exact moment of your cat's birth. This chart will serve as the foundation for interpreting your cat's astrological influences.

- **Use Astrology Software**: There are many astrology software programs and online tools available that allow you to input the birth date, time, and location to generate a natal chart. These tools will provide you with a detailed chart that includes the positions of the planets, the Ascendant, and the houses.
- **Solar Chart Option**: If you don't have the exact birth time, you can create a solar chart by placing the Sun on the Ascendant (1st house). This method provides a general overview of your cat's astrological influences and is commonly used when the birth time is unknown.
- **Manually Create the Chart**: If you're familiar with astrology, you can manually create the natal chart using an ephemeris (a table that shows the positions of the planets at a given time). This method requires a bit more work and understanding of astrology, but it can be a rewarding way to connect with the process.

Step 3: Interpret the Sun, Moon, and Ascendant

Once you have your cat's natal chart, begin by interpreting the Sun, Moon, and Ascendant. These three elements are the most influential in determining your cat's core personality, emotional needs, and outward behavior.

- **The Sun Sign**: The Sun sign represents your cat's core personality, their vital energy, and their basic nature. It's the most straightforward element to interpret, as it reflects your cat's general demeanor and approach to life.
    - **Example Interpretation**: If your cat's Sun is in Leo, they may have a regal, confident demeanor, often seeking attention and enjoying being the center of the household. They may display a strong sense of pride and a playful, energetic personality.
- **The Moon Sign**: The Moon sign reflects your cat's emotional nature, their instincts, and what makes them feel secure. It's an important element to understand your cat's inner world and emotional needs.
    - **Example Interpretation**: A cat with their Moon in Cancer may be very nurturing and affectionate, enjoying close bonds with their human family. They might be sensitive to changes in their environment and need a stable, comforting space to feel secure.

- **The Ascendant (Rising Sign)**: The Ascendant represents your cat's outward behavior and how they present themselves to the world. It influences their physical appearance and first impressions.
    - **Example Interpretation**: If your cat's Ascendant is in Aries, they may appear energetic, bold, and ready to take on challenges. They might be quick to explore new environments and can be assertive in getting what they want.

Step 4: Analyze the Planets in the Houses

Next, analyze the positions of the planets in the houses of your cat's natal chart. Each planet governs different aspects of your cat's life, and the house placement shows where these energies are most expressed.

- **Personal Planets (Mercury, Venus, Mars)**: These planets provide insight into your cat's communication style (Mercury), their affectionate nature (Venus), and their energy and aggression (Mars).
    - **Example Interpretation**: If Venus is in the 4th house (home and family), your cat may find great comfort and happiness in their home environment, often seeking out cozy spots and enjoying the company of their family members.
- **Social Planets (Jupiter, Saturn)**: Jupiter and Saturn influence your cat's growth, discipline, and overall outlook on life. Jupiter brings expansion and optimism, while Saturn brings structure and boundaries.
    - **Example Interpretation**: A cat with Jupiter in the 9th house (travel and exploration) may have a strong desire to explore new environments, showing an adventurous spirit. In contrast, Saturn in the 2nd house (resources and values) may indicate a cat who is more cautious and prefers routine.
- **Outer Planets (Uranus, Neptune, Pluto)**: These planets represent deeper, more transformative aspects of your cat's life, often influencing them over longer periods.
    - **Example Interpretation**: Uranus in the 6th house (health and daily routines) could indicate a cat who occasionally experiences sudden changes in health or behavior, requiring flexibility in their care routine.

Step 5: Consider the Aspects

Aspects are the angles formed between planets in your cat's natal chart, indicating how different energies interact. These interactions can enhance or challenge your cat's natural tendencies.

- **Conjunctions**: Planets in the same sign or degree amplify each other's energy. A cat with the Sun conjunct Mars may be very energetic and assertive, often displaying bold and confident behavior.
- **Squares**: A square aspect (90 degrees apart) indicates tension between planets, which can manifest as challenges in behavior. For example, if Mercury squares Mars, your cat might have a quick temper or be more prone to agitation.
- **Trines**: A trine aspect (120 degrees apart) suggests harmony between planets, indicating ease and natural talent in the areas they govern. A cat with Venus trine Jupiter may have a naturally affectionate and loving disposition, easily bonding with others.
- **Oppositions**: An opposition (180 degrees apart) indicates a polarity between planets, requiring balance. If the Moon opposes Pluto, your cat might experience intense emotional fluctuations, needing extra comfort during stressful times.

Step 6: Synthesize the Chart

After analyzing each element of your cat's natal chart, it's important to synthesize the information into a comprehensive understanding of your cat's personality, behavior, and potential life experiences.

- **Identify Key Themes**: Look for recurring themes or dominant elements in the chart. For instance, if multiple planets are in fire signs (Aries, Leo, Sagittarius), your cat may have a naturally energetic and bold personality. If the water element is strong (Cancer, Scorpio, Pisces), they may be more sensitive and emotionally driven.
- **Understand Strengths and Challenges**: Recognize your cat's natural strengths and any potential challenges indicated by the chart. For example, a strong Mars influence might make your cat assertive and adventurous but could also lead to impatience or aggression in certain situations.

- **Consider the Chart as a Whole**: Think about how the different aspects of your cat's chart interact to create a unique personality. A cat with a Leo Sun (confident and bold) and a Cancer Moon (sensitive and nurturing) might be outwardly regal and playful while also needing plenty of affection and reassurance.

Step 7: Interpret the Transits

In addition to the natal chart, it's important to consider how current planetary transits (the movement of planets through the sky) interact with your cat's natal chart. Transits can trigger changes, bring new opportunities, or highlight challenges in your cat's life.

- **Track Major Transits**: Pay attention to major transits, such as Saturn returns or Uranus oppositions, which can bring significant changes or challenges. These transits can influence your cat's behavior, health, and overall energy levels.
- **Consider Personal Transits**: Look at how transiting planets interact with your cat's personal planets (Sun, Moon, Mercury, etc.). For example, if transiting Mars is conjunct your cat's natal Venus, they may become more affectionate and playful during this time.
- **Monitor for Patterns**: Observe your cat's behavior during significant transits to identify patterns or recurring themes. This can help you anticipate changes in behavior and provide the necessary support during challenging times.

Step 8: Apply the Insights

Finally, use the insights gained from your cat's horoscope to enhance their well-being and your relationship with them. Understanding your cat's astrological influences can guide you in providing the best care, nurturing their strengths, and addressing any challenges.

- **Tailor Care to Their Needs**: Use the horoscope to tailor your cat's care routine, ensuring that it aligns with their natural tendencies. For instance, a cat with a strong Earth influence (Taurus, Virgo, Capricorn) may thrive with a consistent routine and a stable environment.
- **Enhance Bonding**: Understanding your cat's astrological profile can deepen your bond, as you become more attuned to their emotional needs and behavioral patterns. Whether your

cat needs more playtime, affection, or solitude, applying these insights will help you provide a more supportive and loving environment.

- **Support Through Challenges**: Use the horoscope to anticipate and address challenges, such as periods of stress or health fluctuations. Being proactive in providing comfort and care during challenging transits will help your cat navigate these times with greater ease.
- **Celebrate Their Unique Personality**: Every cat is unique, and their horoscope reflects the individuality that makes them special. Celebrate your cat's strengths and quirks, and use the horoscope as a tool to appreciate and understand the rich tapestry of their personality.

Conclusion

Creating a horoscope for your cat is a meaningful way to explore their unique personality, behavior, and life experiences. By following the steps outlined in this chapter, you can cast and interpret a detailed horoscope that offers valuable insights into your cat's astrological influences.

Whether it's understanding their core personality through the Sun, Moon, and Ascendant, analyzing the planets in the houses, or interpreting the impact of transits, astrology provides a powerful tool for deepening your connection with your feline companion. As you continue to explore the astrological influences on your cat, remember that their horoscope is a reflection of their unique journey, guiding you in providing the best possible care and nurturing a deep, loving relationship that enriches both of your lives.

Chapter 41: Astrological Compatibility: Understanding How Different Signs Interact and Affect Your Cat's Relationships with Other Pets and Humans

Astrological compatibility is a fascinating aspect of astrology that explores how different zodiac signs interact and influence relationships. Just as humans have unique personalities shaped by their astrological signs, so do our feline companions. Understanding your cat's astrological compatibility with other pets and humans in your household can offer valuable insights into their interactions, relationships, and dynamics. This chapter provides an extensive and detailed exploration of astrological compatibility, helping you understand how your cat's sign affects their relationships and how you can create a harmonious environment for all.

The Basics of Astrological Compatibility

Astrological compatibility is based on the elements (Fire, Earth, Air, Water) and the qualities (Cardinal, Fixed, Mutable) of the zodiac signs. Each sign has a natural affinity or challenge with other signs, influencing how they interact, communicate, and form relationships.

- **Elements and Compatibility**: The zodiac signs are divided into four elements: Fire, Earth, Air, and Water. Signs within the same element generally understand and complement each other, while signs of opposing elements may experience tension or challenges.
    - **Fire Signs (Aries, Leo, Sagittarius)**: Fire signs are energetic, enthusiastic, and assertive. They tend to get along well with other Fire signs and Air signs, which fuel their energy and creativity. However, they may clash with Water signs, which can dampen their enthusiasm, and Earth signs, which might find them too impulsive.
    - **Earth Signs (Taurus, Virgo, Capricorn)**: Earth signs are practical, grounded, and stable. They are compatible with other Earth signs and Water signs, which provide emotional depth and nurturing. Earth signs may struggle with Fire signs, which can seem too unpredictable, and Air signs, which may be too detached for their liking.
    - **Air Signs (Gemini, Libra, Aquarius)**: Air signs are intellectual, communicative, and sociable. They thrive in the company of other Air signs and Fire signs, which stimulate their minds and inspire action. However, they may find Earth signs too rigid and Water signs too emotional.

- ◦ **Water Signs (Cancer, Scorpio, Pisces)**: Water signs are emotional, intuitive, and nurturing. They connect deeply with other Water signs and Earth signs, which provide stability and grounding. Water signs may struggle with Fire signs, which can be overwhelming, and Air signs, which may seem too distant or unemotional.
- **Qualities and Compatibility**: The qualities of the zodiac signs—Cardinal, Fixed, and Mutable—also influence compatibility. Each quality has its strengths and challenges, and signs of the same quality may experience a balance or clash of energy.
  - ◦ **Cardinal Signs (Aries, Cancer, Libra, Capricorn)**: Cardinal signs are leaders and initiators. They enjoy taking charge but may clash with other Cardinal signs who also want to lead. They generally work well with Mutable signs, which adapt to their leadership, but may find Fixed signs too resistant to change.
  - ◦ **Fixed Signs (Taurus, Leo, Scorpio, Aquarius)**: Fixed signs are determined, stable, and resistant to change. They can provide stability in relationships but may struggle with other Fixed signs who are equally stubborn. They often find balance with Cardinal signs, which provide direction, and Mutable signs, which offer flexibility.
  - ◦ **Mutable Signs (Gemini, Virgo, Sagittarius, Pisces)**: Mutable signs are adaptable, flexible, and open to change. They get along well with other Mutable signs and Cardinal signs, which provide leadership. However, they may find Fixed signs too rigid and unyielding.

Understanding Your Cat's Sign in Relationships

Each zodiac sign influences your cat's behavior, personality, and how they interact with others. Understanding your cat's sign can help you anticipate how they may relate to other pets and humans, fostering more harmonious relationships.

- **Aries Cat**: Aries cats are bold, energetic, and assertive. They are natural leaders and may take charge in their interactions with other pets. They are playful and adventurous but can be impatient or aggressive if not properly stimulated. Aries cats do well with other active, energetic signs like Leo and Sagittarius, but may clash with more passive signs like Taurus or Cancer.

- **Taurus Cat**: Taurus cats are calm, patient, and affectionate. They value stability and comfort, enjoying a peaceful environment. They may be possessive of their space and belongings and can be slow to warm up to new pets or people. Taurus cats are compatible with nurturing, stable signs like Virgo and Capricorn, but may find impulsive signs like Aries or Gemini challenging.
- **Gemini Cat**: Gemini cats are curious, playful, and sociable. They enjoy mental stimulation and are always exploring their environment. They may be more independent and less affectionate, preferring to engage in activities rather than cuddle. Gemini cats thrive with interactive, communicative signs like Libra and Aquarius but may struggle with more reserved signs like Taurus or Scorpio.
- **Cancer Cat**: Cancer cats are nurturing, sensitive, and loyal. They form deep bonds with their human family and may be protective of their home. They can be shy around new people or pets and may need extra time to adjust. Cancer cats are compatible with supportive, stable signs like Pisces and Taurus but may find assertive signs like Aries or Leo overwhelming.
- **Leo Cat**: Leo cats are confident, playful, and love being the center of attention. They enjoy interactive play and may demand attention from their human companions. They can be dominant in relationships with other pets and may clash with equally strong-willed signs. Leo cats get along well with other Fire signs like Aries and Sagittarius but may have conflicts with more passive signs like Cancer or Virgo.
- **Virgo Cat**: Virgo cats are meticulous, intelligent, and health-conscious. They prefer routine and order, often showing a preference for cleanliness and organization. They may be reserved or shy but are deeply loyal to those they trust. Virgo cats are compatible with practical, grounded signs like Taurus and Capricorn but may find more chaotic signs like Gemini or Sagittarius unsettling.
- **Libra Cat**: Libra cats are sociable, balanced, and harmony-seeking. They enjoy interacting with both humans and other pets and may strive to keep the peace in the household. They can be indecisive or easily influenced by others but are generally friendly and cooperative. Libra cats thrive with communicative, interactive signs like Gemini and Aquarius but may find more intense signs like Scorpio or Aries challenging.

- **Scorpio Cat**: Scorpio cats are intense, mysterious, and deeply loyal. They form strong bonds with their human companions and may be protective or territorial. They can be aloof with strangers and may take time to warm up to new pets. Scorpio cats are compatible with other emotionally intense signs like Cancer and Pisces but may clash with more superficial signs like Gemini or Libra.
- **Sagittarius Cat**: Sagittarius cats are adventurous, energetic, and freedom-loving. They enjoy exploring their environment and may have a curious, independent streak. They can be restless and may need plenty of stimulation to stay engaged. Sagittarius cats get along well with other energetic signs like Aries and Leo but may struggle with more reserved signs like Virgo or Capricorn.
- **Capricorn Cat**: Capricorn cats are disciplined, practical, and ambitious. They value routine and may be more reserved or serious in their interactions. They are loyal and dependable but may take time to warm up to new people or pets. Capricorn cats are compatible with other grounded signs like Taurus and Virgo but may find more spontaneous signs like Aries or Sagittarius challenging.
- **Aquarius Cat**: Aquarius cats are independent, quirky, and humanitarian. They enjoy exploring new ideas and may have unique preferences or behaviors. They can be aloof or detached but are generally friendly and sociable. Aquarius cats thrive with other interactive signs like Gemini and Libra but may find more traditional signs like Taurus or Cancer too restrictive.
- **Pisces Cat**: Pisces cats are dreamy, intuitive, and compassionate. They are sensitive to the emotions of those around them and may be very affectionate with their human companions. They can be shy or introverted, preferring a calm, peaceful environment. Pisces cats are compatible with nurturing signs like Cancer and Scorpio but may struggle with more assertive signs like Aries or Leo.

Assessing Compatibility with Other Pets

Understanding the astrological signs of other pets in your household can help you assess their compatibility with your cat. Each pet's sign will influence how they interact with your cat, and recognizing these dynamics can help you foster a harmonious environment.

- **Same Element Compatibility**: Pets with the same elemental signs (Fire, Earth, Air, Water) often get along well, as they share similar temperaments and energy levels. For example, a Leo cat and a Sagittarius dog may both enjoy active play and social interaction, making them natural companions.
- **Opposite Signs**: Opposite signs can either complement each other or create tension, depending on how well they balance their differences. For example, a Taurus cat (Earth) and a Scorpio dog (Water) may complement each other's need for security and emotional connection, but may also have conflicts over territory or possessiveness.
- **Mixed Elements**: Pets with different elemental signs can bring balance to each other, but may also need time to adjust to their differing needs. For instance, a Gemini cat (Air) and a Virgo rabbit (Earth) may need time to adapt to each other's communication styles, with the Gemini cat's curiosity and the Virgo rabbit's need for routine potentially leading to misunderstandings.

Assessing Compatibility with Humans

Just as with other pets, understanding the astrological compatibility between your cat and the humans in your household can provide insights into your relationship dynamics. Each person's sign will influence how they interact with your cat, and recognizing these influences can help you strengthen your bond.

- **Fire Signs (Aries, Leo, Sagittarius) and Cats**: Fire sign humans tend to be energetic, assertive, and confident, making them great companions for active, playful cats. They may enjoy engaging in interactive play with their cats and are likely to appreciate a cat's independence. However, they may need to be mindful of not overwhelming more sensitive or reserved cats.
- **Earth Signs (Taurus, Virgo, Capricorn) and Cats**: Earth sign humans are practical, patient, and nurturing, providing stability and routine for their cats. They may be especially attuned to their cat's physical needs and enjoy creating a comfortable, secure environment. Earth sign humans may need to be mindful of allowing more independent or adventurous cats the freedom to explore.

- **Air Signs (Gemini, Libra, Aquarius) and Cats**: Air sign humans are communicative, intellectual, and sociable, making them great at understanding and interacting with their cats. They may enjoy teaching their cats new tricks or engaging in activities that stimulate their cat's mind. Air sign humans may need to be mindful of providing enough emotional support for more sensitive or affectionate cats.
- **Water Signs (Cancer, Scorpio, Pisces) and Cats**: Water sign humans are emotional, intuitive, and compassionate, forming deep bonds with their cats. They may be especially attuned to their cat's emotional needs and enjoy providing comfort and affection. Water sign humans may need to be mindful of giving more independent or aloof cats the space they need.

Creating a Harmonious Environment

By understanding the astrological compatibility between your cat, other pets, and the humans in your household, you can create a more harmonious environment. Here are some tips for fostering positive relationships:

- **Respect Individual Needs**: Each pet and person in your household has unique needs based on their astrological sign. Respecting these needs, such as providing space for more introverted pets or engaging in active play for energetic ones, will help maintain harmony.
- **Facilitate Positive Interactions**: Encourage positive interactions between your cat and other pets or humans by providing opportunities for bonding, such as shared playtime or grooming sessions. Being aware of potential compatibility challenges can help you mediate and resolve conflicts.
- **Balance Energy Levels**: If your cat and another pet or person have differing energy levels, find ways to balance these energies. For example, provide high-energy activities for an active cat while ensuring a calm space is available for a more reserved pet.
- **Acknowledge Emotional Dynamics**: Pay attention to the emotional dynamics in your household, especially if your cat is sensitive to the moods of others. Providing a stable, nurturing environment will help your cat feel secure, even in the face of emotional fluctuations.

Conclusion

Astrological compatibility offers valuable insights into the relationships between your cat, other pets, and the humans in your household. By understanding how different signs interact and influence each other, you can create a more harmonious and supportive environment for everyone.

Whether it's recognizing the natural affinities between certain signs, addressing potential challenges, or tailoring your care to meet the unique needs of each pet and person, astrology provides a powerful tool for enhancing relationships and fostering a deep, loving connection with your feline companion. As you continue to explore the astrological influences on your cat, remember that compatibility is a dynamic, evolving aspect of your cat's life, guiding them through meaningful interactions and helping them build strong, lasting relationships in their journey of life.

Chapter 42: Health and Wellness: Using Astrology to Promote Better Health and Well-Being for Your Cat

Astrology offers a unique perspective on health and wellness by providing insights into the natural strengths, vulnerabilities, and tendencies of each zodiac sign. Understanding your cat's astrological profile can help you anticipate potential health issues, tailor their care routine, and support their overall well-being in a more holistic way. By aligning your cat's health and wellness practices with their astrological influences, you can create a nurturing environment that promotes balance, vitality, and longevity. This chapter provides an extensive and detailed guide to using astrology to enhance your cat's health and wellness.

Understanding Astrological Influences on Health

Each zodiac sign governs specific parts of the body and has distinct characteristics that influence health and wellness. By understanding the astrological influences on your cat's health, you can take proactive steps to prevent potential issues and support their overall well-being.

- **Elemental Influence**: The four elements (Fire, Earth, Air, Water) provide a broad overview of your cat's natural health tendencies. Each element corresponds to specific qualities that can influence your cat's physical and emotional health.
  - **Fire Signs (Aries, Leo, Sagittarius)**: Fire signs are naturally energetic and active but may be prone to issues related to inflammation, fevers, or overheating. It's important to monitor their activity levels and ensure they stay cool and hydrated, especially in warm weather. Providing a balanced diet and regular exercise will help maintain their vitality.
  - **Earth Signs (Taurus, Virgo, Capricorn)**: Earth signs are generally robust and grounded but may be susceptible to issues related to digestion, weight management, or joint health. These cats benefit from a consistent routine, a nutrient-rich diet, and regular physical activity to prevent weight gain and support joint health.

- **Air Signs (Gemini, Libra, Aquarius)**: Air signs are intellectual and communicative but may be prone to respiratory issues, anxiety, or nervous system imbalances. Ensuring good air quality, providing mental stimulation, and creating a calm environment are key to maintaining their health. Regular check-ups and attention to respiratory health are important.
  - **Water Signs (Cancer, Scorpio, Pisces)**: Water signs are sensitive and emotional, often absorbing the energies around them. They may be prone to issues related to the lymphatic system, fluid retention, or emotional stress. These cats benefit from a stable, nurturing environment, regular hydration, and emotional support to maintain their well-being.
- **Astrological Body Parts**: Each zodiac sign governs specific parts of the body, which can offer clues to potential health vulnerabilities. By being aware of these areas, you can take preventive measures and address issues before they become serious.
  - **Aries**: Head, eyes, brain – Monitor for issues related to the head, such as eye infections, head injuries, or headaches. Ensure regular eye check-ups and protect your cat from situations where head injuries might occur.
  - **Taurus**: Throat, neck, thyroid – Pay attention to throat health, including thyroid function and potential neck injuries. Provide a diet that supports thyroid health and avoid placing undue strain on the neck.
  - **Gemini**: Lungs, arms, hands – Focus on respiratory health and monitor for signs of respiratory infections or allergies. Ensure good air quality and consider adding air-purifying plants to your home.
  - **Cancer**: Stomach, breasts, digestive system – Support digestive health by providing a balanced diet and monitoring for digestive issues such as vomiting or diarrhea. Ensure a calm eating environment to reduce stress-related digestive problems.
  - **Leo**: Heart, spine, upper back – Keep an eye on heart health and monitor for signs of spinal issues or back pain. Provide regular exercise to support cardiovascular health and consider supplements for joint and spinal health if necessary.

- **Virgo**: Digestive system, intestines, spleen – Prioritize digestive health by offering a high-quality diet that is easy to digest. Monitor for signs of digestive discomfort and consider probiotics or digestive enzymes to support gut health.
- **Libra**: Kidneys, lower back, bladder – Focus on urinary health and monitor for signs of kidney or bladder issues. Ensure your cat stays hydrated and provide a balanced diet that supports kidney function.
- **Scorpio**: Reproductive organs, bladder, bowels – Pay attention to reproductive health, especially if your cat is not spayed or neutered. Monitor for signs of urinary or bowel issues, and provide regular vet check-ups to ensure reproductive health.
- **Sagittarius**: Hips, thighs, liver – Monitor joint health, particularly in the hips and thighs. Provide a diet that supports liver health and consider joint supplements if your cat is prone to hip issues.
- **Capricorn**: Bones, joints, knees – Support bone and joint health through a balanced diet and regular exercise. Monitor for signs of arthritis or joint pain, especially as your cat ages.
- **Aquarius**: Circulatory system, ankles, shins – Focus on circulatory health and monitor for signs of poor circulation or leg injuries. Ensure regular physical activity to support circulation and consider massage or gentle exercise to promote blood flow.
- **Pisces**: Feet, toes, lymphatic system – Pay attention to foot health and monitor for signs of swelling or lymphatic issues. Provide regular grooming to prevent foot injuries and ensure your cat stays hydrated to support lymphatic function.

Using Astrology to Tailor Your Cat's Care Routine

By aligning your cat's care routine with their astrological profile, you can create a more personalized and effective approach to their health and wellness. This includes their diet, exercise, grooming, and emotional well-being.

- **Dietary Needs**: Each sign has specific dietary preferences and needs that can support their overall health. Tailoring your cat's diet to their sign can help prevent potential health issues and promote vitality.

- **Fire Signs**: Fire signs benefit from a diet rich in lean proteins and healthy fats to support their active lifestyle. Avoid overly spicy or rich foods that could lead to inflammation or digestive upset. Ensure they stay hydrated, especially in warm weather.
- **Earth Signs**: Earth signs thrive on a balanced, nutrient-rich diet that supports digestion and weight management. Avoid overfeeding, as they can be prone to weight gain. Include fiber-rich foods to support digestive health and monitor portion sizes.
- **Air Signs**: Air signs benefit from a light, easily digestible diet that supports respiratory and nervous system health. Avoid heavy or rich foods that could weigh them down. Consider including foods rich in omega-3 fatty acids to support brain and nervous system function.
- **Water Signs**: Water signs need a diet that supports hydration and emotional balance. Include moisture-rich foods such as wet food or broths to keep them hydrated. Avoid overly salty or processed foods that could lead to fluid retention.

- **Exercise and Activity**: Each sign has different energy levels and exercise needs. Providing the right type and amount of exercise will help your cat stay fit and healthy.
  - **Fire Signs**: Fire signs need plenty of physical activity to burn off their excess energy. Provide interactive toys, play sessions, and opportunities for exploration. Incorporate activities that allow them to chase, pounce, and engage their natural hunting instincts.
  - **Earth Signs**: Earth signs benefit from regular, moderate exercise that supports their physical strength and prevents weight gain. Provide opportunities for climbing, stretching, and gentle play. Focus on activities that build strength and flexibility, such as climbing trees or playing with puzzle toys.
  - **Air Signs**: Air signs thrive on mental stimulation as well as physical activity. Provide toys that challenge their intellect, such as puzzle feeders or interactive toys. Incorporate activities that engage both their mind and body, such as hide-and-seek games or laser pointers.
  - **Water Signs**: Water signs may prefer quieter, more soothing activities that promote relaxation and emotional balance. Provide gentle play sessions, cozy resting spots, and activities that engage their senses, such as playing with water fountains or feather wands. Ensure they have a calm space to retreat to when they need rest.

- **Grooming and Hygiene**: Regular grooming and hygiene are essential for maintaining your cat's health. Tailoring your grooming routine to their astrological sign can help address specific needs and promote overall well-being.
  - **Fire Signs**: Fire signs may benefit from regular grooming to manage their energy and prevent overheating. Brush their coat regularly to remove loose hair and keep their skin healthy. Provide regular nail trims to prevent overgrowth and ensure they stay cool in warm weather.
  - **Earth Signs**: Earth signs thrive on routine and may enjoy a consistent grooming schedule. Regular brushing, ear cleaning, and dental care are important to prevent health issues. Pay attention to their paws and nails, especially if they enjoy outdoor activities.
  - **Air Signs**: Air signs may be sensitive to their environment, making regular grooming and cleanliness important. Brush their coat regularly to remove dust and allergens, and keep their living space clean and free of irritants. Pay attention to their ears and respiratory health.
  - **Water Signs**: Water signs are often sensitive and may require extra care in their grooming routine. Provide gentle brushing, regular baths if needed, and ensure their coat stays clean and free of tangles. Pay attention to their skin health, as they may be prone to dryness or irritation.
- **Emotional Well-Being**: Emotional health is closely tied to physical health, especially for cats. Supporting your cat's emotional well-being based on their astrological sign can help reduce stress and promote a happy, balanced life.
  - **Fire Signs**: Fire signs may need regular social interaction and playtime to stay emotionally balanced. Provide opportunities for active engagement and ensure they feel involved in household activities. Offer plenty of praise and positive reinforcement to boost their confidence.
  - **Earth Signs**: Earth signs benefit from a stable, consistent environment that promotes security and comfort. Provide a routine that includes regular feeding times, play sessions, and rest periods. Ensure they have a safe, cozy space where they can retreat when they need solitude.

- ◦ **Air Signs**: Air signs need mental stimulation and social interaction to stay emotionally healthy. Provide toys and activities that challenge their intellect, and ensure they have opportunities to socialize with both humans and other pets. Offer variety in their routine to keep them engaged and prevent boredom.
- ◦ **Water Signs**: Water signs are emotionally sensitive and may need extra comfort and reassurance. Provide a calm, nurturing environment and be attentive to their emotional needs. Offer affection and comfort when they seek it, and ensure they have a safe space to retreat when they feel overwhelmed.

Using Astrology to Prevent and Address Health Issues

Astrology can also be a valuable tool for preventing and addressing health issues in your cat. By understanding their astrological profile, you can take proactive steps to support their health and address potential vulnerabilities.

- **Preventive Care**: Knowing the health tendencies of your cat's sign can help you take preventive measures to avoid potential issues. For example, if your cat is a Taurus, you may want to monitor their thyroid health and provide a diet that supports metabolism. If your cat is a Gemini, regular respiratory check-ups and maintaining good air quality can help prevent respiratory issues.
- **Monitoring for Warning Signs**: Understanding the parts of the body governed by your cat's sign can help you identify early warning signs of health issues. For example, if your Leo cat starts showing signs of back pain or reduced activity, it may be an early indicator of spinal or heart-related issues. Early intervention can prevent more serious problems and support your cat's long-term health.
- **Tailoring Treatment**: If your cat does develop a health issue, understanding their astrological profile can help you tailor their treatment plan. For example, a Capricorn cat with joint issues may benefit from a treatment plan that includes both traditional veterinary care and complementary therapies like acupuncture or massage, which align with their need for structure and support.

- **Supporting Recovery**: Astrology can also guide you in supporting your cat's recovery from illness or injury. For example, a Cancer cat recovering from surgery may benefit from a calm, nurturing environment with plenty of emotional support. A Sagittarius cat may need mental stimulation and gentle physical activity to stay engaged and motivated during recovery.

Conclusion

Astrology provides a powerful framework for understanding and supporting your cat's health and wellness. By aligning your cat's care routine with their astrological influences, you can create a more personalized and holistic approach to their well-being.

Whether it's tailoring their diet, exercise, grooming, and emotional care to their sign, or using astrology to prevent and address health issues, this chapter offers a comprehensive guide to promoting your cat's health through the lens of astrology. As you continue to explore the astrological influences on your cat, remember that their health and well-being are deeply connected to their unique astrological profile, guiding you in providing the best possible care for your feline companion in their journey of life.

Chapter 43: Daily and Seasonal Routines: Aligning Your Cat's Daily and Seasonal Activities with Astrological Insights

Astrology provides a rich framework for understanding how cosmic cycles influence daily and seasonal activities. By aligning your cat's routines with astrological insights, you can enhance their well-being, support their natural rhythms, and create a more harmonious environment. This chapter offers an extensive and detailed guide to establishing daily and seasonal routines for your cat, based on astrological principles. By following these guidelines, you can ensure that your feline companion enjoys a balanced and fulfilling life throughout the year.

The Importance of Routines for Cats

Cats are creatures of habit who thrive on routine. A consistent daily schedule provides them with a sense of security and predictability, reducing stress and promoting well-being. Similarly, aligning your cat's activities with the changing seasons helps them adapt to environmental shifts and maintain their health throughout the year. By integrating astrological insights into these routines, you can further enhance their connection to natural cycles and support their overall balance.

Daily Routines Aligned with Astrological Cycles

Daily routines are essential for maintaining your cat's physical and emotional health. Astrology can help you tailor these routines to better align with your cat's natural rhythms and the cosmic influences that affect them.

- **Morning Routine**: The morning is a time of awakening and renewal, governed by the Sun's rising energy. This is an ideal time to focus on activities that invigorate your cat and set a positive tone for the day.
    - **Sun Signs (Aries, Leo, Sagittarius)**: Fire signs tend to be naturally energetic in the morning. Engage them in active play sessions or provide interactive toys that stimulate their physical energy. This is also a good time to feed them a nutritious breakfast that fuels their high-energy needs.
    - **Earth Signs (Taurus, Virgo, Capricorn)**: Earth signs may prefer a slower start to the day. Begin with gentle activities, such as grooming or light play, to help them ease into

the day. A hearty breakfast that supports their digestion and overall health is important for these grounded signs.

- **Air Signs (Gemini, Libra, Aquarius)**: Air signs thrive on mental stimulation in the morning. Start the day with interactive toys, puzzle feeders, or activities that challenge their intellect. Feeding them a balanced breakfast that supports their nervous system and respiratory health is key.
- **Water Signs (Cancer, Scorpio, Pisces)**: Water signs may need a nurturing start to the day. Offer comforting activities, such as cuddling or gentle play, to help them feel emotionally secure. A hydrating breakfast, such as wet food or broth, can help keep them balanced and nourished.

- **Midday Routine**: The midday period is associated with peak energy and activity, as the Sun reaches its zenith. This is an ideal time for more vigorous activities and social interaction.
    - **Sun Signs (Aries, Leo, Sagittarius)**: Fire signs are often at their most active during midday. Engage them in outdoor activities if possible, or provide stimulating indoor play that allows them to burn off energy. Social interaction with you or other pets can be particularly fulfilling during this time.
    - **Earth Signs (Taurus, Virgo, Capricorn)**: Earth signs may enjoy structured activities around midday, such as training sessions, puzzle toys, or exploring new environments. This is also a good time to offer a light snack that supports their energy levels and overall well-being.
    - **Air Signs (Gemini, Libra, Aquarius)**: Air signs benefit from activities that engage both their mind and body during midday. Offer a variety of toys or interactive games that keep them mentally and physically stimulated. This is also a good time for social interaction and play with other pets.
    - **Water Signs (Cancer, Scorpio, Pisces)**: Water signs may prefer quieter activities around midday, such as lounging in a sunny spot or gentle exploration. Ensure they have access to fresh water and a comfortable space where they can relax and recharge.

- **Evening Routine**: The evening is a time of winding down and reflection, governed by the setting Sun. This period is ideal for calming activities that help your cat prepare for rest.

- **Sun Signs (Aries, Leo, Sagittarius)**: Fire signs may still have some residual energy in the evening. Offer a final play session to help them burn off any excess energy before settling down. Provide a calming environment where they can relax and unwind.
- **Earth Signs (Taurus, Virgo, Capricorn)**: Earth signs appreciate routine and predictability in the evening. Engage them in comforting activities, such as grooming or cuddling, to help them relax. A small, nutrient-rich meal can help them feel grounded before bedtime.
- **Air Signs (Gemini, Libra, Aquarius)**: Air signs may enjoy a mix of mental and physical activities in the evening, such as playing with puzzle toys or watching birds from a window. Create a peaceful environment that allows them to wind down and prepare for rest.
- **Water Signs (Cancer, Scorpio, Pisces)**: Water signs benefit from soothing activities in the evening, such as being gently petted or curling up in a cozy spot. Provide a quiet, calm space where they can retreat and feel emotionally secure before bedtime.

- **Night Routine**: The night is a time of rest and renewal, governed by the Moon. Ensuring that your cat has a restful night is essential for their overall health and well-being.
  - **Sun Signs (Aries, Leo, Sagittarius)**: Fire signs may need extra encouragement to settle down for the night. Ensure they have a comfortable sleeping area and minimize stimulation before bedtime. A consistent bedtime routine can help them wind down.
  - **Earth Signs (Taurus, Virgo, Capricorn)**: Earth signs generally appreciate routine and stability at night. Provide a comfortable, secure sleeping environment and ensure they have access to their favorite resting spot. A warm, cozy bed can help them feel safe and relaxed.
  - **Air Signs (Gemini, Libra, Aquarius)**: Air signs may be more sensitive to changes in their environment at night. Ensure their sleeping area is quiet and free of distractions. Offering a calming toy or blanket can help them feel more secure as they settle down for the night.
  - **Water Signs (Cancer, Scorpio, Pisces)**: Water signs may be particularly attuned to the energy of the night. Provide a serene, peaceful sleeping environment where they can

feel emotionally secure. Soft lighting or soothing sounds can help them relax and drift off to sleep.

Seasonal Routines Aligned with Astrological Cycles

Just as daily routines are important for your cat's well-being, aligning their activities with the changing seasons can help them adapt to environmental shifts and maintain their health throughout the year. Each season brings its own astrological influences, which can impact your cat's behavior, health, and energy levels.

- **Spring (Aries, Taurus, Gemini)**: Spring is a time of renewal and growth, ruled by the energetic and dynamic signs of Aries, Taurus, and Gemini. This season is ideal for encouraging new activities, exploration, and social interaction.
    - **Spring Activities**: Encourage outdoor exploration if possible, as the warmer weather and longer days provide more opportunities for play and exercise. Introduce new toys or activities that stimulate your cat's curiosity and engage their senses. This is also a good time for a health check-up and refreshing your cat's diet to support their energy levels.
    - **Spring Health Tips**: Monitor for seasonal allergies, especially if your cat is prone to respiratory issues (Air signs). Ensure they stay hydrated, as the warmer weather can increase their water needs. Regular grooming is important to manage shedding as your cat transitions from their winter coat.
- **Summer (Cancer, Leo, Virgo)**: Summer is a time of warmth, vitality, and abundance, ruled by the nurturing and vibrant signs of Cancer, Leo, and Virgo. This season is ideal for focusing on health, well-being, and building strong bonds.
    - **Summer Activities**: Provide plenty of opportunities for social interaction and play, as the energy of summer supports bonding and active engagement. Ensure your cat has access to cool, shaded areas to avoid overheating, and consider introducing water-based play to keep them cool and entertained.
    - **Summer Health Tips**: Monitor for signs of overheating or dehydration, especially in Fire signs. Ensure your cat has access to fresh water at all times and consider adding wet

food to their diet to increase hydration. Regular grooming is essential to keep their coat clean and free of parasites.

- **Autumn (Libra, Scorpio, Sagittarius)**: Autumn is a time of harvest, reflection, and preparation for the colder months, ruled by the balanced and introspective signs of Libra, Scorpio, and Sagittarius. This season is ideal for creating a nurturing environment and supporting your cat's emotional well-being.
    - ◦ **Autumn Activities**: Focus on activities that promote emotional balance and introspection, such as quiet play, grooming, and cuddling. As the weather cools, ensure your cat has a warm, cozy spot to retreat to. This is also a good time to review their diet and make any necessary adjustments to support their health during the colder months.
    - ◦ **Autumn Health Tips**: Monitor for signs of seasonal affective disorder, especially in Water signs, as the shorter days and longer nights can affect their mood. Provide extra comfort and warmth, and consider introducing new toys or activities to keep them engaged. Ensure their immune system is strong by providing a balanced diet and regular vet check-ups.
- **Winter (Capricorn, Aquarius, Pisces)**: Winter is a time of rest, reflection, and conservation of energy, ruled by the disciplined and introspective signs of Capricorn, Aquarius, and Pisces. This season is ideal for focusing on rest, rejuvenation, and maintaining a stable routine.
    - ◦ **Winter Activities**: Provide plenty of opportunities for rest and relaxation, as your cat may be less active during the colder months. Ensure they have access to warm, comfortable resting spots and consider introducing cozy blankets or heated beds. Indoor play that stimulates their mind and keeps them active is also important.
    - ◦ **Winter Health Tips**: Monitor for signs of joint stiffness or discomfort, especially in Earth signs, as the cold weather can exacerbate these issues. Ensure your cat's diet is rich in nutrients that support joint health, such as omega-3 fatty acids. Regular grooming is important to keep their coat healthy and to check for any signs of dry skin or irritation.

Aligning Daily and Seasonal Routines with Lunar Phases

In addition to the Sun's influence, the Moon's phases also play a significant role in shaping your cat's behavior and energy levels. By aligning your cat's activities with the lunar phases, you can further enhance their connection to natural rhythms and support their overall well-being.

- **New Moon**: The New Moon is a time of new beginnings and fresh starts. This phase is ideal for introducing new activities, toys, or routines into your cat's life. Focus on setting intentions for your cat's health and well-being, such as starting a new diet or exercise routine.
- **Waxing Moon**: The Waxing Moon is a time of growth and expansion. This phase is ideal for building on the new routines introduced during the New Moon. Encourage physical activity and social interaction, as your cat's energy levels may increase during this phase.
- **Full Moon**: The Full Moon is a time of heightened energy and emotional intensity. Your cat may be more active or restless during this phase, so provide plenty of opportunities for play and engagement. This is also a good time for grooming and health check-ups, as the Full Moon's energy supports cleansing and renewal.
- **Waning Moon**: The Waning Moon is a time of reflection and release. This phase is ideal for winding down and focusing on rest and relaxation. Reduce stimulation and provide a calm, peaceful environment where your cat can recharge. Consider decluttering your cat's environment and letting go of any old toys or routines that no longer serve them.

Conclusion

Aligning your cat's daily and seasonal routines with astrological insights offers a holistic approach to their health and well-being. By understanding the influence of the Sun, Moon, and seasonal cycles, you can create a more balanced and fulfilling life for your feline companion.

Whether it's tailoring their activities to their astrological sign, adjusting their routine to match the changing seasons, or aligning their daily activities with lunar phases, this chapter provides a comprehensive guide to enhancing your cat's well-being through the lens of astrology. As you continue to explore the astrological influences on your cat, remember that their routines are a reflection of their unique connection to the cosmos, guiding them through cycles of growth, rest, and renewal in their journey of life.

Appendices

Appendix A: Glossary of Astrological Terms

This glossary provides definitions and explanations of key astrological terms and concepts used throughout the book. Whether you're new to astrology or seeking a deeper understanding, this comprehensive guide will help you navigate the astrological terminology and apply it to your cat's horoscope and well-being.

Ascendant (Rising Sign)

The Ascendant, or Rising Sign, is the zodiac sign that was rising on the eastern horizon at the exact moment of your cat's birth. It represents your cat's outward behavior, how they present themselves to the world, and their first impressions. The Ascendant influences your cat's physical appearance and demeanor and plays a significant role in their interactions with others.

Aspects

Aspects are the angles formed between planets in a natal chart. These angles determine how the energies of different planets interact with each other. Aspects can be harmonious or challenging, influencing your cat's behavior, personality, and life experiences. Common aspects include:

- **Conjunction (0°)**: When two planets are in the same zodiac sign and degree, they amplify each other's energy. This aspect can indicate a strong focus or intensity in the areas governed by the planets involved.
- **Sextile (60°)**: A harmonious aspect that occurs when planets are two signs apart. Sextiles indicate opportunities for growth, cooperation, and positive interactions between the planets' energies.
- **Square (90°)**: A challenging aspect formed when planets are three signs apart. Squares create tension and obstacles, requiring effort and adaptation to resolve conflicts between the planets' influences.
- **Trine (120°)**: A favorable aspect that occurs when planets are four signs apart. Trines indicate ease, natural talents, and harmonious interactions between the planets' energies.

- **Opposition (180°)**: An aspect formed when planets are six signs apart, directly opposite each other in the zodiac. Oppositions create a push-pull dynamic, requiring balance and integration of the planets' energies.

Astrological Houses

The astrological houses are twelve divisions of the natal chart, each representing different areas of life. The planets' positions in these houses indicate where the planets' energies manifest in your cat's life. The houses are as follows:

- **1st House (House of Self)**: Represents your cat's personality, physical appearance, and outward behavior. It is associated with the Ascendant.
- **2nd House (House of Values)**: Governs material possessions, finances, and your cat's sense of security and self-worth.
- **3rd House (House of Communication)**: Rules communication, learning, short trips, and interactions with siblings or neighbors.
- **4th House (House of Home and Family)**: Represents home, family, and your cat's emotional foundation. It is associated with the nurturing and protective aspects of life.
- **5th House (House of Creativity and Pleasure)**: Governs creativity, play, self-expression, romance, and leisure activities. It is associated with fun and joy.
- **6th House (House of Health and Service)**: Rules health, daily routines, work habits, and service to others. It is associated with your cat's well-being and care.
- **7th House (House of Partnerships)**: Represents relationships, partnerships, and one-on-one interactions. It governs how your cat relates to others.
- **8th House (House of Transformation)**: Governs transformation, shared resources, sexuality, and deep emotional connections. It is associated with cycles of death and rebirth.
- **9th House (House of Philosophy and Travel)**: Rules higher learning, travel, philosophy, and spiritual beliefs. It governs your cat's exploration and quest for meaning.
- **10th House (House of Career and Public Life)**: Represents career, public reputation, and life goals. It governs your cat's role in the world and their achievements.

- **11th House (House of Friendships and Community)**: Governs friendships, social networks, and community involvement. It represents your cat's connections with others.
- **12th House (House of the Subconscious)**: Rules the subconscious mind, hidden fears, dreams, and spirituality. It is associated with introspection and the unseen aspects of life.

Astrology

Astrology is the study of the movements and positions of celestial bodies, such as planets and stars, and their influence on human affairs and natural phenomena. In this book, astrology is applied to understand and enhance the well-being of cats, offering insights into their behavior, health, and life experiences.

Cardinal Signs

Cardinal signs are the initiators of the zodiac. They are associated with leadership, action, and the beginning of new cycles. The four cardinal signs are:

- **Aries**: Initiates action with energy and enthusiasm.
- **Cancer**: Initiates nurturing and emotional connections.
- **Libra**: Initiates relationships and seeks balance.
- **Capricorn**: Initiates structure and long-term goals.

Celestial Bodies

Celestial bodies refer to natural objects in space, such as planets, stars, moons, and comets. In astrology, celestial bodies are believed to influence various aspects of life, including personality, behavior, and events. Key celestial bodies in astrology include the Sun, Moon, planets, and asteroids.

Elements

The zodiac signs are grouped into four elements: Fire, Earth, Air, and Water. Each element represents a different type of energy and influences the characteristics of the signs within it.

- **Fire Signs (Aries, Leo, Sagittarius)**: Energetic, enthusiastic, and action-oriented. Fire signs are passionate and dynamic.

- **Earth Signs (Taurus, Virgo, Capricorn)**: Practical, grounded, and focused on material stability. Earth signs are reliable and hardworking.
- **Air Signs (Gemini, Libra, Aquarius)**: Intellectual, communicative, and sociable. Air signs are curious and adaptable.
- **Water Signs (Cancer, Scorpio, Pisces)**: Emotional, intuitive, and nurturing. Water signs are sensitive and compassionate.

Ephemeris

An ephemeris is a table or data set that shows the positions of celestial bodies at specific times, usually for each day of the year. Astrologers use ephemerides to calculate the positions of planets and other celestial bodies in a natal chart.

Fixed Signs

Fixed signs are the stabilizers of the zodiac. They are associated with persistence, determination, and resistance to change. The four fixed signs are:

- **Taurus**: Steadfast and focused on material security.
- **Leo**: Loyal and focused on self-expression.
- **Scorpio**: Intense and focused on emotional depth.
- **Aquarius**: Independent and focused on innovation.

Mutable Signs

Mutable signs are the adapters of the zodiac. They are associated with flexibility, adaptability, and change. The four mutable signs are:

- **Gemini**: Adaptable and communicative.
- **Virgo**: Analytical and detail-oriented.
- **Sagittarius**: Adventurous and philosophical.
- **Pisces**: Intuitive and empathetic.

Natal Chart (Birth Chart)

A natal chart, also known as a birth chart, is a map of the sky at the exact moment and location of your cat's birth. It shows the positions of the Sun, Moon, planets, and other celestial bodies in relation to the twelve astrological houses. The natal chart provides a blueprint of your cat's personality, behavior, and life path.

New Moon

The New Moon occurs when the Sun and Moon are in the same zodiac sign and degree, marking the beginning of a new lunar cycle. The New Moon is a time for setting intentions, new beginnings, and initiating projects. For your cat, the New Moon is an ideal time to introduce new routines, activities, or habits.

Opposition

An opposition is an aspect formed when two planets are 180 degrees apart, positioned directly opposite each other in the zodiac. This aspect creates a dynamic tension that requires balance and compromise between the opposing energies.

Planets

In astrology, planets represent different aspects of personality, behavior, and life experiences. Each planet governs specific areas of life and influences the characteristics of the zodiac signs. The key planets in astrology include:

- **Sun**: Represents core identity, vitality, and self-expression.
- **Moon**: Represents emotions, instincts, and subconscious mind.
- **Mercury**: Governs communication, intellect, and thought processes.
- **Venus**: Governs love, relationships, beauty, and values.
- **Mars**: Governs energy, action, and aggression.
- **Jupiter**: Governs growth, expansion, and abundance.
- **Saturn**: Governs discipline, structure, and responsibility.
- **Uranus**: Governs innovation, change, and individuality.
- **Neptune**: Governs dreams, intuition, and spirituality.
- **Pluto**: Governs transformation, power, and rebirth.

Retrograde

A retrograde is an apparent backward motion of a planet as observed from Earth. In astrology, retrogrades are significant periods where the energy of the retrograde planet is turned inward, leading to introspection, reflection, and revisiting past issues. For your cat, retrogrades can manifest as changes in behavior, health, or routine, requiring extra care and attention.

Sextile

A sextile is an aspect formed when two planets are 60 degrees apart. This harmonious aspect indicates opportunities for growth, cooperation, and positive interactions between the planets' energies.

Square

A square is an aspect formed when two planets are 90 degrees apart. This challenging aspect creates tension and obstacles, requiring effort and adaptation to resolve conflicts between the planets' influences.

Sun Sign

The Sun sign is determined by the position of the Sun at the time of your cat's birth. It represents your cat's core personality, vitality, and essential nature. The Sun sign is the most commonly recognized aspect of astrology and provides insights into your cat's basic character traits and overall approach to life.

Synastry

Synastry is the study of astrological compatibility between two or more individuals by comparing their natal charts. In the context of this book, synastry can be used to understand the compatibility between your cat and other pets or humans in your household. By examining the aspects and house placements between charts, you can gain insights into relationship dynamics and potential challenges.

T-square

A T-square is an aspect pattern involving three planets, where two planets are in opposition and both are square to a third planet. This configuration creates a dynamic tension that requires resolution and balance. The planet at the apex (the one not in opposition) often indicates the area where challenges will manifest and where the greatest growth can occur.

Trine

A trine is an aspect formed when two planets are 120 degrees apart. This harmonious aspect indicates ease, natural talents, and positive interactions between the planets' energies.

Water Signs

Water signs are emotional, intuitive, and nurturing. They are associated with sensitivity, empathy, and deep emotional connections. The three Water signs are Cancer, Scorpio, and Pisces.

Waxing Moon

The Waxing Moon occurs as the Moon moves from the New Moon to the Full Moon, increasing in light. This phase is a time of growth, expansion, and building momentum. For your cat, the Waxing Moon is an ideal time for increasing physical activity, social interaction, and learning new behaviors.

Waning Moon

The Waning Moon occurs as the Moon moves from the Full Moon to the New Moon, decreasing in light. This phase is a time of reflection, release, and winding down. For your cat, the Waning Moon is an ideal time for rest, relaxation, and letting go of old habits or routines.

This glossary serves as a comprehensive reference for understanding the key astrological terms and concepts discussed in this book. By familiarizing yourself with these terms, you can deepen your understanding of your cat's astrological profile and apply these insights to enhance their well-being and overall quality of life.

Appendix B: Charts and Tables: Easy Reference for Planetary Positions, Zodiac Traits, and Celestial Events

This appendix provides a comprehensive collection of charts and tables designed to serve as easy reference guides for planetary positions, zodiac traits, and celestial events. These resources will help you quickly find the information you need to interpret your cat's astrological influences and tailor their care accordingly.

Chart 1: Planetary Positions and Their Meanings

Planet	Symbol	Astrological Sign	Governs	Associated Traits
Sun	◇	Leo	Core identity, vitality, self-expression	Confidence, creativity, leadership
Moon	◇	Cancer	Emotions, instincts, subconscious mind	Sensitivity, nurturing, intuition
Mercury	◇	Gemini, Virgo	Communication, intellect, thought	Curiosity, adaptability, reasoning
Venus	♀	Taurus, Libra	Love, relationships, beauty, values	Affection, harmony, attraction

Planet	Symbol	Astrological Sign	Governs	Associated Traits
Mars	♂	Aries, Scorpio	Energy, action, aggression	Assertiveness, courage, passion
Jupiter	�	Sagittarius, Pisces	Growth, expansion, abundance	Optimism, generosity, exploration
Saturn	�	Capricorn, Aquarius	Discipline, structure, responsibility	Ambition, perseverance, boundaries
Uranus	�	Aquarius	Innovation, change, individuality	Rebellion, originality, sudden change
Neptune	�	Pisces	Dreams, intuition, spirituality	Imagination, compassion, sensitivity
Pluto	�	Scorpio	Transformation, power, rebirth	Intensity, depth, regeneration

Chart 2: Zodiac Signs and Their Traits

Zodiac Sign	Symbol	Element	Quality	Ruling Planet	Key Traits	Governs (Body Parts)
Aries	◇	Fire	Cardinal	Mars	Bold, energetic, assertive	Head, eyes, brain
Taurus	◇	Earth	Fixed	Venus	Steadfast, patient, comfort-loving	Throat, neck, thyroid
Gemini	◇	Air	Mutable	Mercury	Curious, sociable, adaptable	Lungs, arms, hands
Cancer	◇	Water	Cardinal	Moon	Nurturing, sensitive, loyal	Stomach, breasts, digestive system
Leo	◇	Fire	Fixed	Sun	Confident, playful, charismatic	Heart, spine, upper back

Zodiac Sign	Symbol	Element	Quality	Ruling Planet	Key Traits	Governs (Body Parts)
Virgo	◇	Earth	Mutable	Mercury	Meticulous, intelligent, health-conscious	Digestive system, intestines, spleen
Libra	◇	Air	Cardinal	Venus	Sociable, balanced, harmony-seeking	Kidneys, lower back, bladder
Scorpio	◇	Water	Fixed	Pluto	Intense, mysterious, loyal	Reproductive organs, bowels, bladder
Sagittarius	◇	Fire	Mutable	Jupiter	Adventurous, optimistic, freedom-loving	Hips, thighs, liver
Capricorn	◇	Earth	Cardinal	Saturn	Disciplined, ambitious, practical	Bones, joints, knees

Zodiac Sign	Symbol	Element	Quality	Ruling Planet	Key Traits	Governs (Body Parts)
Aquarius	◇	Air	Fixed	Uranus	Quirky, independent, humanitarian	Circulatory system, ankles, shins
Pisces	◇	Water	Mutable	Neptune	Dreamy, intuitive, compassionate	Feet, toes, lymphatic system

Chart 3: The Four Elements and Their Influence

Element	Signs	Key Characteristics	Health Focus
Fire	Aries, Leo, Sagittarius	Energetic, enthusiastic, action-oriented	Monitor for inflammation, overheating, and fevers
Earth	Taurus, Virgo, Capricorn	Practical, grounded, focused on material stability	Focus on digestion, weight management, and joint health
Air	Gemini, Libra, Aquarius	Intellectual, communicative, sociable	Pay attention to respiratory health and mental stimulation

Element	Signs	Key Characteristics	Health Focus
Water	Cancer, Scorpio, Pisces	Emotional, intuitive, nurturing	Ensure emotional support and monitor fluid balance

Chart 4: Lunar Phases and Their Influence

Lunar Phase	Description	Ideal Activities for Your Cat
New Moon	A time for new beginnings and setting intentions	Introduce new routines, toys, or habits
Waxing Moon	A period of growth, expansion, and building momentum	Increase physical activity and social interaction
Full Moon	A time of heightened energy and emotional intensity	Engage in active play, grooming, and health check-ups
Waning Moon	A period for reflection, release, and winding down	Focus on rest, relaxation, and decluttering old routines

Chart 5: Qualities of the Zodiac Signs

Quality	Signs	Key Characteristics	Interaction Style
Cardinal	Aries, Cancer, Libra, Capricorn	Leaders, initiators, action-oriented	Prefer to take charge, initiate change
Fixed	Taurus, Leo, Scorpio, Aquarius	Stabilizers, determined, resistant to change	Provide stability, maintain routines, resist change
Mutable	Gemini, Virgo, Sagittarius, Pisces	Adaptable, flexible, open to change	Easily adjust to new situations, adaptable

Table 1: Major Celestial Events and Their Influence

Celestial Event	Description	Influence on Your Cat
Solar Eclipse	Occurs when the Moon passes between the Earth and the Sun, blocking the Sun's light	Major changes, revelations, heightened energy

Celestial Event	Description	Influence on Your Cat
Lunar Eclipse	Occurs when the Earth passes between the Sun and the Moon, casting a shadow on the Moon	Emotional highs and lows, intense emotional experiences
Mercury Retrograde	A period when Mercury appears to move backward in its orbit	Communication breakdowns, routine disruptions, increased introspection
Venus Retrograde	A period when Venus appears to move backward in its orbit	Changes in affection, relationships, and comfort-seeking behaviors
Mars Retrograde	A period when Mars appears to move backward in its orbit	Fluctuating energy levels, increased aggression, and assertiveness
Jupiter Retrograde	A period when Jupiter appears to move backward in its orbit	Changes in growth, exploration, and overall happiness
Saturn Retrograde	A period when Saturn appears to move backward in its orbit	Reevaluation of discipline, boundaries, and responsibilities
Uranus Retrograde	A period when Uranus appears to move backward in its orbit	Sudden changes, unpredictability, increased independence
Neptune Retrograde	A period when Neptune appears to move backward in its orbit	Heightened intuition, vivid dreams, increased sensitivity

Celestial Event	Description	Influence on Your Cat
Pluto Retrograde	A period when Pluto appears to move backward in its orbit	Deep transformation, emotional release, and power dynamics

Table 2: Zodiac Signs and Compatibility

Sign	Compatible Signs	Challenging Signs
Aries	Leo, Sagittarius, Gemini	Cancer, Capricorn

Sign	Compatible Signs	Challenging Signs
Taurus	Virgo, Capricorn, Pisces	Leo, Aquarius
Gemini	Libra, Aquarius, Aries	Virgo, Pisces
Cancer	Scorpio, Pisces, Taurus	Aries, Libra
Leo	Aries, Sagittarius, Gemini	Taurus, Scorpio
Virgo	Taurus, Capricorn, Cancer	Gemini, Sagittarius
Libra	Gemini, Aquarius, Leo	Cancer, Capricorn
Scorpio	Cancer, Pisces, Virgo	Leo, Aquarius
Sagittarius	Aries, Leo, Libra	Virgo, Pisces
Capricorn	Taurus, Virgo, Scorpio	Aries, Libra
Aquarius	Gemini, Libra, Sagittarius	Taurus, Scorpio
Pisces	Cancer, Scorpio, Capricorn	Gemini, Sagittarius

Table 3: Seasonal Activities for Your Cat

Season	Astrological Signs	Ideal Activities	Health Focus
Spring	Aries, Taurus, Gemini	Outdoor exploration, new toys, social interaction	Monitor for seasonal allergies, ensure hydration
Summer	Cancer, Leo, Virgo	Playtime, social bonding, water-based activities	Prevent overheating, ensure fresh water, groom regularly
Autumn	Libra, Scorpio, Sagittarius	Quiet play, grooming, preparing for colder weather	Support emotional well-being, immune system health
Winter	Capricorn, Aquarius, Pisces	Rest, indoor play, cozy environments	Monitor for joint issues, ensure warmth, provide a rich diet

This appendix serves as a quick reference for understanding the key astrological concepts and their application to your cat's daily and seasonal routines. Whether you're looking to interpret planetary positions, understand zodiac traits, or plan activities based on celestial events, these charts and tables offer valuable insights to help you align your cat's life with astrological wisdom. By using this information, you can create a more balanced, harmonious, and fulfilling environment for your feline companion.

Appendix C: Recommended Reading: Books, Articles, and Resources for Further Exploration of Astrology and Feline Behavior

Astrology and feline behavior are rich, intricate fields of study that offer endless opportunities for exploration and discovery. Whether you're a seasoned astrologer, a cat lover eager to deepen your understanding of your feline companion, or someone new to both fields, this appendix provides a curated list of books, articles, and resources to support your journey. These resources cover a wide range of topics, from the fundamentals of astrology to the nuances of cat behavior, offering valuable insights and practical guidance.

Books on Astrology

1. **"The Only Astrology Book You'll Ever Need" by Joanna Martine Woolfolk**
   - This comprehensive guide covers the basics of astrology, including how to create and interpret a natal chart. It's an excellent starting point for anyone new to astrology and offers detailed explanations of each zodiac sign, planetary influence, and aspect.

2. **"Parker's Astrology: The Definitive Guide to Using Astrology in Every Aspect of Your Life" by Julia and Derek Parker**
   ◦ A classic in the field, this book provides an in-depth look at astrology, including the history, techniques, and applications of astrological practice. It's highly visual, with detailed charts and diagrams that make complex concepts accessible.

3. **"Astrology for the Soul" by Jan Spiller**
   ◦ Focused on the concept of the North Node, this book explores karmic astrology and how your astrological chart can guide personal growth and fulfillment. It's particularly useful for those interested in the deeper spiritual aspects of astrology.

4. **"Planets in Transit: Life Cycles for Living" by Robert Hand**
   ◦ This book offers a detailed exploration of planetary transits and how they influence different areas of life. It's an essential resource for understanding how current astrological events impact your natal chart and can be applied to interpret your cat's life cycles as well.

5. **"The Twelve Houses: Exploring the Houses of the Horoscope" by Howard Sasportas**
   ◦ An in-depth exploration of the twelve houses in astrology, this book explains how each house influences different areas of life. It's a valuable resource for those looking to understand the specific domains governed by each house in an astrological chart.

6. **"Astrology for Cats: Unlocking the Mysteries of Your Feline Friend's Personality" by Liz Allen**
   ◦ Specifically focused on feline astrology, this book offers insights into how each zodiac sign influences your cat's personality, behavior, and needs. It's a must-read for cat owners interested in applying astrology to their pet's care.

Books on Feline Behavior and Care

1. **"Cat Sense: How the New Feline Science Can Make You a Better Friend to Your Pet" by John Bradshaw**

- Drawing on the latest scientific research, this book offers insights into cat behavior, evolution, and psychology. It's an essential read for understanding your cat's natural instincts and how to meet their needs in a domestic environment.

2. **"The Cat Whisperer: Why Cats Do What They Do—and How to Get Them to Do What You Want" by Mieshelle Nagelschneider**

   - A practical guide to understanding and modifying cat behavior, this book provides step-by-step advice on addressing common issues like aggression, litter box problems, and anxiety. It's written by a renowned feline behaviorist and offers practical solutions grounded in a deep understanding of cat psychology.

3. **"Total Cat Mojo: The Ultimate Guide to Life with Your Cat" by Jackson Galaxy**

   - Written by the star of Animal Planet's "My Cat from Hell," this book offers a comprehensive guide to living with cats. It covers everything from basic care to addressing behavioral issues and is filled with practical advice, personal anecdotes, and a deep love for cats.

4. **"Think Like a Cat: How to Raise a Well-Adjusted Cat—Not a Sour Puss" by Pam Johnson-Bennett**

   - This book offers insights into the mind of a cat, helping you understand their needs, behaviors, and how to create a cat-friendly home. It's an essential resource for anyone looking to build a strong, positive relationship with their feline friend.

5. **"The Trainable Cat: A Practical Guide to Making Life Happier for You and Your Cat" by John Bradshaw and Sarah Ellis**

   - This book challenges the notion that cats are untrainable and offers practical techniques for training cats in a way that respects their natural instincts. It covers everything from basic commands to solving behavioral problems.

6. **"The Domestic Cat: The Biology of Its Behaviour" by Dennis C. Turner and Patrick Bateson**

   - An academic exploration of cat behavior, this book delves into the biology, social structure, and psychology of domestic cats. It's a valuable resource for those interested in a deeper, scientific understanding of feline behavior.

Articles and Journals on Astrology and Feline Behavior

1. **"The Astrological Journal" (Journal of the Astrological Association)**
   - This journal offers in-depth articles, research papers, and discussions on various aspects of astrology, including how astrology can be applied to animals and pets. It's a great resource for staying up-to-date with the latest developments in the field.
2. **"International Journal of Feline Medicine and Surgery"**
   - A peer-reviewed journal that publishes research on all aspects of feline health, including behavior, medical conditions, and surgery. It's a valuable resource for understanding the latest findings in feline medicine and applying them to your cat's care.
3. **"Understanding Feline Emotions: The Role of Stress in Feline Behavior" (Journal of Veterinary Behavior)**
   - This article explores how stress impacts feline behavior and offers strategies for reducing stress in domestic cats. It's particularly useful for those dealing with anxiety or behavioral issues in their cats.
4. **"Astrology and Animal Behavior: The Celestial Influence on Pets" (Astrology.com)**
   - An online article that explores the influence of astrology on animal behavior, including how planetary positions can affect your pet's mood, health, and daily activities. It's a good starting point for understanding the basics of pet astrology.
5. **"The Role of Environmental Enrichment in Feline Behavior" (Journal of Feline Medicine and Surgery)**
   - This article discusses the importance of providing a stimulating environment for cats to prevent boredom and behavioral issues. It offers practical advice on how to enrich your cat's environment, which can be aligned with astrological insights.

Online Resources and Websites

1. **Astro.com**
   - A comprehensive website offering free natal chart calculations, daily horoscopes, and in-depth astrological articles. It's a valuable resource for both beginners and advanced astrologers.
2. **The American Federation of Astrologers (AFA)**
   - The AFA offers a wide range of resources, including books, courses, and certifications in astrology. They also have a section dedicated to astrology and pets, providing insights into how to apply astrological principles to animal care.
3. **The International Society for Astrological Research (ISAR)**
   - ISAR provides access to a global community of astrologers, along with resources such as webinars, conferences, and publications. It's an excellent resource for those looking to deepen their knowledge of astrology and connect with other professionals.
4. **Jackson Galaxy's Cat Mojo Website**
   - This website offers a wealth of information on feline behavior, care, and training, based on Jackson Galaxy's philosophy of understanding cats as individuals with unique needs. The site includes articles, videos, and a community forum.
5. **The Conscious Cat Blog**
   - A blog dedicated to feline health, behavior, and lifestyle, offering articles, reviews, and tips on how to keep your cat happy and healthy. It's a great resource for practical advice and inspiration on living harmoniously with your cat.
6. **The Feline Behavior Solutions Website**
   - Run by a certified feline behavior consultant, this website offers online courses, articles, and personalized consultations to help cat owners address behavioral issues and improve their cats' quality of life.

Courses and Workshops

1. **Astrology University**
   - Offers online courses and webinars on various aspects of astrology, including natal chart interpretation, transits, and astrological compatibility. Some courses also touch on how to apply astrology to understanding animal behavior.
2. **The Cat School Online**
   - An online school offering courses on training and understanding cat behavior, with a focus on positive reinforcement techniques. These courses can complement your astrological insights by providing practical strategies for behavior modification.
3. **Animal Communication Workshops (Offered by Various Instructors)**
   - These workshops teach the basics of animal communication, helping you understand your cat's needs and emotions on a deeper level. Combining these skills with astrological knowledge can enhance your ability to care for your cat.
4. **International Society of Astrological Research (ISAR) Conferences**
   - ISAR hosts conferences that bring together astrologers from around the world to discuss the latest research and techniques. These conferences often include sessions on applying astrology to animals and pets.

Documentaries and Films

1. **"The Secret Life of Cats" (National Geographic)**
   - This documentary explores the behavior, biology, and instincts of domestic cats, offering insights into what makes them tick. It's a great companion to understanding the practical aspects of feline behavior alongside astrological influences.
2. **"Astrology and Animals" (Astrological Society of London)**
   - A documentary that delves into how astrology can be applied to understanding animal behavior, including interviews with experts and case studies. It provides a visual introduction to the concepts discussed in this book.
3. **"Jackson Galaxy's My Cat from Hell" (Animal Planet)**

◦ While not specifically focused on astrology, this series offers valuable insights into cat behavior and practical solutions for common problems. Watching the series with an astrological perspective can provide additional layers of understanding.

Conclusion

This appendix serves as a gateway to further exploration of astrology and feline behavior. Whether you're interested in deepening your understanding of astrological principles, learning more about your cat's behavior, or finding practical advice on caring for your feline companion, these books, articles, and resources offer valuable insights and guidance. As you continue your journey, remember that both astrology and feline behavior are complex, evolving fields, and there is always more to discover. By integrating these resources into your practice, you can enhance your ability to support your cat's well-being and strengthen the bond you share with your beloved pet.

<u>Message from the Author:</u>

I hope you enjoyed this book, I love astrology and knew there was not a book such as this out on the shelf. I love metaphysical items as well. Please check out my other books:

-Life of Government Benefits

-My life of Hell

-My life with Hydrocephalus

-Red Sky

-World Domination:Woman's rule

-World Domination:Woman's Rule 2: The War

-Life and Banishment of Apophis: book 1

-The Kidney Friendly Diet

-The Ultimate Hemp Cookbook

-Creating a Dispensary(legally)

-Cleanliness throughout life: the importance of showering from childhood to adulthood.

-Strong Roots: The Risks of Overcoddling children

-Hemp Horoscopes: Cosmic Insights and Earthly Healing

- Celestial Hemp Navigating the Zodiac: Through the Green Cosmos

-Astrological Hemp: Aligning The Stars with Earth's Ancient Herb

-The Astrological Guide to Hemp: Stars, Signs, and Sacred Leaves

-Green Growth: Innovative Marketing Strategies for your Hemp Products and Dispensary

-Cosmic Cannabis

-Astrological Munchies

-Henry The Hemp

-Zodiacal Roots: The Astrological Soul Of Hemp

- **Green Constellations: Intersection of Hemp and Zodiac**

-Hemp in The Houses: An astrological Adventure Through The Cannabis Galaxy

-Galactic Ganja Guide

Heavenly Hemp

Zodiac Leaves

Doctor Who Astrology

Cannastrology

Stellar Satvias and Cosmic Indicas

Celestial Cannabis: A Zodiac Journey

AstroHerbology: The Sky and The Soil: Volume 1

AstroHerbology:Celestial Cannabis:Volume 2

Cosmic Cannabis Cultivation

The Starry Guide to Herbal Harmony: Volume 1

The Starry Guide to Herbal Harmony: Cannabis Universe: Volume 2

Yugioh Astrology: Astrological Guide to Deck, Duels and more

Nightmare Mansion: Echoes of The Abyss

Nightmare Mansion 2: Legacy of Shadows

Nightmare Mansion 3: Shadows of the Forgotten

Nightmare Mansion 4: Echoes of the Damned

The Life and Banishment of Apophis: Book 2

Nightmare Mansion: Halls of Despair

Healing with Herb: Cannabis and Hydrocephalus

Planetary Pot: Aligning with Astrological Herbs: Volume 1

Fast Track to Freedom: 30 Days to Financial Independence Using AI, Assets, and Agile Hustles

Cosmic Hemp Pathways

How to Become Financially Free in 30 Days: 10,000 Paths to Prosperity

Zodiacal Herbage: Astrological Insights: Volume 1

Nightmare Mansion: Whispers in the Walls

The Daleks Invade Atlantis

Henry the hemp and Hydrocephalus

10X The Kidney Friendly Diet

Cannabis Universe: Adult coloring book

Hemp Astrology: The Healing Power of the Stars

Zodiacal Herbage: Astrological Insights: Cannabis Universe: Volume 2

Planetary Pot: Aligning with Astrological Herbs: Cannabis Universes: Volume 2

Doctor Who Meets the Replicators and SG-1: The Ultimate Battle for Survival

Nightmare Mansion: Curse of the Blood Moon

The Celestial Stoner: A Guide to the Zodiac

Cosmic Pleasures: Sex Toy Astrology for Every Sign

Hydrocephalus Astrology: Navigating the Stars and Healing Waters

Lapis and the Mischievous Chocolate Bar

Celestial Positions: Sexual Astrology for Every Sign

Apophis's Shadow Work Journal: : A Journey of Self-Discovery and Healing

Kinky Cosmos: Sexual Kink Astrology for Every Sign

Digital Cosmos: The Astrological Digimon Compendium

Stellar Seeds: The Cosmic Guide to Growing with Astrology

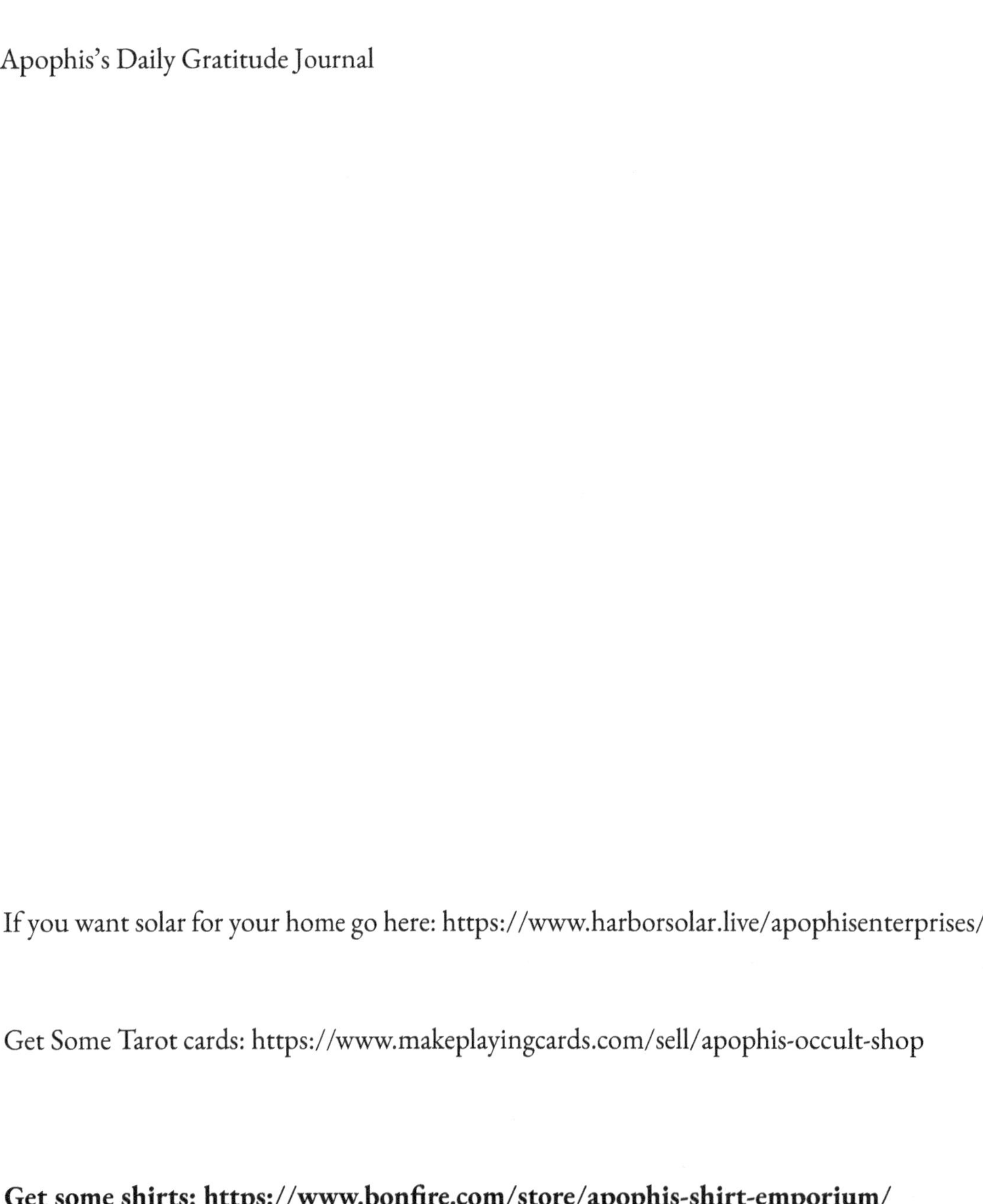

Apophis's Daily Gratitude Journal

If you want solar for your home go here: https://www.harborsolar.live/apophisenterprises/

Get Some Tarot cards: https://www.makeplayingcards.com/sell/apophis-occult-shop

Get some shirts: https://www.bonfire.com/store/apophis-shirt-emporium/

<u>Instagrams:</u>
@apophis_enterprises,
@apophisbookemporium,
@apophisscardshop
Twitter: @apophisenterpr1,
Tiktok:@apophisenterprise
Youtube: @sg1fan23477, @FiresideRetreatKingdom
Podcast: Apophis   Chat   Zone: https://open.spotify.com/show/5zXbr-CLEV2xzCp8ybrfHsk?si=fb4d4fdbdce44dec
Newsletter: https://apophiss-newsletter-27c897.beehiiv.com/